The Black Matador, "Sugar"

By: Odie Hawkins

authorHOUSE®

AuthorHouse™
1663 Liberty Drive
Bloomington, IN 47403
www.authorhouse.com
Phone: 1-800-839-8640

Published by AuthorHouse 2/11/2013

ISBN: 978-1-4817-0661-2 (sc)
ISBN: 978-1-4817-0662-9 (e)

Library of Congress Control Number: 2013901149

Cover art by: Tony Gleeson, www.tonygleeson.com
Cover design by AuthorHouse
Author Photo by: Nima Razfar, www.nimarazfar.com

Dedicated to Manie Barron and to those who are different.

CHAPTER ONE

Matador Juan Negro, "Azucar"

"The brother's nickname was "Mouse" and I met him through my cousin David on the Near Northside. What was I doing on Wells and Oak Street that balmy afternoon? Ahh yes, "Mouse"had copped the latest Sun Ra's ALBUM. And a really nice bag of Chicago Light Green.

Several of us avant garde music lovers had assembled in "Mouse's" family apartment to smoke a few joints and intoxicate ourselves with Sun Ra's "Beyond", or whatever he was playing. "Mouse" mentioned that he was about to give up his delivery boy gig at Carnegie Drugstore in the Drake Hotel, right over there on Michigan and Oak Street.

I seemed to be the only one who had heard what he said. "Gopher" was giggling uncontrollably at a chord that Sun Ra hit from six different angles. David, my cousin, was simply shaking his head at the audacity of Sun Ra's "Arabic approach" to the theme in the piece. "Skinny" had cupped his ears in his hands to better scoop up Sun Ra's most discordant musings. "Beyond" was circling the turn table.

"'Mouse', when're you giving up your gig?"

"Tomorrow. I've got to move on."

"Could I get it?"

"Yeah, the White folks don't care, all they want is a delivery boy. I think we all look the same to them anyway. Can you get over here by 4:00 p.m. tomorrow?"

"I'll be here."

"Mannn, did you hear the way Sun Ra just bent that note?"

———◆◆◆———

"Hilda, Frank, this is Chester Simmons, he's taking my place."

"O.K., we've got some stuff to deliver right now."

Simple as that. I had a beautiful little gig as a delivery boy on Chicago's Gold Coast, working every other day. I managed to pull my friend Johnny Fox aboard after the alternate boy left. Dream job, lovely circumstances.

We could alternate days. Or work five and five. The only thing the pharmacist and the people on the other side of the store, in the cafeteria, cared about was the prompt delivery of the drugs, sandwiches and ice cream. "Mouse" had left me with two pieces of advice – "You can make a lot of change if you hustle hard and don't steal too much."

I hit the ground runnin'. My delivery route was basically from Oak and Michigan Avenue to Sheridan Road and the area adjacent to the Drake Hotel. Every other day it was like I had taken a bus from a swamp to the Rivera. The contrast were unreal. I lived in the Almo Hotel, 3800 Lake Park Avenue, which may have sounded like a ritzy place to live. It wasn't.

The Almo rented rooms by the hour to the hoes from around the corner in the red light district. Prostitution was semi-legal in our neck of the woods, as well as drug selling and using.

Me, Momma and my sister lived in three rooms on the third floor; the transients, meaning the hookers, did their thing on the first and second floor. And the fourth floor was reserved as a R&R space for relaxing pimps and off duty hoes. It was what you might call a "mixed residence."

It was also a very dangerous place to live. Anything might happen at any time. Example coming right up. A sailor had his money ripped off while he's spending his half hour with "BiBi". He comes back the next night with fifteen or twenty of his mates to tear the place up. Big pachanga downstairs, the police came and wore their night sticks out on the sailor boy's heads.

An hour later, Miss Kitty, the quiet little ol' lady in the front room (#101) blasts a couple holes in this dope friend who was trying to break through the transom of her apartment. Mr. Jackson in the basement is caught trying to rape the little Brice girl. Several of the Brice men take him out in the alley and stomp his balls up into his belly, leaving him impotent for life. No one mourns his fate.

Several ex-cons, bringing their perverted senses of sexuality to the scene, try to rape me in a dark corner on the second floor. I wouldn't let it happen by kicking, punching, biting and kicking, punching and biting some more. Til one of them holding his battered eyeball, decided that my **ass** wasn't worth the trouble.

"Leave that lil' nigger alone'fore he kills somebody".

These men saluted me respectfully as I went in and out of the building every day because, number one, I hadn't screamed like a lil' bitch when they tried to get at me. And number two, I didn't snitch on them. I felt secure. I was a football player and a boxer, I could use my feet and my fists very well, but I never turned my back on these pedophilic gentlemen.

Hoes giving blow jobs on the dark stairs was a common occurrence. Sex was rampart, in all kinds of forms. I impregnated my first girl on the bathroom floor, on the Southside of the building. She wasn't a hoe, or even a loose piece, she was simply a tall, skinny yellow girl with alcoholic parents, who was hungry. Psychologically, she may have been hungry for love, affection and all that. But she was also physically hungry and she gave me what my screaming hormones wanted, in exchange for these ham sandwiches and ice cream that I was bringing home from Le Drugstore.

People sat on the cool front steps of the Almo drinking beer and wine all day and half the night, but there were no parties going on, just alcoholic fixes to keep the shakes from rattling their caged minds. The dope fiends shot dope in the toilets, the hoes hoed, the pimps pimped, the hard working people worked hard and we conexisted somehow. The only thing I had in common with the rich White folks I delivered drugs and sandwiches to on the Near Northside, the Gold Coast, was that we shared a common view of Lake Michigan.

They could see the lake from their windows, we had to go up to the fourth floor to see it, the same lake, different windows. I didn't spend a lot of time staring at the lake; I was into the petty hustles that my delivery boy job offered me. I was making more money in tips than many of the people in our building were spending on booze and dope. Here is the way I did it.

I jumped on the stick promptly at 4:00 p.m. (on the alternate days I worked, unless me and Fox had made other arrangements: "Hey, Chester, why don't you work four straight and I'll work four straight?" "Cool with me").

First thing to do was grab for the wrapped packages on the take out counter. This was always a little tricky because I had to get stuff in the right geo-money-tip order. Codeine laced cough syrup to Mr. Julian, way up the Outer Drive would be a quick two dollar tip. But Mrs. Tratt, of Tratt and Tratt, would be worth a five buck tip for a quick response to her call for a half pint of paregoric. Which druggie should be first?

I had no idea, when I first started, what these drugs were. I knew something about coke, smack, smoke, booze and a few pills. But paregoric? What the hell was that? It didn't take long to find out. Me and Fox compared notes.

"Fox, what's with this codine shit, and this paregoric?"

"It's dope, man, White folk's dope."

It didn't take much longer to see that they probably had as many dope heads on the Gold Coast as they had everywhere else, but they didn't have to deal with a dealer, they could order their poison direct from the drugstore. It was a revelation.

Petty Hustles: The fake Frenchman in the gourmet shop around the corner from the drugstore – "Le Petit Pavilion" – paid me to take his horse racing bet to Louie the bookie, the butcher at the Italian place two blocks away two dollars.

Louie the bookie asks me to deliver a small package of something to this woman in apt #104, 215 Chestnut, one of those exclusive New Yorky looking buildings with the tent draped across the entrance.

"Uhh package from Louie for Miss Fawn La Doe."

Buzzzzz…

Mizz LaDoe answers the door in a gauzy pink see through gown. She snatches the package from my hands and pushes a five spot down into my shirt pocket. Louie has already given me two to make the delivery, so I'm $7.00 ahead of the game. When I think back on it, I was probably delivering as much cocaine and high grade marijuana as one of the Mexican cartels, but I didn't even give it a second thought at the time.

Back to the drugstore for more deliveries. They had a policy of giving the delivery boy bus fare for deliveries to Sheridan Road. What was it? A mile or something? I took the bus fare, went through the tunnel to Oak Street beach and jogged back and forth, glancing at all the semi-naked white women en route. I didn't have any real social interest in the scene, I just saw the whole area as a place to "graze", make tips. On dozens of occasions, White women **and** men, hit on me.

"You're cute, you know that?" Little chuck under the chin from this boozed out, middle aged blonde with the full blown boobs. Never mind that, gimme a nice tip.

"Are you gonna be my regular delivery boy?"

"I really can't say, sir, we alternate."

"What's your name?"

"Chester Simmons."

"Well, Chester, you just give me your schedule of days on and I'll just order when you're on duty. Do you know who I am?"

"I've seen you on T.V."

"Do you like my show?"

"I haven't had a chance to really watch it, I'm too busy working."

"Well, that's too bad, here's a five spot, don't forget where you got it from."

"No Sir, I won't."

I discovered fifty different ways to dodge devious homosexual advances, the easiest way was to play dumb.

"Chester, I have some absolutely gorgeous photos I'd like to show you, would you like to take a peek?"

"Uhh huh."

Gorgeous photos? Men doin' it to each other?

"Well, what do you think?"

"You ain't got no photos of no fine ladies, you know, chicks with big titties 'n stuff?"

"Uhhh, no, I'm afraid not, I don't do that kind of photography. Here ya go, lad, see you next time."

"Thanks, Mr. Gorgeous Photos."

These were definitely not Almo Hotel thug-ruffians, so it was fairly easy to fend them off. I was definitely young, definitely Black, but certainly not dumb. Some of the ladies had a bit of a problem trying to process those elements. Especially the middle aged types.

"Chester, would you like a lil' hug?"

"No thank you, I might get in trouble."

"I won't tell if you don't tell."

"Sorry, Miss Lucy, I'm from Mississippi and where I come from delivery boys don't be huggin' they customers."

"Oh, you poor boy." Five dollar pity tip.

The young ones were the hardest to reject, the sophisticated teenagers who had been everywhere and done everything.

"C'mon in, Chester. You wanna have a Martini with me?"

"I don't drink."

"I got some great Moroccan hash, you wanna a hit?"

"I don't smoke."

"Well, what do you do?"

"I deliver packages from the drugstore, this one is $12.85."

"You wanna come back over after you get off? I could slip you up the back way. I'd like the talk with you about a couple things. You see, I don't believe in racial prejudice'n all that crap. That's for the ol' folks. Incidentally, my folks are gone for the weekend."

"You get anything smaller than a twenty? I don't have any change."

"Oh, that's awright, keep the change."

Wowwww! Bonanza! -- $12.85 for the package -- $7.15 for me.

"Uhhh, look, I don't know about comin' back over here after I get off. Maybe we could do it another time."

"You promise?"

"I don't make promises."

It was fairly easy to resist the temptations offered because I couldn't see any of it going anywhere. They wanted to see what it was like to do it to the delivery boy and then what? The worst case scenario in the back of my mind, despite the fact that I wasn't **directly** from Mississippi, was that we might get caught and I would have the rape charge draped around my neck. The other part of it was that I preferred colored girls/women over non-colored women. Hard to say where that came from, but there it was.

Back to Carnegie Drugs.

"Chester, go up to the kitchen and get these items." The kitchen of the Drake Hotel where the Caféteria got it's pastrami, cheese, ham bacon, pastries from. I loved the kitchen. It was like going to a football field long assembly line of foods. I would push my small flatbed dolly up one side and down the other, collecting goodies. Each station off the aisle featured something delicious.

On the right, pushing east; George the Greek, the bread man. George toasted and baked all kinds of stuff. If it was bread, he had it.

"So, what the fuck you vant now?"

"Here, here's the order slip."

He loads me up with buns, rolls, sour dough slices, rye slices.

A few yards away Müller and Heinzmann, the Germans who fried, baked, grilled, roasted every kind of meat I could think off.

"Vhat do you tink, Herman? You tink ve take heem and make a nize roast braun boy hahhahhah!"

It took awhile to get used to the crude humor of these two, to get used to the crude humor of the kitchen period, but I soon discovered their humor was a way to blow off steam.

Working in front of hell fire all day was not romantic or easy.

The salad bar. The big French woman who made such delicate little Japanesy looking salads, but always seemed to be in a foul mood.

"Naw what?! Cawn't you see that I'm busy?!"

"Here's the order from the cafeteria."

"Gotdamn! Doo Doo! Pee pee fuck!" Weird ass cusser.

Then, pushing back west, to my favorite person in the kitchen, the Mexican pastry guy, the one they called "Cantinflas." It took me awhile to find out why they called him "Cantinflas", but that'll come. And how "Cantinflas" changed my whole life around.

———◆———

"Hey keed, you got the rubbers, the onion skins?"

"Huh?"

"Oh! I thought you was the other guy."

A quick call to Johnny Fox to check the pastry cook's credentials – "Fox, what's the story with this funny lookin' little dude up in the pastry section?"

"Oh, that's 'Can-tin-flas', give him what he wants, he's cool." And thus began my relationship with Jośe Mangual, a.k.a. 'Cantinflas'".

Jośe wanted these onion skin thin condoms that we were "liberating" from the drugstore and I fell in love with these exquisite pastries that he was concocting in the pastry section.

"Wowww! Can-tin-flas, this is delicious as hell, what do you call it?"

"I call it Bomba de Nata de Cantinflas."

"Huh? What's that mean?"

"It cannot be no translacion, it's my creation."

"Well, all I can tell you is that it's delicious as hell."

That's the way it started. I came up to the kitchen to collect supplies for the cafeteria, supply "Cantinflas" with these onion skin thin condoms and feast on these delicacies that Jośe was making.

"Hey, Cantinflas, what do you call this one?"

"I tell the White peoples that she is called 'Brown Mountain', but **we** call it 'Sweet Brown Titty.'"

Very interesting dude. If you came up to the pastry section during his "down time" you might catch him reading a book. I had never found any of the other chefs reading anything heavier than a scratch sheet or a Playboy Magazine.

"Hey, Cantin-flas, what're you reading?"

"Octavio Paz, very difficil, you got the skins?"

So far as I was concerned it was a fair trade off, onion skin thin condoms for Bombas, or what he was making that day. Fox wasn't quite as pleased with the situation as I was; "Chester, look, man, I think the dude is cool too, but I think he's takin' advantage of us."

"How so?"

"Well, we're supplyin' him with these super thins and he's just givin' us cupcakes. I suspect he's re-sellin' these things to his own community and cleanin' up. He couldn't be fucking that much."

I had to agree with my friend Fox, but I didn't really give a shit whether "Cantinflas" was black marketeering or not. I valued the Bombas de Natas' way above the condoms. Of course, I would have to believe that Jose was a super sonic stud to be using all of these condoms every week, but, like I said, I put my taste buds above consideration for his sex life, real or otherwise.

Fox stopped his supply from happening, and that was that, nobody could complain to anybody about anything. Which left me and "Cantinflas" facing each other head to head. We broke it down to four thins per Bomba. He would bake me a wonderful cake to take home for twelve thins, if that's what I wanted, from time to time.

We weren't the only one's doing "corrupt" stuff. Everybody on the scene was doin' the do. "Pierre", the maitre d' of the store around the corner from the Carnegie Drugstore, Le Petit Pavilion, was doing what he had to do to get over. I was shocked to have him call out to me one evening as I was passing the gourmet shop on my way home.

"'Eh kid, you want to take some wine home?"

Wine? Home to the Almo Hotel. I was going to be a national – Almo Hotel-hero.

"Yeahh, sure."

Problem. The wine had arrived with the labels scraped in half, or the corks had been screwed in assbackwards. In any case, I arrived at the Almo Hotel with twelve bottles of excellent Beajolais Villages to peddle and, after the first bottle had been sold, no one would chance a second bottle because the word had been passed – 'that shit Chester got is sour as vinegar."

Actually it wasn't, but my neighbors and been alcoholized on sweet-sweet wines and anything that wasn't sweet was bitter.

It didn't matter a whole lot to me, I just kept doing what I was doing. It gave me a real good feeling to come "home", to our three rooms in the Almo, with twenty or thirty dollars, a bag full of turkey sandwiches, a couple quarts of melted peach melba ice cream and a few onion skin condoms. The condoms didn't go over big in our neighborhood. Most of the hoes didn't even require their Johns to use condoms. Then was then.

"Lulu, how do you stop yourself from gettin' pregnant?" I asked.

"See this?" She held up a simple, small bathroom sponge, "you wet it, stick it up in there and it catches all of them sperms." Something to be learned every day, all I had to do was ask. Back to the gig. Back to the pasture of big tips.

"Hey keed, you ever seen Cantinflas?"

"I thought you was Cantinflas."

"Hah hahhah, nawn keed, I ain't Cantinflas. They just call me Cantinflas 'cause I look like hemm, you wanna see the reel ting?"

"Yeah, sure."

"Got four skins?"

"Be right back."

There was really no problem to open up the bottom drawer on the left in the back room and take as many condoms as I wanted. The pharmacists didn't seem to care about the damned things. It was like they were dealing with something nasty or something. Maybe they were Catholics or something. In any case I was always careful not to take more than four at a time.

Four super thins for two tickets to the World Playhouse Theater in the Roosevelt University Building on 12th and Michigan Avenue.

"My cousin Manuel get these teekets for me, he work, a janitor in the Theater – 'eh José, they have a Cantinflas movie these weekend – but I cannot go I gotta do fuckin' pastry for these banquet. Go, enjoy."

Two tickets to the World PlayHouse Theater. Who could I take to see this Cantinflas thing with? I had to cross off a whole bunch of names in order to get to Sandra M…

The biggest reason was that I knew it was a foreign movie, this Cantinflas thing and who did I know that would dig a foreign film? I wasn't sure that Sandra M. would dig the movie, but I was lustin' after her a little so this would give me a chance to take her to an expensive movie and make my play at the same time. I called her and talked sweet bullshit for a half hour before she agreed to meet me at the Theater the next day.

"'Ca-tin-fast'? Who is that? I ain't never heard of nobody named 'Ca-tin-fast'".

"Cantinflas, he's a comedian. He's funny as hell."

"Really?"

"O yeah, make you laugh yourself silly."

"O.K., see you at six. If you stand me up I'll never speak to you again."

"See you in front of the Theater at six."

I made a mental note to be sure to take a couple of onion thins in my wallet. My teenaged plan, driven by lust demons, was to take in the movie and then steer Sandra M. into the Maryland Hotel on 63rd Street. They would rent a room to anybody. **<u>Anybody</u>**. All you had to do was sign a phoney name of the register and slip $10.00 through the slot at the bottom of the Plexiglas window. I thought about going to my place, the Almo, after the show, but I didn't want to tarnish my image, everybody thought I was an angel. Well, most of them did anyway.

———◆◆◆———

CHAPTER TWO

Friday evening six p.m. Sandra M. shows up promptly. Big hipped, heavy bosomed girl, chocolate skinned. She was already showing signs of being a middle aged housewife at fifteen. Or was she sweet sixteen?

"Hi Chester."

"Hi Sandra."

We got the biggest container of popcorn they sold and tripped on into this beautiful designed theater. Roosevelt University had been designed by Frank Lloyd Wright (I found out years later) and the theater was a reflection of his genius.

The theater was about three fourths full and most of the people were speaking Spanish.

"Ain't nothing but Mexicans up in here," Sandra whispered to me. I shrugged. What could I say? Mexicans had a right to go to the movies too.

Of course the Cantinflas film, an import from Mexico was subtitled. It took a minute or two for me to adjust to the idea but Sandra started squirming.

"I hate movies where you have to read what the people are sayin."

I ignored her squirming, her comments, and focused on the

character and the story. Cantinflas wore his pants low on his narrow hips, had a short suit coat, a crazy looking little hat and these two wisps of a mustache at each side of his mouth. And he was funny.

"Chester, this shit is boring." Sandra M. announced and slumped down into a serious nap. I wasn't bored and I didn't go to sleep. Mario Moreno, Cantinflas was the Mexican Charlie Chaplin, but since I hadn't seen Chaplin at that point in time I had no frame of reference for him.

I simply responded to the "Cantinflas vibe". There were times during the movie when I laughed 'way after the Mexicans laughed, but it didn't seem to matter. At one point, Sandra M. popped her left eye open and looked at me strangely – "Chester, you speak Mesican?"

"No."

"Then what're you laughin' at.?"

"This guy is funny." That's all I could think of saying to her. She propped her fist under her chin and snoozed on. I woke her up after the delightful little film was over and made a mental note not to ever have anything else to do with her. If she couldn't enjoy a guy as funny as Cantinflas, then she definitely would be a dud in bed.

———◦◦◦———

José Mangual, our Cantinflas in the pastry section of the Drake Hotel Kitchen, got his cookies out of hearing me describe what the film had been about. And looked real surprise when I started talking about the comic bullfighting scenes in the Cantinflas film.

"You got eet, keed! You got eet! I know these movie! It's one of his best! Oldie but guudie!"

"They say Cantinflas really want to be a matador, but the guy so fonny they don't take him serious. You know wot I'm sayin'? So, you wanna see real bullfight pichers?"

It wasn't too many weeks after that, that he called out to me – "Hey keed, you wanna go see a pelicula about the corrida?"

"Yeah sure."

"I get teekits for you. O.K?"

"Sure"

"Uhh, four onion skins?"

"No problema."

Four onion skins = two tickets. I didn't even bother to search around for somebody to go with me. Two tickets to see a flick about bullfighting. I would go by myself and save the other ticket for a souvenir.

No Sandra M., no bucket of popcorn this time; nothing to distract me from absorbing the life story of "Manolete", Manuel Rodriguez y Sánchez. The narration for the documentary was in English. Eat your heart out Sandra M. "Manolete", this tall, slim, sad eyed man seemed to be doing a dance that linked him to the bull's movements by the large cape he used at the beginning, and then the smaller, half moon shaped cape he used to make the kill.

What I saw made me think of some kind of magic. How could a hundred and fifty pound man control the movements of a thousand pound bull with a couple capes?

During the course of the documentary there were a few times when we got a taste of what could happen when the man lost control of the bull, the bull gored the man. It wasn't simply a well choreographed thing, that was obvious from the way the bull threaded his right horn into Manolete's left thigh as he went in for the kill.

Realistically, the film showed "Manolete" being gored several times. The narrator explained. . .

"The matador was gored seriously in the left thigh in his fight against a cathedral of a bull named "Primitivo", in the bullring at Seville. Ten days later he was pitting his skill and courage against another cathedral named "Mozambique" in the bullring at Malagá when he was wounded by one of the cathedral's antlers. The damage was done to his right buttock. Once again, as in Seville, he received his fifty-seven stitches without any anesthesia. His explanation was – "Anesthesia slows down the healing, I must be ready for my next fight in Madrid next week."

I was absolutely hypnotized by the whole scene, by all of it. I was even fascinated by the grainy textured scenes of the matador "Manolete" dying on the gurney in the infirmary of the bullring at Linares, after his femoral artery had been severed by the bull called "Islero". He killed "Islero" as "Islero" killed him. I don't know why but that struck a chord in me.

From that point on Cantinflas was sure to have his four 'skins. All he had to do was give me the names of the theatres where they were showing bullfight movies or documentaries.

After "Manolete", there was "The Life of Luis Procuna", Arruzza, Matador", Manuel Capetillo:, "Dominguin-Ordoñez". I can remember dozens of times when I was the only non-Spanish speaker in an audience of Spanish speakers, but I didn't give a shit; I was on the scene to check out the matador, not to have social interactions.

Maybe, I say, maybe, one of the things that got all up in me was that these young dudes; Mexicans mostly, but Venezuelans, Peruvians, Spaniards, were willing to put their nuts on the line. That had a crazy-macho appeal to me. It was either the bull's balls or his balls. The art of what they were doing and the way they were doing it began to appeal to me more and more.

Shit, most of them were only twenty or so, it was definitely not an ol'man's game. I started reading seriously about this art they called "Tauromarquia"/bullfighting. I was in a bubble by myself.

———————◆◆◆———————

"Cantinflas" looked forward to me coming up into the kitchen so that we could have these bullfight debates.

"So, who you think was the best – Dominguin or Ordoñez?"

"Hemingway liked Ordoñez more than he liked Dominguin. He said that Dominguin was too cold, too scientific, that his neck was too long."

"Awww fock Hemin'way! Fock that ol' man! He don't know everything! When Luis Dominguin got gored in the cojones n' got sewed up with no aesnasticos, he prove heemself to be a Superior man. You know wot I'm sayin?! Wot did Hemin'way do? He commit suicide."

We did a lot of that, me'n "Cantinflas"; lots of ying yang about whether Josélito was more masterful with the muleta than with the capote. Or whether Gaona was a greater killer than Frascuelo.

"Eeets all about the keel, keed, eets all about the keel. The matador can do many nice passes, you know wot I'm sayin'? But if he don't do the keel good – nada."

We argued in a friendly way because, well, who else knew anything about this stuff but us? We went back 'n forth about a lot of peple, but the one matador we didn't argue about was the great Manuel Rodriguez y Sanchez, "Manolete">

"From all I've read, they say "Manolete" didn't do a circus full of pases, but each one he did was done with "icy perfection".

"Si, that's what they say. That uncle had templé and sandunga up the ying yang."

Templé y sandunga. It took a long time to find out what those words meant.

Seems like I walked around for months with a weird secret burden on my head. Little donging bells had gone off in my head from the first time I saw the "Manolete" documentary. I could remember walking up the aisle of the World PlayHouse Theatre thinking, I'd like to do that.

It was just a random thought that banged around in my head for months. It seemed that the bubble I was in grew smaller and smaller. I felt like I was about to explode at times. I wasn't thinking about going into the boxing ring, playing major league baseball (I was too short – 5'10"— to think about baskeball) or soccer even. I was thinking about bullfighting. The thought seemed so out of the box. I couldn't even bring myself to talk about it. People, my friends, my family would've understood if I said that I wanted to be a musician, a drug dealer, a pool shark, a pimp, a biznessman, anything but a matador. When the pressure on my head got too great I decided to talk to the one person I thought would understand me – José Mangual, "Cantinflas".

"Eh keed, you know lotsa matadors get the horn in the cojones? They get the horn in the face. The bull ain't nuthin to play 'round with. You know wot I'm sayin'?"

I answered his skepticism in a completely cool way (had "Manolete" showed me cool, or not?). . . . "Cantinflas, amigo, I'm gonna get off into this because it's ordained for me. Dig it?"

"Cantinflas" made the sign of the cross on himself. And never offered me another ticket to anything at the World PlayHouse Theater. It was on me after that, everything. I had been enchanted, if you wanted to see it that way, by the bullfight.

Suddenly, Spanish #102 became important. Señora Jimenez, our Spanish hard knot, became one of my best friends.

"Please, eberybody, lissen to Señor Simmons' pro-noun-ciation care-forly."

But she couldn't do very much for me concerning the corrida puro. I smirked at her when I found out that she was a Cuban.

"Uhhh, Señor Simmons, I can gift you the proper pro-nun-ciations for the terms you are talking of, but I am a Cubana, I cannot say what the Andalusian, or the Galician pro-nunciations of those terms would be. It is the same with Mexico. So, why are you interested in the bullfight, for God's sake!"

———— ◆ ————

"BOBO"

"Hey, it was some crazy shit, believe me. Here we are, about fifteen or so, chasin' pussy, playin' baseball, football, handball on the building next to the Almo Hotel where he lived, and he's doin' all of this shit with us. O.K.? And better than some of us. But then he starts wavin' a half blanket around, like it was 'sposed to mean something; callin' out – "eh toro! 'eh hey! eh toro!"

To be frank about it. Some people thought he had lost his marbles, but they didn't know nothin' about bullfightin' or bullfighters.

None of us did at that time."

———— ◆ ————

JOHNNY FOX

"After he explained what he was about it didn't seem all that crazy to me. If you wanna be good at something, you have to practice. He wanted to be a bullfighter, so he had to practice. I understood that. It got to a cut off point with me when he asked to charge this large bath towel he was waving – "eh hey toro eh hey!"

"Eh hey, my ass!. You gotta pay me, man. I anin't gonna be chargin' into no towel for nothin', dig?"

———— ◆ ————

LEO ANDERSON a.k.a. "RAUL"

"I felt that I understood Chester better than most did because I had copped to the tango after going to see Valentino ten times. Doin' the tango was a funny bit too, for a lot of my friends, til I started teaching the tango at the Ida B. Wells Social Center and coppin' these middle aged Black school teachers 'n shit.

It was about that time that I started callin' myself "Raul" and wearin' a beret. Somehow it just seemed more natural to have a name like "Raul", rather than Leo. It also had something to do with the fact that I was a shade under six feet, thin as a rail...back then, and was light beige with semi-curly hair, what they used to call "good hair". I kept telling Chester – "hey man, if you really serious about this bull fight thang, you oughta change your name. From all I've read and heard about this scene, all of the dudes have names like "El Candi", "El Fandango", "El Hoochi", "El Loco" or something like that."

He took me up on my suggestion and the next thing I know he was calling himself "El Mongo", like the great conga drummer, Mongo Santa Maria. I was one of the few people he shared his bullfight name with because some of the folks in our 'hood thought he was a lil' bit weird, goin' out in the vacant lot behind the building he lived in, swirlin' this big blanket/cape around himself.

That was what he called his "Capote". And then he had a smaller half moon shaped piece of the same cloth he called his "muleta".

He could do some fascinatin' shit with both of these pieces of cloth. I can think back to some summer nights, late, when people would be sittin' out on their back porches drinkin' a lil' beer, smokin' a joint or two, tryin' to catch a breeze off the lake and "El Mongo" would be down there, swirlin' his "capote" around like mad.

"Hey, why don't you come up here'n fan that thing around? Hahh hahhah."

People laughed at what he was doin', but you would have to be crazy to think that he wasn't serious. He **was** as serous as a heart attack. I could definitely appreciate his energy, his devotion 'n all that. But where in the fuck could you find a bull to fight in Chicago?

The tango was workin' good for me. I had graduated to givin' "private lessons" to a few of the middle aged school teachers, but where would your money come from fightin imaginary bulls in the vacant lot?"

— ◆ —

MOMMA

"I think every mother wants to see her child succeed, but you have to be realistic about things. You'd have to be blind to **not** see that Chester was head-over-heels into this bullfight thang.

Chester, I must've asked him a dozen times by the time he was fifteen, "What're you plannin' to be, what're you goin' to do with your life?"

'I want to be a bullfighter, Momma.'

"That's what he told me. A bull-fighter."

"Chester, there ain't no bulls around here, and you damn sure can't make no livin' wavin' a piece of cloth around. You better go on down and fill out that post office application. They're hirin' for the Christmas rush, and after you graduate, you could go from part time to regular."

Don't get me wrong, it wasn't like he was a bad boy messin' with drugs and all that kind of thing. And he was always hustling; even cashin' empty bottles 'n cans into the re-cycle center to bring money into the house, but he had a definite fixation on the bull fight thing.

I just threw up my hands at one point and took him and his sister on that *loong* bus ride to see his Daddy at Joliet. I thought maybe Chester, Sr. could talk some sense into his head. Chester, Sr. was doin' time, but I have to give him credit, he was doin' everything he could possibly do to maintain a relationship with his kids. He wrote Chester and Louise long letters, talked with them on the phone as often as possible, and once a month, sometimes more often, we would take that *loong* bus ride to Statesville Penitentiary.

We had pretty much settled matters about Louise, she was either goin' to become a nurse or somebody's wife, maybe both. The problem was Chester wavin' these pieces of cloth around, talkin' about being a bull-fighter.

— ◆ —

CHESTER JR.

In 1968 I was five years old, just beginning to be aware of the world when my Daddy got busted for dealing coke. Ten years, ten loonng years was his sentence. I can't honestly say I missed the shit out of him, or anything like that, at first, because he wasn't exactly a homebody even before he got his dime.

I don't think the hammer really fell on my head 'til we, Momma, Louise, my sister, and me made a second visit to see Daddy at Statesville Penitentiary in Joliet, Illinois. It had to do with all of these bars everywhere, gates clanging open and closed. I was in jail, my Daddy was in jail and he was going to be there for awhile.

Jail scared the shit outta me! The gates opening and closing like there was some kind of invisible hand operating stuff. I was scared, but Daddy just seemed to be angry and defiant. Defiant, that's the best word I can think of to describe the way he was.

His eyes looked like snake's eyes, the flanges on both sides of his nose flared out like Puff the Magic Dragon, and when he smiled, he looked like he had just chewed on something bitter.

"Fuck these motherfuckers!"

I can definitely remember him saying that more than once during our early visits. Momma always seemed to be trying to cool him out.

"Chester, you better behave yourself…nobody lives forever and I know damned well you don't want to get more time tacked onto the time you're already serving." Thank God this was before the three strike/twenty-five-to-life sentences started happening.

When I was 'round about eight or so I started noticing a change happening with Daddy. It wasn't like he had become a punk or anything – he was still hard – but he didn't spend our whole visiting hour ranting about The System; or "White mother fuckers". Or why he had to do ten years for dealing cocaine – 'Shit! All of the fuckin' politrickians do coke and everybody knows it!"

"Chester, don't talk like that around the children, please baby."

Yeahhh, it was 'round about the third year that he seemed to have mellowed out.

"What're you plannin' to be when you grow up Chester? And how about you, Lil' Sistah?"

He had never asked me, asked us questions like that before. And he seemed to be really interested in our answers.

What did I want to be? I don't think, at eight, that I had even wasted a stray thought on anything that abstract. And I'm sure the question busted Louise between the eyes too because she was two years younger than me.

What did I want to be? Well, as a thoughtful young rascal I pushed it back and forth in my head a whole bunch of times, but I remember telling him – "Uhhh, I wanna be a fireman or a cowboy." Louise answered – "A nurse".

CHESTER SR.

I was on the downhill slope of a ten year bit for "Possession of cocaine with intent to sell." Intent, my ass. I was caught dealin', straight up. One of the things that some people have to get straight is that everybody in the pen ain't innocent. Now then, havin' said that…

I had done my share of petty dirt (breakin' 'n enterin', a couple robberies without a weapon, outright stealin') and a few short term bits, but that dime they stuck on me turned me completely around. A decade, ten long years, "a dime" for dealin' coke. That rally turned my lil' crime filled mind completely around. I started havin' nightmares about dyin' in the pen, away from my wife and kids. It got real heavy on me 'round about my third year.

I think that's when I made that commitment to myself, not to Jesus, Allah, Buddha, or nobody else but me. That's it, your criminal career is over. I had a woman who had stuck with me through my madness, a couple of beautiful kids. A lot to be thankful for.

I had a year to go, before the gates would swing open for me. Meanwhile, as some of the cons say, I had made the time serve me, rather than the other way 'round. I had my G.E.D., I had gotten into every program they had on the premises, and I knew as much about the computer as anybody. I was going to open up a shop when I got out, repair computers, make some honest money, go straight.

When Lillian told me that she was bringin' Chester Jr. up for me to talk with him about becomin' a bullfighter I didn't know what to think. I had a couple long talks with this dude we called the "Ol' Wise Man."

This was a brother servin' triple life for killin' a whole bunch of people -- "They were scum, they were supposed to be killed" – and had probably read every book in our library. It would be hard to imagine anything that he didn't know somethin' about.

"Bullfightin', huh? Well, first off I wouldn't put it in the same category as first degree murder. Or a whole bunch of other stuff I can think of. And so far as I know, it's not illegal in the state of Illinois. As a matter of fact, I don't even think they have a statue concerning the bullfight in Illinois.

If the kid is determined to fight bulls he's gonna have to go where people fight bulls; Mexico, Spain, Venezuela, Peru, places like that. Interesting profession, it's one of the few that I can think of, other than gang warfare, where the participant is running the risk of dying whenever he goes to work."

After a few hours of conversations like that with the "Ol' Wise Man" I felt that I had a leg to stand on. The whole thing still struck my funny bone in a kicky kind of way. Who in the hell would want to run the risk gettin' his nuts ripped out by an angry bull? For what?

As a model prisoner I was given the privilege of having a picnic on the lawn behind the bricks. We got right off into it with the tuna fish sandwiches. Lillian looked good enough to nibble on, but I had other stuff to deal with.

"So, son, you want to be a bullfighter, huh?"

"Uhh huh…"

"I guess you know that that means you're gonna have to leave the U.S., go to where they have bullfighting – Mexico, Spain, Venezuela, Peru, some place like that."

He sat up straight and blinked real hard a few times. It was obvious that he hadn't thought that far into the thing.

"Are you prepared to put America behind you?"

I loved the innocent expression on his face when he answered; "I'll be honest, I hadn't really thought about that, about, uhh, leavin' the country."

The "Ol' Wise Man" had loaded both barrels for me and I fired straight at Chester's head. I could see that he was serious, so I had to hit the target the first time around.

"Well, that's what you'd have to do 'cause you know you wouldn't be able to make a thin dime killin' these hamburger machines up in here."

Lillian, Louise and Chester smiled. I was making a point. I aimed a little lower.

"In addition to leavin' the States, there are a whole bunch of other things you should consider: number one, you're an African-American and if you went to, let's say to Mexico you might have a hard time because you're an American and they're not too happy about having foreigners comin' to take their jobs away."

He was taking it all in, and I could see that he was trying to figure out how to defend himself. I was relentless on his ass. The "Ol Wise Man" had primed me well.

"Look, Chester, don't get me wrong I would be the last person in the world to piss on your parade but we have to keep reality in plain sight here. I've talked with a couple of the Latino brothers here who knew something about bullfighting and they're telling me that dudes have to go through apprenticeship periods...."

"They call them novilleros."

"Oh, so, you're learning a little Spanish too."

"You have to, in order to be able to understand the terms'n stuff."

Louise was picking at the hem of her dress and looking somewhat pissed off because I was paying so much attention to Chester Jr. I felt bad about that, but I had to get this situation squared away.

"So, let's say you wind up going to Spain after you graduate from high school. Remember, you promised me and your Mom that you would get that piece o' paper..."

He nodded in agreement. He didn't look pleased at what I was saying but he **was** listening.

"Now how do you get to Spain, Mexico, Venezuela, Peru, any of these places? Last I heard it still costs money to travel from one country to another. And if you manage to get there, who will take you on, manage you and all that because, as you know, bullfighting, like prize fighting, is a business.

So, let's say I'm a Spanish bullfight manager. Would I want to take on a fifteen year old African-American guy over a fifteen year old Spanish guy? And finally, I'll just say this and drop the whole thing. What about the bulls themselves? It's one thing to see a bull in a pasture with his harem around him, it's another thing to get into an arena with a fighting bull who wants to tear your ass up. Do you have the heart for that?"

He looked me straight in the eye when he said, "I won't know 'til I get there Dad, I won't know 'til then . Look, Dad, Mom, I know you guys mean me well, that you have my best interests at heart, but haven't you always told me that I should follow my dreams, be the best I could be, no matter what it was?"

Me and Lillian nodded our heads like bobble headed dolls. What else could we do?

"And Dad, how many stories have you told me about my Grandfather, Big Chester, about how he had gone to different places in the world on rusty freighters when he was a young man?"

The minute he mentioned my Dad's name to support the argument he was making I knew that my stuff was shot down, my whole program shredded.

"Remember, Dad?"

"Yeahhh, I remember. But you have to also remember that then was then and now is now. And he was just doin' some adventurous traveling. He wasn't fighting bulls."

"But didn't he hang out with that great ol' bullfighter named Ernesto Suarez, 'El Encanto'?"

"Yeah, that's what he said…"

"And what about the presidential candidate, Mom? The Shirley Chisholm woman. What if she had let them talk her out of runnin' for president? She didn't make it but we'll always have to give her credit for trying. And we all know that some day we're gonna have another Black person run for president. What should we tell him or her? Don't go for it because it's impossible: Haven't y'all always told me? -- nothin' beats a failure but a try."

Lillian tried to make some kind of weak argument about how dangerous it was to be fighting bulls. He stabbed that one to death with this statement. Never will forget it.

"Mom, in all the bullfight books they always say – '…the fighting bull gets his size and strength from his father and he gets his fighting heart from his mother."

And that's pretty much where we had to leave it. It didn't seem to make a whole lot of sense to spend the whole two hours of visiting time trying to block his dreams. We turned our attention to Louise and her thoughts about becoming a nurse.

"That's a good idea, sis, then you can take care of me when the bulls get me." Chester Jr. joked.

It was one of the best visits we ever had and when our time was up, as I was hugging Lillian goodbye, I whispered in her ear.

"Baby, I think the boy is serious."

"I **know** he's serious."

I had twelve more months to go, one of the longest periods of time in my life and I think I must've spent some part of each day thinking about Chester Jr., about his dream of becoming a bullfighter.

Sister Louise

"I don't know where he got this notion from, to become a 'bull-fighter'." A boxer maybe, or somethin' like that, but a 'bull-fighter'? Who in the hell ever heard of a 'bull-fighter' comin' off the Southside of Chicago?

I thought, after we made this visit to see Daddy in the joint, that he had been talked out of the idea of being a 'bull-fighter', but nope, that ain't what happened.

Next thing I know he was back out there swirling that damn blanket/cape around again. It got to be almost embarrising. One of my girlfriends named Perline, who kinda liked him a lil' bit asked me, 'Don't he ever get tired of twirlin' that damned cape around?'"

What could I say?

"It don't look that way does it?"

HERB, friend

"One of the things I found out about Chester growin' up in the same neighborhood, right around the corner from each other, is that he was persistent as a pit bull. Once he locked onto somethin' he wouldn't let go."

------◆-◆------

Chester, himself. . .

"I guess the best description I could offer of myself at that point in time would be obsessive. I grabbed every book I could find that said anything about bullfighting, bullfighters. I had facts and figures about who had done what and where; but who could I talk with about this? Nobody. Well, other than Cantinflas.

I felt like somebody who was in a strange kind of bubble. I was in a world that was completely different from all of the people around me. And, to tell the truth, I did feel a lil' weird at times, 'specially in the winter time when I would go over to the lakefront park with my homemade capote, the large cape; and my muleta, the smaller half moon shaped cape that I draped across a broomstick pretending that it was a sword.

It was all imaginary, the thousands of people screaming 'Olés!' as I performed my slow statuesque veronicas and media veronicas with the capote, bringing the horns of a huge black bull closer and closer to my side.

I wrapped my wool scarf around my ears to keep them from freezing as I pretended that the treacherous winds whipping in off Lake Michigan were forcing me do more dangerous passes, forcing me to cope with Nature as well as this cathedral of a bull who was trying to stab me to death with his huge wide spread horns.

Lots of other stuff was happening while I was doing serpentinas and chicuelinas antiguas on the strip of park bordering the lake. But it was like – hey, it's over there, it ain't got nothing to do with me, even if I only thought of it in a peripheral way. Like out of the corner of my eye.

The Black Matador, "Sugar"

The biggie was Dad getting out of the slams. He hit the streets whirling like a dervish.

"I'm forty-two fuckin' years old, I've just spent the last ten locked up, I don't have a minute to waste."

The first thing he did was pull us out of the Almo Hotel.

"This is not a good environment for nothin' or anybody." We were **not** kickin'n scream'n when we moved into this two bedroom apartment over on Bowen Avenue. We were still in the ghetto but the edges were not quite so rough. Dad had been sending out job applications and stuff during his last six months in jail and landed a nice gig in a computer repair shop downtown.

"I can't complain, the pay is decent, the ol' White guy who owns the place likes to go fishin' a lot and he trusts me. What more can I ask for? Gimme a couple years and I'll have my own shop."

A couple other things were happening too. I got fired from my delivery boy gig. I suspect that they had discovered that I was stealing more onion skins than they were selling, in addition to all of the other lil' corrupt shit that I was doing. Hilda, the major league blonde/racist/pharmacist was the only one given the pleasure of 'releasing' me.

"Sorry Chester, you won't be needed here tomorrow."

Johnny Fox, my alternate, was given a similar dismissal.

"You know I was expectin' somehin' like this, 'specially after we mentioned somethin' about a delivery boy's union, but I didn't expect it to be this cold blooded."

I was temporarily at sea before the post office crooked it's finger at me. I was outright happy because the post-office saved me from a confrontation with my Dad. The prison experience had turned this dude into an outright dickhead. He was working his ass off in the computer repair shop. He had Louise in an apprentice nursing program and Momma was doing an online course in 'Business Practices.'

"Lillian, you're gonna be the one runnin my shit when we get this Small Business loan, so you may as well get into how stuff is done."

He didn't give me a hard time, but he made it plain that I would be expected to pull my share of the load. He did it in a cool way.

"Chester, you've been the man of the family since I've been away, but now I'm back and everbody is goin' to have to follow my lead."

I thought he came across a bit too authoritarian. I mean, where was he when I was growin' up? Don't misunderstand, I could understand where he was comin' from, but he sorta grated on my left nerve by being so self righteous. Like I said I was outright happy when the post office called me in. People were congratulating me---"Ohhh, Chester, you got a good gig now, all those benefits 'n what not."

"Mannn, your credit reference are gonna go sky high!"

So I had to fold my capes up for a little while to do the zombie thing at the post office. The pay ($15.00 something an hour) was quite decent for the time, but the pay couldn't compensate for the boredom I suffered. Seventeen-and-a-half year's old, fresh out of high school (my school mates screamed "O yea!", O yea!" "O yea!" when I received my diploma. They were being sarcastic about my love for the corrida).

Now what? After six months of sitting on a collapsible seat, pushing letters into the proper boxes, hour after hour, I was beginning to understand why so many of the regulars came to work drunk, or went across the street for the half hour "lunch hour" to try to drink themselves into a stupor. Or drop enough Dexedrine tabs to stay awake for their eight hour shifts. The boredom of the post office was bad, but my scene at home was getting worse. Like I said, Dad had landed on the ground whirling like a dervish. The problem with me is that he was an authoritarian dervish.

"Chester! do this! Chester do that! Chester, go do that! Chester, c'mere! Do this!

Mom seemed to like to see her man in charge an all that, and Louise wasn't far behind, but he pissed me off. Here's somebody I haven't seen in ten years and now he's ordering me around like a servant or something. I was working, I was bringing money home. Why would he have to treat me like a punk?

It popped to the surface real hard one evening. Luckily there was nobody home but the two of us, just me and Dad. He had been home almost two years and had plans for the family.

"Chester, you're out of school now, you're down at the post office part-time and, if you're lucky, you could wind up working full time in the next year or so.

Yeah, I know you hate workin' at the post office, its about as exciting as watchin' ice melt, but you got good benefits and a strong union. Lots of dudes would like to have a gig like that."

I didn't say anything, I just sat there listening, trying to figure out where this was going to go.

"We haven't talked about you goin' to college because it seems that what you're most interested in is somethin' that they don't teach in college…"

I started to speak but he shut me down with an impatient gesture. I was beginning to hate that too. He could talk to me but I couldn't talk to him.

"Now what I'd like to have you do is come in with me. Ol' man Gelman has practically given me the day to day operations of the shop. No doubt in my mind that he's gonna be retirin' pretty soon and I'll have the shop. He's already hinted that he'll sell me the shop outright, or I'll have a major interest in it. It's got a damned good location, the money is comin' in good, I know that from dealin' with the books…."

"Dad, I don't want to be a computer repairman."

I could see from the way he was clenching his jaw muscles that he was becoming real agitated.

"Awright, Chester," he started in real cool, "you hate workin' in the postoffice and you don't want to become a computer repairman. So, what do you want to do:"

I felt like screaming, but I made my cool match his cool.

"I want to be a matador, a bullfighter."

The gloves fell off, it was on. It was Dad and me…

"Goddamnit, boy! What the fuck are you talkin' about?!" This is the U.S. of America! Ain't no fucking' bulls to fight up in here! Can't you see that?!"

"Yes, I can see that there are no bulls to fight here, so I'll have to go to where the bulls are!"

"Chester, don't be talkin' this crazy shit to me! Do yourself a favor and drag your head out of the clouds and stop daydreamin', stop talkin' this stupid shit about bulfightin'; I'm tired of hearin' this crazy shit!"

"It ain't crazy shit, Dad. It may sound crazy to you because you've never had dreams, your thing was stealin' and robbin' until you got caught sellin' coke. I have a dream, why don't you give me a fuckin' break?!"

We were seated at opposite ends of the kitchen table and I could see that he was getting ready to come around the table and kick my ass. Or, he was going to **try** to kick my ass. I had already made a decision to jump up and snatch one of Mom's twelve inch butcher knives and stab the shit out of him. I was damned near eighteen years old, I was a man already, I was not going to take a "spanking"/

Fortunately for me, for him, Momma and Louise came in and prevented a crime scene from happening. I'm pretty certain that they snagged the fringes of what might've happened, but everybody played it cool.

"Let's have somethin' to eat, I'm starved," Momma said, and stared from one angry face to another. I could tell, from the last angry glare that Dad flung my way, that I was going to have to exit the scene as soon as possible. Or, be forced to stab him to death because I was definitely not going to take a "spanking".

<hr />

That's pretty much the way it went for a couple months. I mean, that's what the level of tension was between us. I made it my business to be out of the pad when I knew Dad and I might be on the premises at the same time. I didn't want us to have to have another go 'round with each other. It was time for me to go, I felt that. It was like the old bull and the young bull, couldn't be but one or the other on the scene at one time. The problem/dilemma I had was about how to fully support my exit. I didn't want to jump out there, fall on my ass and be forced to have to ask for a bailout.

The solution hit me like a sock full of rocks. Get a roommate, somebody to split expenses with. Yeahhh, that would do it. I did a quick survey of all the dudes I knew who might be elgible.

Johnny Fox. "Hey, I can dig where you're comin' from Chester, I definitely can. The only reason I haven't decided to take that step is because, well, right now would be a bad time for me. I just started junior college and both of my parents have promised, if I make it through the two years of the junior college bit they'll help me go on to the college of my choice"

"So, you're saying that you want to stay at home until you graduate from college, four years from now?"

"It ain't like I'm tryin' to take advantage of them or something, I'll be able to pay them back in spades when I get my degree."

"What're you plannin' to major in?"

"Uhh, I haven't quite decided yet. It looks like a toss up between criminal law an Phys. Ed."

BoBo. "When the brother approached me about doin' the roommate bit. I have to admit I was tempted. But then, he started layin' out all these rules'n regulations that we would have to follow and I thought, oohh no, not me. He made it sound like we were gonna be a boot camp or something; beds have to be made, we would take turns cleanin' up the pad once a week, no orgies'n shit.

I thought, hey, what's the point of havin' two dudes sharin' a pad if we couldn't do our thang. You know what I'm sayin'? I had to say thanks, but no thanks."

Herb. "So, what do you think, man?"

"I would've been down for it last week, Chester, but I just joined up, I'm goin' into the Army."

"Into the Army, for what?"

"Well, they got good benefits and the recruiter says I'll get a chance to see the world."

"Did the recruiter tell you you could get your ass shot off?"

"Shit, that could happen right here, right now."

"Raul" was like my last hope. And he let me down hard. Well, in one way, but he made up for it in another way.

"Nope, not me, pal. I'm about a month from shackin' up with this middle aged woman I met in my tango class. She's tryin' to convince me that she's twenty eight, but I saw her driver's license, she's pushin' thirty five.

"Frankly, it doesn't really matter, it's time for me to get out there and do the survival tango, no matter what. Is that what's happenin' with you? Family pressure?"

"Something like that."

"Raul" stroked his little Van Dyked chin for a couple seconds.

"Chester, look, you're just about the only dude I would do this for…"

"Uhhh, what's that Raul?"

"Well, I got a couple loose chicks in my tango class over at the Center who are just dyin' to get into what they call " a relationship". Dondisha Phillips is about twenty-five I think, a kindergarten teacher, fresh outta Yazoo City, Miss'ssippi. Big ol'chit' lin fed sister with about much grace as an ox. Every time we dance, and I do that lean back movement with her I'm afraid I'm gonna drop her. Or else she's gonna fall on me."

"You say you got a couple in your class?"

"Yeahhh, the other one is from Lou'siana, jet black hair, sorta slanted eyes, beautiful body. I think she mentioned she used to be a gymnast when she was younger. She's a social worker. Light beige skinned."

"Doesn't sound like a bad catch to me."

"Raul "stroked his chin hairs again."

"Well, you'd think that, just from looking at Condizza."

"That's her name?"

"Yeah, Condizza R. Le Forté. I don't know what the R. stands for. The only problem with her is that she seems to have some emotional issues."

"What's that mean:"

"I'm not sayin' the sister is crazy or anything like that, but she's definitely a lil' bit neurotic. I think it's got something to do with her Creole background.

After class is over we do a lil' socializing, that's how I hooked into Stella."

"This is your middle aged woman?"

"Correct, Stella McMillan. We're standin' around talking, I had the pick of the patch 'cause I'm the only man on the scene. We had one other brother for awhile, but he was so gay it was hard to tell which one was supposed to be wearin' a dress. Can you do the tango?"

Can I tango? "I don't think so, I never tried."

"No problem I'll teach you. You're gonna have to do the tango to get at Dondisha or Condizza."

———◆———

It took a week to get the basic steps down, but because of my work with the capote and the muleta, I didn't have any problems with the look you're supposed to have doin' the tango, those arrogant gestures 'n stuff. I had that down cold. "Raul" even complimented me." Well, Chester, I have to tell you, you damned sure look like a tango dancer. Now, let's get into some of these triple back steps, some of my personal shit."

For the next two weeks, every moment that I wasn't at work, I was at Raul's, picking up "Raul's" pet stuff. Funny scene happened one Saturday afternoon. Me and "Raul" really had it goin' on. I was pretending to be the lead, the male and "Raul" was playin' the female role. He was leanin' back in my arms with his back arched all up and everything, with this smoldering, sultry expression on his face, when his Dad walked in. I would give a zillion bucks to have recorded/photographed the expression on his Dad's face. O my God! My son is a goddamned Sissy!

I have to say that that was the only conclusion his Dad could reach coming from where he was comin' from. But, strangely enough, he didn't say a word to either one of us; he just staggered through our front room-tango dance scene, shaking his head from side to side.

So, now I've seen it with my own eyes, my son's a fuckin' sissy. "Raul" didn't seem to be too disturbed.

"See", he whispered to me as he went to change the music, "that's the way he thinks. That's one of the big reasons why I'm getting' outta here."

"Uhh, Raul, my brother, I can definitely understand where you're comin' from."

"O.K., so, now lets get back to this sexy ass drag pattern again. Thing you have to remember is that the tango was originally an African dance…"

"An African dance?"

"You heard me. An African dance that was co-opted by the European immigrants to Argentina. I did my research. Originally, believe it or not, this was a dance between two males. Can you get ready for that?"

I had to nod – no, no, no. "Raul" was deeper than I thought he was.

"O yes, robust, muscular, masculine shit between two males. I did the research. Now, how it got to the way it is, between male and female, I don't know. Maybe it was a European adaption of the original. In any case, it is what it is. Now, let's go back to that improvisational phase. When I introduce you to my class I want them to see you as my equal, or almost. It'll speed your game up. Dig?"

"Raul" was moving me fast, but I could understand where he was comin' from.

"If I said – "Oh, incidentally, this is my friend, Chester from duh' hood", they would look at me like I was crazy. But if I brought you on the scene as "Chester Simmons", who happened to learn the tango in Argentina, then that would open up another door. I would suggest that you immediately take your ass to the library and find out all you can find out about Argentine Tango".

"Raul" did something intensive with me every day. --- "You have to make the bitch feel like you wanna fuck her every time y'all dance, or else the whole thang will play off as a, what do you call it? As "caricature"? Tango may not be real, but it's got to look real. Somebody might even get some pants after it's all over; everything depends on what the vibe is. Dig?"

I didn't resist anything. When "Raul" said, "awright, Chester, fuck the bitch right there, in front of everybody. Make her **feel** that dick you wanna put in her. But more important than anything else, make the audience feel your performance."

I didn't have a real big problem understanding what he was tryin' to promote. The problem was tryin' to make it seems real, dance after dance.

"'Chester, that's the challenge. You've got to make the audience feel your hard-on, or else the shit is **not** gonna work. I don't wanna try to brag on myself or anything, but in our classes, and when we do performances, when we wind up, just about everybody, male and female, thinks that I'm fuckin' my partner. You have to cultivate that feelin. Dig?"

I was dazzled by "Raul's" expertise, but he shoved it right back at me.

"Chester, hey look, my brother, maybe if you weren't into this bullfightin' thang, I wouldn't be able to teach you shit. But since you are, you can see aspect of the dance that I can't see, Dig?"

I couldn't see shit for a long while; I was comin' to "Raul" to learn how to do what he called "The Survival Tango."

But there were many aspects of the bullfight that seemed to have a lot to do with his type of tango. First, shit was semi-rough; it was like – "c'mere, bitch! Gimme what I want!"

I translated that to a bull who didn't want to cooperate, one of these creatures who had established a "querencia", a place where they wanted to be and there was nothing you could do with your cape to lure them out of that position.

That was the way I saw Condizza R. Le Forté and Dondisha Phillips. Both of them had established a "querencia", and it was my job to get them to come out, to charge the matador, so that I could do something with their bullish heads.

"Raul" was a great help. He played his role out for me after our second class.

"Awwww Chester, Chester, Chester, my man, you got 'em goin', my brother! You got em goin', my brother! You got e'm goin!"

"What's that mean?"

"It means, after you finished that intermediate step lean back, that Miss Creole, Condizza R. Le Forté, was just about ready-ready to fling her panties in your face. And then you did the same thing with Dondisha. Now they both want to fling they panties in your face."

"So, now what?"

"You have to figure it out."

CHAPTER THREE

I chose Dondisha Phillips, rather than Condizza R. LeForté. It was a haarrrd decision to make. I liked Condizza, I really did. And I sneaked away with her a couple times after we finished our tango classes, but it didn't take but a moment to realize that the sister had "issues', as "Raul" described then.

"Chester, why do we have to come here, on the Southside, to have a glass of wine? Why can't we go over on the Northside, with the White folks, where people really understand wine?"

"Uhh, 'scuse me?"

"You know what I'm saying. Black people don't really have the palate for fine things…"

"Uhh, Condizza, don't you think you're being a bit prejudiced, a bit too judgmental?"

"I don't think so."

I think that did it for me, I've never liked dogmatic, hard edged people, the ones who have never made a mistake, who are never wrong. I did it as diplomatically as possible, but I did it, I edged Miss LeForté off of my romantic screen. Like I said, it was a haarrrd decision to make because, well, the girl did have a fine body on her. But I could foresee endless problems with her mindset and I wasn't quite ready for that.

Dondisha Phillips ragged on me for a few minutes when I invited her to have dinner with me.

"Why me, I thought you were into light skinned women?"

I had to put on my knee pads for a little while to overcome Dondisha's negative shots at me, but I managed to do it by meeting her at my favorite Thai restaurant.

"This is nice, Chester, real nice."

She liked the atmosphere and all, but I don't think she cared all that much for the food.

"Chester, what kinda gravy is this?"

"That's coconut milk."

"Milk? I didn't know you could cook with milk."

Warm chocolate skinned, beautiful lips, eyes, face, earrings. A damned kindergarten teacher from Yazoo City, Miss'ssippi. By the time I started on my second Singha beer I was really warming up to her. It was easy to do because she was, how shall I say this? So simple and down to earth. "Raul" had whispered some important stuff into my ear.

"Chester, you gotta remember two important things about Dondisha; number one, she's from Yazoo City, Miss'ssippi and number two, she's a kindergarten teacher. That means she's square as a brick and she spends most of her wakin' moments around lil' munchkins barely two feet tall."

I took careful notice of the way she was, the way she behaved. She was a full grown woman, no doubt about that; with these gorgeous chocolate bulbs straining to pop out of her low cut dress. I was looking at enough cleavage to run a Mack Truck through. And when she bounced up to go to the ladies, I took a harder look at these two lovely globes rotating under her purple satin dress. What was she? About 5"6'? About a hundred and forty? The image that came to my mind was of ripe grapes. Her breasts were ripe grapes, her buttocks, her cheeks, but if she wasn't careful the grapes were going to bust wide open and she would be a big fat mess.

My estimated time for this to happen was about three-five years. She was twenty-five. Yeahhh, she would be ripe for another three-five years and then pop! She would be big as a house. I was thinking so hard I didn't notice her easing back into the seat across from me.

"Chester, what are you thinking about?"

"I was just thinking of what a fine woman you are, Dondisha."

It was a beautiful thing to see this reddish tinge suddenly blaze up under this warm chocolate. She was blushing. I had gotten to first base; it was time to try for a home run. I reached across the table to hold both of her well manicured hands in mine. Her soft palms were warm and sweating a little.

"You know, guys like me, who barely made it out of high school, seldom have a chance to have a date with beautiful, educated sisters like yourself."

She tightened her grip on my hands and gave me her intense kindergarten teacher's look.

"Oh, Chester, you can't go around thinking like that. Having an education ain't the whole thing. Lots of people have degrees but they don't have any Mother Wit. I'm one of those people who happen to believe that the greatest gift a person can have is to be able to look another person in the eyes and tell the truth."

The Moment of Truth. I couldnt've said it any better myself. I liked Dondisha. "Raul" was right, she was square as a brick and as down to Earth as could be. By the time she finished her second beer and started in on her banana pudding, she was laughing just a wee bit too loud; playfully patting me on the cheek and her Miss'ssippi drawl had become darker. She made me think of front porches with magnolia bushes growing up on each side of the steps, corn bread, sweet potato pies baking, pecan trees in the back yard, people moving slowly through the humidity, Miss'ssippi.

———◆◆———

We stood in front of the restaurant for a few minutes, trying to decide what to do next.

"Dondisha, you want to go dancing somewhere?"

She threaded her arm through mine and smiled up at me "Not tonight, I've had enough dancing for this week."

We exchanged understanding smiles; "Raul" had danced our socks off during our Monday and Wednesday evening tango classes.

"Well, why don't I just take you home? I'll go back in the restaurant and call a taxi."

"We don't need a taxi, I'm parked over here."

She lived in a nice apartment complex in Hyde Park, miles away from our place on Bowen Avenue. We just made aimless chit chat on the way to her place. It was obvious that neither of us had given any serious thought to me going home. I was about to round the bases. Miss'ssippi, home run.

-------◆◆◆-------

The pressures were building. Dad was rolling his eyes at me about one thing or another; Mom was on my case about staying out late so often.

"Now Chester you can't be hangin' round out there in the streets. When you get off from work, bring yo' ass on home."

I was about to go crazy with impatience, and from trying to juggle so many things at one time. I was spending as much time as I could at Dondisha's place, but I had to take it slow. I had already made it clear to her that I was right on the cusp of leaving my family and going off on my own. I was trying to tie that psychological knot around her head that would lead her to saying, "Well, why don't you come in with me?"

It was August already and, as everybody knows, September is the beginning of the Big Chill in Chicago. I couldn't stand the idea of spending another winter in the same apartment with Mom, Dad and my sister. I decided to do some drama to speed matters up between me and Dondisha.

"Raul" had moved in with his middle aged woman and was "living happily-ever-after." "It's real sweet, Chester, real sweet. I can't think of nothin' sweeter than layin up behind this big ol' soft body every night. I can tell, just from lookin' at her, that you got Dondisha's nose wide open. So, wass up?"

"It's only a matter of time, 'Raul', only a matter of time."

Dramatically, this was my play. I made one of those "desperation-urgency" calls to Dondisha at just about the right time of evening. I knew she would be on her second bowl of Hagen Däaz Vanilla ice cream, watching the evening comedy shows.

"O hi Chester…"

"Dondisha, I need to talk with you, I need to see you…"

"What's wrong, baby, you sound upset."

"It's me and my Dad…"

"You want me to come pick you up?"

"No, I'll be over in about a half hour."

"O.K., you had anything to eat?"

"Uhhh, no, not this evenin'."

"Well, don't worry. I got some greens 'n corn bread for you."

"Sounds good, see you in a little while."

I filed around the edges of my game on the way to her place. I wanted my story to be air-tight. Me and my Dad had finally gotten into it and he kicked me out. I had no where to go. Could I spend a few days at your place?

Lovely down-home girl. She met me at the door with a plate of greens and corn bread in one hand and a spare set of keys in the other hand.

"Chester, don't worry 'bout nothin', you can stay here with me 'til you get yourself together."

I breathed a deep, deep sigh of relief. I was over; I couldn't wait to tell "Raul" the good news.

———◆◆◆———

"Don't tell me that the tango ain't magic! Look at us, we're all hooked up just because of the tango. I look at all those crazies goin' over to Budland and Mambo City every Friday and Saturday night, shakin' their asses and sweatin', doin' the Funky Dog like maniacs."

"Hey, 'Raul', don't knock the Funky Dog, it's got its place too."

"Yeahhh, I guess you got a point there, home. So, how's the domestic life treatin' you?"

"Couldn't be sweeter, man, couldn't be sweeter."

Well, after only six weeks of knock down/drag out love making, what else could I say?

———◆◆◆———

I got the feeling that Dad wasn't too terribly pissed off to see me take my blankets/capes and my attitude out of his house. The good part of it is that we didn't part on an ugly note. He slipped me a hundred dollar bill and whispered, "Chester, you're really lucky when you can find somebody who's in your corner, stay focused and keep your nose clean."

Momma was quietly outraged and she let me know it.

"I think it's tacky to be shackin' up with somebody. I thought we had raised you better than that."

I guess, to keep her ranting down, I lied about my situation.

"Actually, we're just doin' what you might call a trial thing, our intention's to get married."

"When?"

"In the Spring. Yeahhh, in the Spring, probably around June."

"Well, let's see…"

Dondisha

"I ain't good at lying. I felt like my knees were about to give out the first time Chester held me in his arms in the tango class. It would be hard to put my finger on it, but there was just something about the way he carried himself. He was such a *man*.

Yes, indeed, he was such a *man*. I had my eye on him from the beginning., but it seemed that he was more attracted to this high yaller neurotic named Condizza R. LeForté. Fortunately, I was mistaken. I almost blew the whole thing.

He invited me to dinner and I almost turned him down because I didn't feel too good about being seconds. I have to admit I was wrong about him. Maybe he was just feeling his way along. I hate to admit it but I gave in to him the first time we went out. I just couldn't help myself, he brought my love down so hard.,,

I knew he was younger than me, eighteen to my twenty-three; which didn't exactly make us May – December or anything. I gave myself a good talking to about the possibility of us developing a relationship. Don't push it, just go with the flow, don't push it…

I knew, after a little while, that he wasn't getting along too well at home. He told me all about his father coming home from prison, acting like a dictator and all. I was feeling him, no doubt about that. So, when he called on me, with nowhere to go, I felt like my secret prayers had been answered."

"Dondisha was a square, no doubt about that, but she had a lot of what she called "Mother Wit". We were into our second week of being together when she suggested that we both get AIDS/HIV/STDs testing.

"Chester, look I know you ain't got nothing and I ain't got nothing either, but I don't think it would be a bad idea to get tested. I mean, let's face it, we're up in here together and I know you don't want to be pulling a condom on every time we make love."

"But, what about you getting pregnant?"

"I went on The Pill the day after we went to the Thai Restaurant."

The AIDS testing and all of that was sort of like getting married. What it signified is that we were goin' to be faithful to each other. I had never been a big time bed jumper so I was cool with that. In addition, I liked the idea of us being down front about stuff.

I don't know what we had been doin' before we took our test, which came out negative on all sides; but thereafter our sex lives ballooned to another level. It got to the point where we would start undressing each other the minute we found ourselves in the same room. What made it so sweet is that we had roughly the same hours -- 9 – 5 p.m.

If I got home before she did I would throw something together for us. I was into baked fish, rice, pasta without tons of meat sauce on it, what some people call health food cookin'. Dondisha was comin' from another place. I had to ask her to stop frying everything – "Dondisha, why don't you bake the chicken sometimes? It tastes pretty good like that."

At 5'10" and 155 pounds I was concerned about gaining weight. Whoever heard of a fat bullfighter?

I loved this lovely thing we did at 10 p.m., but I wasn't prepared for the Hagen Däaz and pound cake she wanted to put into my mouth afterwards.

"Dondisha, I'm not hungry, baby."

"Makin' love gives me an appetite…"

We had little snags happen here and there, but basically things were on track. Financially, we were doin' well. She made a nice salary and as we edged into November the post office started giving us lots of overtime. I paid the utilities bills, brought groceries, made sure that we had tickets to concerts and stuff. I also had myself a little savings account. I put a bit in it every other week, just to be able to say I had something on the side.

In addition to a full fledged sex life, we had a pretty well developed social life; the tango on Monday and Wednesday, going out to parties and stuff on the weekends. But, like I said, we had little snags going on, from time to time.

The first big snag happened in December. I got in after a twelve hour day at the mind numbing post office and she had fried a chicken, made a thick macaroni and cheese casserole and had opened a bottle of this too sweet wine that I hated.

"Chester, there's food on the stove, if you want something to eat. I'm in here."

I was hungry but I didn't want any fried chicken, macaroni and cheese or too sweet wine. I strolled through the apartment, feeling out of sorts, and she was curled up on top of the white eider down cover, "dressed" in her favorite red velvet night gown with the spaghetti straps straining to hold her full breasts in check.

"You ain't hungry?"

"Naw, I had a late lunch at work."

I went into the bathroom, undressed, put on my pajama bottoms, brushed my teeth, came back out and slipped under the cover on my side of the bed.

"Night, Dondisha."

"Uhh, good night, Chester."

I could feel her get up and slide under the cover beside me but I was too worn out to care about it. I knew what she wanted, but I had decided – sleep tonight, sleep comes first.

———◆———

I took a close look at the raccoon circles under "Raul's" eyes and eased over to him just before our Monday class started.

"Wass up, brother? You look a bit whipped about the eyes."

He gave me this little lopsided smile.

"I could say the same about you."

We exchanged lopsided smiles. You too huh? Uh huh. No words

were exchanged to explain what was happening, all we had to do was look at us and look at our ladies. Dondisha and Stella were flitting around like butterflies while we were draggin' our ass, nookied out.

"Raul's" tango was beginning to look a bit baggie at the knees and I hadn't waved my cape around since I moved in with Dondisha. Me and "Raul" made a silent agreement that evening, we've got to break out of this sexual slavery thing. I don't know what "Raul" did, or how he did it, but I just basically told Dondisha….

"Look, girlfriend, much as I like it, I can't come up in here every night snatchin' your panties off. You know what I'm sayin'?"

She did a lil' pout, but she nodded – yes. I know what you're sayin'. Aside from putting a little breathing space between our sex acts, I took a closer look at Dondisha's booty and thighs. That thing that I had predicted about her ripe grape shape was happening, Dondisha was getting fat.

Some people might've said it was because she was happy, pleased with our life together. I saw it was a result of undisciplined gluttony. I made a cold bloodied decision to talk to her about eating so much of the wrong kinds of food and exercising. I would wait another month, until the New Year kicked in, two weeks away. No need to hurt her feelings any sooner than necessary.

The first Sunday of the New Year found us sprawled out in bed, bright winter's sunlight shining in through the bedroom window.

I was reading the Sunday paper, watching Dondisha out of the corner of my eye. She was making her second trip to the kitchen for a large slice of pound cake. Pound cake. I had to smile at the thought of the name. Some honest baker had put the right name on that delicious, rich piece of butter and flour.

The announcement flared up at me as though the print was an inch high. The announcement in the T.V. section of the paper, in English and Spanish, was that station KMEX number 34 was going to begin showing bullfights from Mexico and Spain. Bullfights from Mexico **and** Spain!

"Dondisha! They're goin' to start showing bullfights on KMEX, 34, starting next Friday."

She came to the doorway of the bedroom, pound cake crumbs on her full breasts, looking puzzled.

"Whose gonna do what?"

"They gonna be showing the bullfights from Mexico **and** Spain, startin' next Friday from 8 p.m. to 12 p.m. on KMEX 34."

"Ohh." That's just about as much surprise as she could manage about the announcement. O well…

———◆———

I was damned near in a state of high anxiety on the Friday of the first scheduled fight. I read the latest blurb/article in the T.V. section over and over; scared to death that they would announce a cancellation. Or that I had misread the date or something.

The article stated that the first fight would be a broadcast of two old fights, and on succeeding weeks they would show the most recent fights as well as profiles of matadores, their managers, wives, children, bull ranch owners, people who were connected to La Fiesta Brava in some way. I tried to keep my cool, but it was hard. I was about to have everything I wanted, needed, brought right into my house.

Matador-like, I couldn't eat before the fight. Some matadors don't eat before a fight, just in case they have to be operated on, they will have it done on an empty stomach. I couldn't eat because I was so nervous.

"Chester, I made some gumbo, you mean you can't eat because of a T.V. show?"

I tried to explain as patiently as I could.

"Dondisha, this is not just a T.V. show, this is a bullfight, mano-a-mano, between Luis Procuna and Manuel Capetillo, two great Mexican bullfighters."

"Ohh…"

I have to give her credit for being a good soldier though. That evening, at exactly 8 p.m., as I leaned forward to stare at every inch of our huge "Sports size" T.V., she slumped on the sofa beside me, gobblin' buttered popcorn by the fist full.

One of the things I loved about the KMEX bullfight broadcasts, they didn't do a lot of chit chat. When the gates across from the president's box opened, the announcers told you what was happening but they didn't put any spin on it. They didn't try to sell you a bill of goods. I guess they figured if you had tuned in on this good stuff there was no need to try to take it over the top. I tried to explain this stuff as it was happening so Dondisha wouldn't be left completely out of the action. I didn't try to explain **everything**, just enough to have her make some sense out of the scene. I invited her to ask questions.

"Are the bulls trained?"

"Trained? What do you mean – trained?"

"You know, the way you train animals. Like right there, the way that man – what's his name?"

"Luis Procuna."

"The way that Pro-cuna is making him follow that cape around."

Just the two of us in the apartment but I felt like howling with laughter. It took all of my self control to keep from screaming with laughter. Were the bulls trained? Who could ever think something like that? Ask a question that absurd?

"Uhh, no, baby, the bulls are wild. What you see the man doin' with the cape is an effort to direct the bulls's horns, the bull's focus away from his body so that he won't get gored."

She spilled some of her popcorn as she sat up straight.

"O my God! You mean that man is down there with a real live-honest-to goodness wild bull?! Bulls are dangerous. I've seen 'em down home, out in the pastures. They would have signs on the fences, telling us to keep out."

"And those were almost domesticated bulls; what you're lookin' at are fightin' bulls, bulls bred to fight."

"Ugggh! That's ugly, that man on the padded horse with the blind folds on, stabbing the bull in the neck like that." She was right, the picador business was ugly, but necessary.

"That man is called a picador and he's trying to weaken the bull's neck muscles. So that when it's time for the bullfighter, the matador, to make the kill, the bull's head will be low enough for him to go over the right horn and…"

"Look! Look at that! What're they doing?

"Those are the bandilleros, the men who place the bandilleras, the barbed sticks, in the bull's neck. But check it out, Procuna is gonna place his own sticks."

I wanted to tell her, Procuna can place the sticks as well as anybody; maybe it's a Mexican thing – "Armillita Chico", Fermin Espinosa, Carlos Arruza, 'Carnicerito de Mexico", José Gonzalez, Procuna. . .— but I didn't have a chance, Procuna was on the job.

Even to Dondisha's untrained eyes it was obvious that Luis Procuna had lived up to the Mexican reputation for being a "master" of the sticks. She was especially drawn to the way the matador did his little quarter circle movements to draw the bull into an attack.

"He's thinks he's cute, huh?"

"Maybe, Maybe so, but there's a purpose for his cute behavior. See! See that!"

Procuna had met the bull at a perfect intersection; he pushed the sticks in, pushed off and went one way and the bull went another way. It was a beautiful placement of the sticks. Dondisha was focusing on the activity. I glanced at her. Hmmm. . .maybe I have a possible aficionado here.

Procuna went over to the barrier circling the ring and broke the last pair of sticks in half.

"What's he doing?"

It took me a few seconds to figure it out. Procuna took a position about fifty yards from the bull and just stood there, completely still. The bull looked at him, jerked his big bull head from side-to-side, as though to say – aha! Now I got yo' ass right where I want you!

The bull took four or five tentative steps in Procuna's direction before he jumped into a full charge mode. Procuna slowly began to lean to his left, but was still remaining stock still. He was going to place a pair of half-sized banderillas al quiebro. I had only seen this done in still photos in some of the bullfight books. I felt myself leaning to my left with the half sized banderillas in my hands. I felt the terrible fear of being punctured by this monster's horns, I felt the urge to run, to throw the sticks in the bull's face and jump over the barrera.

Dandisha screamed and hid her eyes behind her hands – "He's gonna kill him!"

I held onto my courage and at just the right moment Procuna/I faked to the left with my left leg. Procuna faked to his left and as the bull thundered past us, following the fake, he reached over the horns and placed the short sticks into the bull's big hump of a neck. The crowd ole'd til it was hoarse.

Dondisha peeked through her fingers – "What happened?"

"The bullfighter did something incredibly brave and we, he survived."

The fight went into the muleta, the small, moon shaped cape phase. By this time Dondisha was shaking her head with disbelief and resumed her popcorn eating.

"I can't believe this man is doing all this stuff with this little piece of cloth draped across a stick."

"Just wait 'til you see Capetillo."

It was obvious that Manuel Capetillo was going to have to do some spectacular stuff in order to prove that he belonged in the same bullring with Luis Procuna. And he did it, he pulled it off by doing some hair raising passes with the muleta. I wouldn't've believed them if I hadn't been there, that was the feeling I had.

He did four arrucinas that had the hair on the back of my head stiffening up. The arrucina, the pass where the bull fighter holds the muleta behind his back with his right hand and offers the bull the barest edge of the cloth as a lure. If the bull doesn't go for it, the horn is going to go right into the man's chest, or belly.

Manuel Capetillo didn't stop there, he went on with this pass where he turned his back on the bull, cited the bull for the charge and, just as the bull came full steam, he slowly changed the muleta over to the other side of his body. He did that six times in a row. I had big beads of sweat on my forehead at the conclusion of that series.

Both of the men made quick kills of all three of the bulls that they fought, which was really a blessing because nothing can put as bad a taste in your mouth as to see a half dead bull staggering around, hemorrhaging out of his mouth.

Matador, killer of bulls. Luis Procuna and Manuel Capetillo had given me a deeper feeling for the corrida, the bullfight. I settled back at the end of it and whispered to Dondisha, "that's what I want to be, Dondisha. I want to be a bull fighter."

She didn't hear me, she was sound asleep.

CHAPTER FOUR

DONDISHA

"Chester was the first brother I ever met who was interested in the bullfights. As a matter of fact he was the first person I'd ever known who was interested in the bullfights period.

The first time we sat down to watch this stuff together I didn't know what to think. Well, one of the things that came to my mind is that it was just a lil' bit crazy to be down in a bullring, in the first place, swirling a cape around. Seems to me that that was just asking for trouble.

But I decided to give it a chance. If Chester wanted me to sit with him and watch the bullfights on Friday night; I would sit and watch the bullfights. I didn't have anything for it or against it. I grew up on a farm and I watched animals get slaughtered all the time, so the blood part didn't disturb me all that much. But I have to admit, it did trip me out a bit to watch some of the things these men did. I asked him, "They don't have any Black men doing this, do they?"

"A few, "he answered, "always a few."

We could negotiate this thing about the bullfights, but then he started getting on my case about gaining weight. I didn't like that too much. O.k., so I had gained a couple, a few pounds since we got together, but it wasn't like I had become obese or anything."

———◆———

"After the first fight I almost held my breath waiting for the next one. I was afraid that there wouldn't be a next one; maybe the animal rights people would bomb KMEX or the show would be yanked, for any reason.

I went back and forth to work, I ran errands,went to our tango sessions.

"Raul", they're shown' bullfights on KMEX, Friday nights from 8 to 12."

"Wow! Never thought I'd see the day that would happen in Chicago, you must be in 7th Heaven."

"You better believe it."

"Oh, did I tell you? I went to an audition for a show about the tango, me and Stella."

"What happened?"

"We danced our asses off! You should've seen the way the producer's jaws dropped when we got into our dip'n swirl stuff. One of 'em even applauded after we finished our number but they rejected us. Well, I can't say they completely rejected us, they put us on an "auxiliary list." That means that we might be called if these two White couples that they picked should drop dead or something."

'Raul" actually sounded bitter, the first time I had even heard him sound that way.

"Look like you're gonna have to go where they do the tango, in order to get the recognition you deserve."

"Chester, you know something? I've been thinkin' real hard on that, real hard. Well, let's get busy, we need to polish up those backsteps. You and Dondisha are doin' pretty good, but it can get better."

———◆———

"I was damned near suffering from acute anxiety all day Friday, the second Friday of the bullfight series. This was another oldie, from Spain this time. The program listed Julio Aparico, Miguel Baez, "Litri" and Antonio Borrero, "Chamaco", three of Spain's best. They weren't in the Manolete, Belmonte, Josélito category, but they were pretty far up there.

Each of the toreros were fightin' in the usual rotational pattern;

the senior man had the first bull the second man the second bull, the third man the third bull and then back to the senior man for the fourth bull and so on. The fight had been filmed in the great old bullring in Madrid, the Plaza Madrid. From the Plaza Mexico one week to the Plaza Madrid the next week. It couldn't get any better than that.

By the time 8 p.m. finally came around I was beside myself. Once again the gate across the arena from the president's box opened, the horseman in his 17th century outfit, all lace and ruffles, pranced this beautiful black horse across the ring to get the president's permission to start the event, backed his horse up to the gate and led the matadores across the ring Julio Aparicio, Miguel Baez, "Litri", Antonio Borrero, "Chamaco" and their cuadrillas, the men who assisted them, did a majestic parade across the arena, strutting would be a better description. It's called sandunga in Spanish, arrogance. I had to smile when Dondisha asked me, between spoons of Hagen Däaz, "What're they saying now?"

I had been so into the program from the beginning that it didn't even occur to me that the announcers, with those cognac - Cuban cigar rich voices, were speaking in Spanish. What was happening, the form and shape of things was so clear to me that they could've been speaking English.

"Oh, they're just telling us stuff about the bullfighters, where they came from, stuff like that."

"So, you can speak Spanish?"

"Uhh, not really. I can pronounce the words of the guy's names, the movements, stuff you need to know to understand what's happenin'."

"That's a good way to learn Spanish." *The school teacher speaking.*

"Yeahh, I guess so. Well, here we go – the first bull goes to Julio Aparicio."

Once again the ritual was unfolding. I had arrived at that conclusion that the first time I saw the bullfight, the Manolete story at the World PlayHouse Theater. It was spectacle, it was theater, it was Ritual.

Aparicio was leading what the Spanish called "una auténtica

catedral", an authentic catherdral of a bull, away from the picadores with graceful chicuelinas antiguas.

"That's really pretty", Dondisha murmured, "the way he's wrapping himself in that cape."

I nodded in agreement. It **was** pretty and I knew how to do it just as well. I made a promise to myself to get back with my capework that weekend.

Aparicio gave the work of doing the bandérillas to members of his cuadrilla and, after they had done a workman like job of jabbing the sticks in, he opened up the muléta phase of the fight with six pases de pecho.

"You couldn't make me stand stock still like that and have a full grown bull like that pass under my arm pit"

"Yeahh, baby you got that right. The pase de pecho opens you up to a horn to the heart." Dondisha shook her head in disbelief.

Aparicio did passes on his knees, he did really close work, winding the bull's huge body around him with his muleta and, to show his control of the "cathedral", he switched the muléta to his left hand and started doing "naturales", those slow garden gate opening passes seeming to pull the bull's nose around with the bottom of his muleta. It was bullfighting at the sublime level.

He didn't kill well. It took him four thrusts of the sword to place it in the right spot, but the crowd granted him two ears anyway.

"What's he going to do with those?"

I was becoming slightly annoyed with Dondisha's questions because I got the feeling that she was asking to be asking. Maybe to make me think that she was more interested in the bullfight than she really was.

"Oh, he'll probably keep them in his den or some place, to remind him of the great day he had in the Plaza Madrid."

"Oh."

"Litri", Miguel Baez, placed himself in front of the gate where the bulls charged into the ring, on his knees, his capote spread out in front of him like a giant fan. The gate opened and this huge brown monster, only slightly smaller than the previous one, charged straight out at "Litri". And at the last second, with beautiful time, "Litri" deflected the charge by swinging the capote over and around his head. The bull's right horn missed his right eye by inches.

I edged up to the screen a little. This was great schooling, a great way to study timing, geometry, psycho-logical stuff. The thing about timing was blowing my mind. Nothing could happen before it was time for it to happen. The bullfighter had to wait it out, he had to "aguantar". Like "Litri" did when the bull stopped halfway through a charge. He had to stick it out, refuse to give ground. And finally the bull finished his charge.

Sweat was running down from my armpits by the time "Litri" went in for the kill. Suddenly the bull lifted his head just as the man was going to in over the right horn. "Litri" went up into the air like a rag doll and the bull went at him the second he hit the ground. "Litri" landed on his side and started rolling away from the bull, covering his head. I imagined that that was a maneuver that bullfighters practiced a lot. I made a mental note if that ever happens to me, roll, roll, roll.

It all happened in seconds but suddenly all the members of the "Litri's cuadrilla and the other matadores were in the ring, flashing their capes in the bull's face, distracting him. "Litri" rolled out of danger, brushed himself off and took up the muleta and the sword again.

He performed a few more close passes with the bull, maybe to get his nerve back up, positioned the bull and pushed the sword in up to the hilt between his shoulder blades, the bull dropped to the ground as though it had been shot.

I turned to get Dondisha's reaction to the drama that had just happened but she had gone to the kitchen for another bowl of butter pecan ice cream. I could hear the refrigerator door slam shut. O well. "Litri" got an ear.

"Chamaco" had his work cut out for him. After Aparicio and "Litri", what could he do? That was the question that I shared with the thousands of fans in the seats in the Plaza Madrid.

It didn't take but a few passes for us to see that "Chamaco" was determined to do or die. Aparicio and "Litri" had worked close to their bulls, "Chamaco" looked like he was glued to the bull at times. His "suit-of-lights", his traje de luces, was smeared with the bull's blood, a testimonial to how close he was working with the bull.

"Chamaco" was dealing with a huge, wild hooking animal. I could see from looking at this monster's hooking right horn, that he was going to be hell to kill. I jumped ahead to "the moment of truth". What would I do? How could I take myself over that treacherous right horn when the moment came?

I stood up and imagined that I was going in over that terrible right horn. The solution would be to make the beast's head go down as low as possible when it was time for the kill.

"Chamaco" did all kinds of things, he even performed that "mirando al publico" stunt, looking at the audience as he led the bull through a beautiful pattern of passes. I was almost certain that he was going to get a horn up his ass a few times when he was doing behind the back stuff. But he survived. The crowd in the bullring was screaming "Olé!" for everything he did.

And then it was time for the moment. He stepped to the center of the ring with his bullfighter's hat in hand and made a slow, graceful turn, dedicating the bull to us, to the aficion. I felt that.

The KMEX camera focused right where it was supposed to be at all times, did a glance around the audience. The camera showed people praying. One of "Chamaco's" people called from the fence, the barrera, surrounding the ring.

"Cuarteà, matador, Cuarteà!"

"Cuarteà?" He was telling him, don't go in over the horn, deflect the bull with the cape in the left hand and stick the sword in as you dodge to the left. It would be dishonorable to do something like that, but under the circumstances, with a bull who looked like an assassin with his right horn not many hip people would've held it against him.

"Chamaco" lured the bull's head way down and went in over that dangerous right horn in the honorable way. The bull staggered a bit, hemorrhaging from his heart muscle being cut, and dropped. The crowd erupted. I even shouted "Olé". Dondisha rushed in to see what was happening. It had already happened.

"What was that all about?"

"Chamaco just finished a beautiful faena."

"Oh."

Dondisha plopped down on the sofa and curled up in the corner, spooning ice cream into her mouth mechanically. I wanted to ask her – how in the hell can you sit up in here stuffing yourself full of ice cream when Julio Aparicio, "Litri" and Chamaco are doing all of this fantastic stuff? But I couldn't bring myself to say anything that cold to her. After all, the sister had opened her door for me, the least I could do was to be polite and grateful.

The second part of the rotation started, Aparico again. If the first three fights were exceptional, then it was obvious that these three matadores were out to try to "give each other the bath" their second bull around.

It was like going to a Master bullfighting class. One man or the other answered the questions I had in the back of my head about how to do this or that, which bulls were the best to try certain things with. During "Litri's" second bull I could see that he had drawn one of those bulls they called "nuns", the ones who run so smoothly and so evenly that they look like they're running on rails. "Litri" did a whole series of long range passes with this "nun".

One of them was from something like thirty yards away. The bull charged, running faster than a race horse, straight at "Litri's" cape. But just as the bull was about to run into his side, he slowly shifted the muleta behind him without even glancing at the bull's horns swooshing past his behind.

I could feel my own ass muscles tighten up, like I was doin' involuntary Kegels. "Litri" was positioning the bull's front hooves to a parallel position so that the space between the shoulder blades would be opened wider, to allow him to slip the sword in more easily for the kill, when I noticed that Dondisha had gone to bed. O well…

"Chamaco" didn't do quite as well with his second bull as he had done with the first one, but he still gave me a lot to study and think about. Finally, at midnight, it was over. I remoted the T.V. off, slumped back on the sofa, and re-played the whole evening of fights back through my brain.

I thought a lot about my size; 5'10, 155 pounds, slim but muscular. I would definitely have the advantage of height and reach over all of three of the men I had just seen. I doubt if any of them had been taller than 5'8" or so. But what they lacked in stature, they made up for it with heart.

I remembered Dad asking me – "Do you have the heart for that?"

I stared up at the sky, dark blue and cold, a typical January night in Chicago. Yeah, I got the heart, I know I have. Dondisha was snoring by the time I got in bed.

◆ ◆ ◆

By the time the following Friday, rolled around, Dondisha excused herself – "I got a lil' headache, I'm gonna take a hot bath and an aspirin."

I gave her a peck on the lips and settled down to watch three great Mexican toreros: Joselito Huerta, Fernando de los Reyes, "El Callao" and José Ramon Tirado.

No need to lie about it, I had become what some people might call…obsessed. It seemed that the only thing that had any meaning for me was the Friday night bullfights. I went to the post office, put in my robotic overtime. We went to "Raul's" tango class on Monday and Wednesday.

"Chester, my brother, I got to tell you, you're bringing in a whole 'nother dimension to your tango. Is that from the bullfights?"

"Could be", "Raul", could be. But I'm not sure I know what you mean?"

"Well, it would be hard to define. What I see is a certain definite sense of purpose, and a kind of arrogance. I like that."

He was telling me that I had sandunga and templé, two words that couldn't be defined by English because English doesn't have those kinds of attitudes, not towards the bullfight anyway or life in general.

"Thanks", "Raul", I hear what you're sayin'."

"The **big** problem, as I see it, is that your partner isn't reaching up to your level."

There was something about the way he said "big problem" that made me cringe a bit. No doubt about it, my dance partner was a "big problem" and getting larger by the week. I didn't really know what to do about Dondisha's King Henry the Eighth appetite. I mean, after all, I was a "guest" in her space.

Once again, I decided to put all problems off to the side and study the Friday night fights. After the first Friday I had gone into the closet and pulled out my capote and muleta out.

I didn't have a lot of time to go through my repertoire of pases, but I took advantage of every stray moment I had to get in the middle of the front room and do various cape movements.

It took a few days to make my wrists strong and flexible again. I hadn't realized how heavy the capote was, or the muleta, draped across a sawed length of broom slick. Dondisha stood off to the side, checking me out at first, and after that she just wandered past, nibbling on something. I didn't give a shit whether I had her attention or not. I knew that I was going to have to have strong wrists and a decent repertoire of cape movements whenever I had the opportunity to face the bulls.

Josélito Huerta, Fernando de Los Reyes, "El Callao" and José Ramon Tirado, the Mexicans. I settled in place, poised to critique the matadores to the bone. The announcers seemed to be speaking more clearly to me all the time. I couldn't understand every word, but it seemed that their words were creating a more complete picture of the scene the harder I listened.

One of them said, "Joselito Huerta was excellent as a novillero both in Mexico and Spain, but as a real matador he has had better luck in Spain." Maybe it was the bulls.

"El Callao", Fernando de Los Reyes, was dedicated, willing, but lacked "that spark". That's what one of the announcers said.

"José Ramon Tirado could give us a thrilling afternoon if he hasn't been out with the college girls too late." I was beginning to understand and relate to the announcer's enthusiasm and cynicism. The announcers were not promoting baseball heroics or pumping up seven foot tall Black millionaires pushing a basketball around, they were talking about the bullfights that they were showing us.

"Josélito Huerta has plunged deep inside of himself to explore a new level of sensitivity. The ferocious animal with the antlers called "Missionero" deserves enormous applause for having helped the matador discover himself."

"Fernando de Los Reyes, "El Callao", from Huamantla TLaxcala, on this occasion, might have done himself and the noble citizens of Huamantla, Tlaxcala, a favor by remaining in his bed today. His corrida was somewhat sleepy."

I was smiling from what I had seen and from what I had understood of the bullfight announcer's sarcastic comments, when I took notice of Dondisha standing behind me, her arms crossed on her full breasts, not eating anything, thank God.

"I really can't see what's interesting about this, to tell you the truth. The same ol' thing happens all the time. The man kills the bull."

"But sometimes the bull kills the man."

"I haven't seen that happen yet."

"Well, would you like to see that happen? And how many bullfights have you seen anyway?"

She glared at me and drifted away to our bedroom like a malevolent shadow. Awww shit! I done really screwed up now.

I remained in place after the last sword had been plunged into the last bull's heart, thinking. Well, maybe I had been a bit insensitive. Dondisha certainly hadn't welcomed me into her space just so I could watch the bullfights.

I went into our bedroom. Dondisha was curled up on her side of the bed. I curled myself up behind her and nibbled on her left ear lobe, slipped my right hand under her full bloomed right breast. She resisted my urgency for a few minutes before she turned around to face me.

"Chester", she purred into my ear, "I was beginning to think that you didn't love me any more."

"Didn't love me any more". The statement almost caused me to lose interest in the whole "investigation". What did love have to do with it?

———◆———

CHAPTER FIVE

The bull shot out of the gate as a huge monster, hooking madly at the matador, at me. It didn't seem to matter what the matador did, no matter how cleverly the man used his brain and his cape to deflect the bull's charges, he (the bull) was always trying to get at the bull fighter from different angles.

Matador me came to the faena, the part of the bull fight where the bull fighter shows his ability to work closely with the bull, with a confidence that demonstrated that he had sandunga and templé up to the yang yang.

Dondisha nudged me gently.

"Chester, Chester, you were having a bad dream…"

I opened my eyes and stared at her. Was I having a bad dream? Well, it was definitely an interesting dream, no doubt about that.

"I'm gonna make us a couple of omelletes. You want a cuppa coffee?"

I nodded no, watched her ease out of bed with her red silk gown clinging to every enlarged curve. I laced my hands behind my head and stared up at the high domed ceiling above me.

It was Saturday. What did we do on Saturday? What did we have planned for this Saturday? Well, we'd certainly have to do a bit of grocery shopping, pay a few bills, do a few of the things you never had time to do during the course of the week. And maybe later we would take a trip over to my parent's house (Dad had managed to buy a place in South Shore).

I was dressed and pulling my long cape case out of the closet by the time Dondisha finished making her six egg omellet.

We were a long, six blocks from the Midway, the green border section that separated Hyde Park from the areas to the south of us. The Midway consisted of a series of depressed quadragles, perfectly placed to play soccer games, punt a football or practice my veronicas, media veronicas and naturales. Dondisha was bringing in her tray full of goodies as I headed for the door.

"Chester, don't you want some breakfast?"

"I'll have some when I get back."

"Where are you going?"

"Out onto the Midway to work with my capes."

"But it's cold out there."

"I know. I won't be long."

I can close my eyes for a hot minute, even now, years later, and visualize the bewildered expression on Dondisha's face. It was about 10 degrees above zero, normal for a January day in Siberia-Chicago; and I was going out to swirl my capes around. And that's exactly what I did. Out there, with only a few anxious graduate students from the University of Chicago pausing to check me out. I worked my way through about ten of the movements that could be done with the capote, the large cape. And then, ten with the muleta, the smaller cape. I wanted to create the impression of a garden gate being opened ever so slowly.

And then I went back to the capote, to do variations of the first ten movements I had done. It was bone chilling cold, but thank God, no wind. After a half hour of serpentinas and manoletinas, I had to take my gloves off. I had gotten so hot I didn't even feel the cold. Maybe I was in that state of mind that people talk about when they're deep into their Tai Chi, or Zen Buddhism, when they allow their bodies' total freedom to regulate their controls. Walking back home I felt a strange calm. I had done what I needed to do, that was the important thing.

I had to smile when I let myself in and paused to listen to Dondisha talking on the' phone. It only took a couple of sentences to figure out that she was talking to my mother.

"Mzzz Simmons, he's out there right now, as cold as it is, with his bull capes . . . .

I walked right past her as though I hadn't heard a word. What sense would it make to talk about what I was doing? She wasn't in my mix, she didn't share my passions.

Momma

"I felt sorry for the po girl, I really did. I could tell from the way that she talked about him that she really loved him; but she was beginnin' to feel alienated because of his interest in this bullfight stuff.

It was on the tip of my tongue a half dozen times to say to her --- well, at least he doesn't have a couple stray women out there somewhere. But I couldn't say that; how would that sound to say to your prospective daughter-in-law, it's better for him to be at home with the bulls than be out there with the girls?

We became close friends over the course of a bunch of conversations all focused on Chester and his bullfight thing. But we also exchanged a few recipes and circled around the idea of her and Chester getting married. He hadn't proposed yet."

DAD

"Despite the fact that Chester was a real pain in the ass, in some ways, I had to admire his stubbornness. The young man was determined to be a bullfighter, of all things, and he was not even open to the possibility of that **not** happenin'.

I snuck up on him a half dozen times with arguments that were so tight water couldn't even flow through them. He listened hard, analyzed my point and came back at me.

"Dad, look, you wanted to be a crook, a lawbreaker, a drug dealer, at one point in your life you wanted to be . . . ."

"And it cost me ten years of my life behind bars."

"And it cost you ten years, but at least you can say, I did what I thought I wanted to do. I think that's very, very important."

Chester was deep. I couldn't begin to imagine many 18 year old dudes who had a mind like his, who were as focused as he was."

------◆◆◆------

BoBo

"We didn't see Chester around the hood a lot after he shacked up with this school teacher over there in Hyde Park. I felt pretty good about the brother, like he was movin' onward and upward.

Johnny Fox was still in school. Somebody told me that he had made a deal with his parents to finish two years of junior college, and they would sponsor him for the last two years at a four year college. Herb had joined the Army and was out there somewhere.

"Raul" was still doin' that sex dance they called the Tango. He had hooked into one of those middle aged "sugar Mommas" and was workin' it, if you know what I mean?"

Me? Well, ain't no sense pussy footin' around about it, I had discovered that *heron* , or maybe the *heron* had discovered me, hard to say which way it was. In any case, I was hooked, bad."

------◆◆◆------

"RAUL"

"I was really bent a lil' bit outta shape after those racist-snake dogs denied me and Stella first place in that dance competition. Stella may have been only average, but I'm here to testify that I did enough tango for both of us, believe me.

I think it was Chester who first planted the seed, the idea of goin' overseas to do my thing. Argentina would have to be the place, no doubt about it. I had all the confidence in the world that I would be a success down there. I had also given the brother some good advice about his bullfightin' career.

"Chester, you're gonna have to go where the bullfights are happenin', they are not happenin' here, a blind man could see that. You could spend a century swirlin' your cape around in the air and never come close to the action."

I checked him out at a distance, watchin' to see how his relationship was gonna play out with Dondisha. I didn't have anything against Dondisha, other than the fact that I could see that she had limited imagination. Like Stella.

The first time I mentioned goin' to Argentina to Stella. She just absolutely shut down on me. "No", that's all she said. "No". And I wasn't in a position to argue the point with her so I had to let it go. But I didn't push the thought out of my head."

SISTER LOUISE

"I thought, for a hot minute, that my brother had recovered his good senses when he hooked up with Dondisha.

But that didn't happen, he was still hooked on this crazy idea of fightin' bulls. I had to sign off on the whole thing because I had been accepted in this nursin' program. All I had to do was maintain decent grades and I would be allowed to get into this program that this lady in Maryland had set up.

Far as I could understand it, this lady, everybody called her 'Queen Jewel', had set up a model hospital in Antigua, West Indies, and she was recruitin'. What it meant was this, if you passed the correct standards 'n stuff you could get a nice scholarship to do nursin' in Antigua.

To be honest, I didn't even know where Antigua was, but the deal looked good and I didn't have anything better goin' for me.

I felt sorry for Chester, you know what I'm sayin'? Everybody knows that the world needs nurses, but how many bullfighters do we need?"

DONDISHA

"We were in the middle of February, Black History Month, and we had been invited here and there, to celebrations and what not, but we couldn't go anywhere, do anything, if it was happening on Friday night.

"'Dondisha, look, you can go if you want to, that's on a Friday night, bullfight night.'"

'Chester', I asked him, 'What's the deal with you? All you wanna do is sit here and watch these people stab these damned bulls to death.'

"' Well, I think that's better than sittin' here eating ice cream by the pint.'"

I had to leave him alone because we were on the verge of getting kinda nasty with each other. And I really didn't want that to happen. I had a couple of friends who were like living in a constant state of warfare, they argued all the time.

I decided to try to reason with Chester because I thought it important that we should make our relationship work.

'Chester, can we talk?'

"'Yeahh, sure, what about?'"

'It's about me and you.'

"'What about me and you?'"

'Well, it's quite obvious that we don't see eye to eye on some things.'

He nodded in agreement.

"'So, what do you think we should do?'"

'I think we oughta compromise. . .'

"'By compromise, you think I should stop watching the bullfights on Friday nights?'"

'Well, do you have to watch them **every** Friday night?"

"'That's the only time they come on, Dondisha.'"

'But do you have to watch them **every** Friday night? I mean, couldn't you miss watching them some Friday nights?'

You should've seen the way his bottom lip turned down, the cold expression that came on his face.

"'Dondisha, listen to me close because I'm not goin' to repeat myself. I'm watching the Friday night fights, I'm **studying** the styles, the ways the men fight the bulls. This is the only way I have of getting into the core of this art, don't you understand that?'"

'No, I do not understand that. What is the point of doing all this studying?'

"'The point of it is that it's going to make me a better bullfighter.'"

' 'Scuse me?'

"'You heard me, all of this studying is going to make me a better bullfighter.'"

'A better bullfighter?'

"'You heard me, I didn't stutter.'"

'Chester, are you telling me that you plan to become a bullfighter?'

"'Yes'", he answered and clamped his jaws tight as a bear trap.

I couldn't do anything but just stare at him for a few minutes. And then I started crying, I couldn't hold back the tears. I felt so sad I didn't know what to do. Chester looked sane and he sounded sane, but I was certain that he was in the middle of a nervous breakdown and I didn't know what to do about it.

He came over and wrapped me in his arms.

"'What're you crying about?'"

'I'm crying because I'm afraid for you, I don't want to see you get hurt. I don't want to lose you.'

He held me away from him by my shoulders and looked me dead in the eye.

"'And I don't want to get hurt either, that's why I'm studying the bullfights every Friday night.'"

Chester had obviously lost his mind and I felt that I had to help him, or get help for him. I turned to his Mom and Dad. They agreed to meet with me and discuss the problem. I made a date to go over to meet with them on Friday night; what better time could I pick? I told Chester I was going over to a girlfriend's house for a baby shower.

'See you later.'

"'Yeah, baby see you later.'"

Very nice people, Mr. and Mrs. Simmons. I know Mrs. Simmons didn't like it at first, that me and Chester were living together but she softened up after we talked on the phone a few times and exchanged a few recipes. They welcomed me like I was their for real daughter-in-law. We sat at the dining room table and had cups of coffee and slices of Mrs. Simmons' German Chocolate cake.

"'Dondisha, we don't really believe Chester is crazy, you know like schizophrenic or anything like that. But we think he's fixated on this idea.'"

'But why, Mr. Simmons, why?'

Mrs. Simmons looked real tired as she slowly turned her cup around in the saucer.

"'That's a good question, honey, a damned good question. We both have sat here for hours, tryin' to figure out where he got this notion from.'"

"'The closest we've come to explainin' it comes from two places, from two sources. Number one, he went to see a documentary down at the ol' World PlayHouse Theater, something about a bullfighter named Manolo, or something like that.

And number two, he's always been fascinated by the travel stories that his grandfather, my Daddy, passed on to me. One of the stories was about him traveling to Spain and hangin' out with a bullfighter named 'El Cante'. Now, whether he did that for real or not, I can't say. I **can** say this for sure – my father loved to stretch the truth to the outer limits.'"

'So, what do you think I ought to do?'

I could see both of them frowning, thinking hard on the question. Mr. Simmons gave me the best answer.

"'Dondisha, if you really love the guy, just hang in there. I'm pretty certain that this wild idea is gonna have to die a natural death. Just think about it, the possible lack of bulls to fight is definitely going to play a part in him giving up on this idea of becoming a bull-fighter.'"

I hugged both of them on the way out. I was feeling better about things already. All I would have to do is be cool and wait 'til my man came back to his senses."

MO' DONDISHA...

"I spent the last two weeks of February and all of March watching bullfights with Chester. I even cut back on my Hagen Däaz consumption. I couldn't tell him how much he had hurt me when he talked about me getting fat. And I stopped that fried chicken thing. Well, to be truthful, I had to have me a 'burger'n some fries from time to time, but I reduced my consumption by half. I mean, who wants to sit up in front of a television, piling pounds on with buttered popcorn and ice cream whilst your man is nibbling on pumpkin seeds?

I had taken a couple #101 Spanish classes, so I wasn't totally at sea when these announcers started talking about this and that. Over the course of about six weeks, watching the bullfights on Friday nights, I can't say that I became a bullfight expert but I can say I saw César Girón, his brothers Rafael and Curro Girón...the brothers from Venezuela."

" 'O.K. Dondisha, you've been asking me – "'Where are the Black guys in bullfighting?'" What would you call those brothers?'" I had to admit that they looked like 'Raul'.

I saw old style dudes, according to Chester, and new style dudes. It was hard for me to tell the difference between one or the other. But I did make an effort to record their names in my head.

" 'They can't show us Juan Belmonte, Gaona, Cagancho, Francisco Arjona, 'Cuchares', Rafael Gomez, 'El Gallo', Silverio Perez and some others because there were no videos back when they were fighting. My Daddy used to talk about how Sugar Ray Robinson's greatest fights were never seen because T.V. came late in the game.'"

Well, we didn't see some of the people I mentioned, but the announcers talked about them. And Chester talked about them. And compared them to a lot of the modern fighters, people like Antonio Ordoñez. Juan Flores, "Brilliante Negro', Alfredo Leal, somebody named 'El Cordobes', Domingo Ortega. And they even showed a couple women – Conchita Cintron and Patricia McCormick.

By the end of March I was just about sick of watching the bull fights, to tell the truth. But Chester was really into it. He was always getting books about the bullfight an then he started listening to that flamenco music. I didn't like the bullfight very much, and I hated the flamenco music, it sounded like people being tortured or something.

———◆◆◆———

"I was really shook up when I got on the scale and saw that I had gained five pounds over the course of the winter. Five pounds! I started runnin' and fastin' every chance I got. And started doin' some serious work on my capote and my muleta. . .

I had seen Manuel Capetillo and Luis Miguel Dominguin swing the muleta in front of a hard charging bull as though they were slooowly opening a gate. I couldn't figure that one out for a bit. How could they move the cape so sloolwly while the bull was charging so fast?

The secret was in their wrists, the way they moved the cape actually forced the bull into the rhythmic flow they had established. I wanted to scream Halleluya! I've found the key to this garden gate swinging stuff.

I needed a mirror to work in front of, to perfect my thing with the capote. "Raul" was the answer, the Ida B. Wells Center had a room with mirrors on three sides.

"Yeah, c'mon. You can do your thing before or after the tango classes."

Damn! Why hadn't I thought of that before?! I decided to do it for an hour after the tango classes. I wanted to create sculptures with the capote, ice cold veronicas that would have the bulls bury their horns in the capote, but never touch it. I got busy.

I got as deeply into "Raul's" tango class as I possibly could. First off, I could easily see how the tango, with all the fancy footwork would be a great help in helping me perform the cape movements. Sometimes "Raul" would stay a few minutes after class to check me out, but most often it would just be me and Dondisha. She would review a few of her tango steps or read a magazine looking bored as hell.

I didn't give a shit about her attitude or any of that. I was working stuff out in the mirrors. All I had to do was imagine a thousand pounds of bull charging me and I would work out a way to avoid being gored. It was all about domination, who was going to be the boss of the arena, me or the bull?

On more than one occasion it took me two hours to work out the solutions for some of my problems. By the end of April, after having studied some of the great ones on Friday nights, during the course of the winter, I felt very much at ease with my cape work, with the capote and the muleta.

The big bump in front of me was the kill. How could I call myself a matador if I didn't know how to kill a bull?

I <u>understood</u> the anatomy of the bulls from studying one dozen books detailing the insides of a bull. I knew that the right placement of the sword thrust, right between the bull's withers, would sever the bull's aorta and he would hemorrhage to death right away. I knew the five most common ways of killing: (1) receiving/recibiendo, when the man waits for the bull to come to him; (2) "flying feet"/a volapié, when the man goes to the bull; (3) simultaneously/a un tiempo, that's when the bull and the man move toward each other at the same time; (4) when the bull and the man meet as the bull is about to charge; (5) when the bullfighter and the bull meet as the man is about to advance, aguantando.

I had the theory stuff down pat, but I didn't have a bull to kill. Strangely enough the problem was practically solved by a chance conversation I had with my Dad. Seems that he and Mom weren't feeling so mean and evil towards me for "shackin up" with Dondisha. As a matter of fact, they had almost become down right cordial. I put in my weekly-parental-How-y'all-doin'-call?

"So, how's that bullfight thang goin?" my Dad asked me. I couldn't tell if he was being sarcastic of sincere. I decided to give him the benefit of the doubt.

"Well, Dad, I really feel that I'm on top of the cape work, you know, with the large cape and the muleta."

"That's the small, fan shaped one?"

"Yeah, the muleta. My problem is finding bulls to practice killing on." He laughed.

"Well, I think we told you, ain't too many bulls to kill in Chicago…"

"I know, I know. But that's a matador's job, to kill the bull. You can do all the great cape work in the world, but if you're not a good killer, the whole thing goes out the window."

Dad was real quiet for a few moments. Seems like I could hear him thinking. And when he spoke he sounded very serious. He wasn't humoring me.

"Chester, I think I might be able to help you solve your problem."

"Huh?!"

"I said, I think I might be able to help you solve your problem."

Coming from Dad, that really meant something. Since his jail time, he had cleaned his own clock. I had to respect that.

"What I need to have you do is give me some idea of the dimensions of the bull ring, and what the bullfighter does when he's setting the bull up for the kill."

I laid it all out for him, all the way up to what Hemingway called "The Moment of Truth". I could just see Dad working the mouse around, making stuff happen on his computer. He asked me questions about this and that and I gave him the answers. Finally, after about half an hour, he said, "I'm at the shop, you want to come down here 'n take a look at this."

"Give me the address, I'll be there within the hour." The shop was on Michigan Avenue, right down the street from the Art Institute.

Dondisha was correcting papers, designing games on her computer or doing the work a kindergarten teacher does on Saturday. She gave me that look that I was beginning to hate, a combination of pitiful puppy and serious anger.

"Be back in a bit, got a meeting with Dad down at the shop."

She looked somewhat pleased about that, I don't know why.

CHAPTER SIX

One of the things I always liked about Chicago is that the place is compact, you can go from the Southside to the Northside in fifteen minutes, if there are no traffic jams.

I thought about Dad on my way downtown. The dude had done his dime and landed on the outside, runnin'. "Gelman's Computers" had given him a lot of traction. He had bought a nice home in South Shore and he was doing well. I admired his spunk, his "git up 'n go" the old folks used to call it.

"Can I help you, Sir?"

The young White boy looked like a typical nerd, complete with a pair of large sized, black rimmed glasses and a hair style that looked like he had just taken his finger out of an electric socket.

"I'm here to see Mr. Simmons…"

"Oh, you must be Chester. He told me you'd be in. He's upstairs, please come with me."

Huge place, it looked like the inside of an airplane hanger. Computers everywhere, busy. I had never thought enough about what Dad was doing to pay him a visit; to know where he worked. One thing was damned certain, if he was running all of this he was on top of his game.

"Uhhh, Mr. Simmons, Chester is here, sir."

"Thank you, Jeffrey."

I took a good look at my ol' man. Clean cut, sharp, expensive slacks, a vest and a bow tie. Usually, whenever I saw him at home he was in jeans and a sport shirt. He gestured for me to follow him through this large office where about six people were working.

"Let's go back here where I have my own set up."

He led me into a combination office/workshop and made a 'phone call – "Debbie, I'm going to be in a meeting for the next hour, hold all of my calls. And if any emergency comes up, call Jeffrey. Thanks Debbie."

I was awe stuck, my Dad was duh Man.

"Dad, where's the owner?"

"Mr. Gelman? He's in Florida right now. And he'll probably be going to the South of France from there, he likes the sunshine."

"And he's left you in charge?"

"You got that right, son, I'm the man in charge". We smiled at each other about that. I'm the man in charge. An ex-convict with a beef sheet as long as his arm.

"O.K., let me show you what I've done and tell me what you think."

He took a seat in front of this extra large computer screen, pushed the on button and five seconds later we were in the center of a bullring, minus a crowd. I sat beside him, no slow boot-up here.

"Now, let me explain what I've done here. I'm calling it the acupuncture concept."

"The acupuncture concept?" I was totally puzzled.

"Yeahhh, it'll make sense to you in a minute. Here come Seenyor your bull."

A beautiful simulation of a well muscled bull burst into the ring. After he raced around the ring, looking for something to fight, the way real bulls do, he was suddenly facing me, facing the matador. Dad motioned me to take his seat.

"Awright, it's all yours now. I didn't make any effort to get with that horse and spear stuff, or somebody playing with those sticks. You made the point that the kill is the most important part. So, what we have is a bull for you to kill. Here's where the acupuncture concept comes in. I found out about this from reading about how the Chinese teach little kids about acupuncture.

They take dolls and teach the kids meridian points. If the kids pin the wrong meridian point, water will drip. So, now we have this bull in front of you, waiting for you to place the sword properly.

If you do it correctly he's going to hemorrhage and go down just the way a real bull would go down. If you don't hit the right spot, he'll race around and pause to give you another shot at it. What do you think?"

I was dumbfounded. My father had created a virtual reality for me. I jumped up to hug him. He took my show of affection in a kind of "awww shucks" kind of way, the way men act when they're not used to being hugged by other men.

"Now, the next component is to put virtual reality goggles on you, so that you'll be right down there with Seenyor Bull. But for right now, I thought it be a good way to get into this. Go 'head, give it a shot."

All I had to do was pretend that I was holding the muleta in my left hand and my sword in my right hand. I would distract the bull with the muleta and do the crossover, slipping the sword right into the place between the shoulder blades. It didn't work out. The bull was racing around the ring again.

Dad started doing a little tweaking.

"Damn, Chester, I just saw what you did, what you're trying to do. That's some dangerous shit. You're trying to get the bull to follow your cape as you cross your arms to put the sword in. Right?"

"That's the way it's done."

"O.K., let me add this feature: Let's say you don't do the crossover thing properly, then the bull gets you, right?"

"Right."

"Now, this feature will show when you haven't led the bull through this crossover maneuver well enough. In effect it will show that the bull has snagged you if you haven't done the procedure well enough. Does that bother you?"

"It's what happens…"

"As we develop the program more completely we can add sound effects and what not. What is it that people yell when the bull-fighter has done something good? "'O yeahh!'"…"

"Olé!"

"Well, it'll be a simple matter to add that. O.K., you wanna give that bull another stab?"

A simple matter, mouse the bad boy into focus, line him up so that the space between his withers, his shoulder blades will be open to receive my sword. The sword sank into that muscular hump like it had melted into a brown mound of butter. The big problem is that I hadn't created the proper crossover-follow-through. Maybe I had killed the bull but there was the strong possibility that his right horn had ripped me up, from my right knee to my nuts.

Dad took it all in at a glance.

"Hmmm, looks like you did one thing right, but you didn't do the other thing quite right."

I didn't say anything, but I have to admit, for the first time since I had picked up the cape, I felt a little queasy. Or should I say – scared? If this computer bull was able to get at my balls that easy, what chance would I have against a fully live-not-in-the tech beast? Dad saw my feelings.

"Whoaaa Chester, don't go there. This program is new to your head, you can't get down on yourself for not being able to master the situation from the git go."

"But, Dad, you have to understand, the real bull may not be open to the idea of me tryin' to do it 'til I get it right."

"I can dig where you're comin' from, that's why you're doin' what you're doin', right here 'n now."

He was right. And I didn't have to belabor him with questions, all I had to do was get it right. Make the bull follow the muleta away from my body as I stuck the sword down into his body. It all seemed so simply simple. But it wasn't, it was simply complicated.

After twenty wayward thrusts; muleta, muleta, muleta must lead the bull's right horn away from your right thigh. And your left thigh. And all of the points in between.

I was beginning to feel more determined to do the right thing, it would prevent me from being de-balled.

Dad left me after forty-five minutes, satisfied that I knew what I was doing, and what was at stake.

"Chester, I've got to go back to work, Dondisha called a few minutes ago, you want to return her call?"

"I will, Dad, I will. But right now I'm doing something else."

What the hell could I say to Dondisha about what I was doing? She was calling to try to get me to come home and eat some greens 'n thangs. I was dealing with life or death realities.

It took me exactly forty two thrusts of the sword, accompanied by a perfect distraction of the muleta, to say that I had made my first, perfect kill.

Dad had come back upstairs at exactly the right moment to see me do it. I didn't have to hear the "Olés" out loud, I could hear them in my head. Dad came over, patted me on the shoulder and whispered . . .

"Don't tell your mother I had anything to do with this, o.k.?"

I nodded yes, yes, yes, in agreement. But all I could think of was how Mr. Chester Simmons Sr., had revolutionized the bullfight. Well, he had revolutionized **my** bullfight. The adrenalin rush of plunging a real sword into a real bull would have to wait for awhile, maybe the virtual reality goggles would take care of that.

I leaned back in my seat after making my first, perfect kill. This is a technology that the picadores could use to improve the thrust of their lances into the bull's neck.

The banderilleros, the guys placing the sticks, would definitely benefit from this kind of analysis, this kind of practice. I had to laugh at my thoughts – here I am, a pure amateur whose never done anything but swing a cape around and I'm already thinking about how I can revolutionalize something that's been around for centuries.

Stuff really began to get intense that May. I was working at the Post Office part time, the holiday overtime was long gone, which meant that I had a lot more time to practice my cape work and line the bulls up on my computer. I had broken my kill pattern down to eight out of ten. I was aiming for ten out of ten.

There were times when I was almost surprised to see Dondisha come in the door. If it hadn't been for our Monday and Wednesday tango classes I doubt if she would ever have been in my arms.

A plan started ballooning in the back of my head. It wasn't working out between me and Dondisha and I was beginning to feel real bad about us. I had to do something. I did a careful accounting of my resources. Almost three grand in my savings account, not much, but better than nothing. I tried to pick a good way to say what I had to say to Dondisha, a good time.

There was no good way, no good time. It was on the third Friday in May and I had just watched one of those great bullfights between Andrés Blando, with his super arrogant ass, Luis Briones and Jaime Bravo. Never will forget the beauty of their performances. It came from the giant Plaza Mexico. I had seen so many fights from that arena I felt I knew the place.

Dondisha was curled up in bed, reading Ebony, as usual.

I stood in the doorway of the bedroom for a few seconds, looking at her. We had been together since the previous September and she looked like she had pads on under her cotton nightgown.

She had given me an opportunity to move out of my parent's house, she had tried to be a good woman to me. I felt that I owed her something for all that; but I didn't feel that I owned her my life, my future.

"Dondisha, put the magazine down a minute."

I don't know what she saw on my face, what she read from my expression, but she suddenly looked scared and sad at the same time. I sat beside her on the bed.

"Dondisha, I'm goin' to Mexico."

She shook her head as though she was trying to shake the words out of her ears.

"You're going where?"

"I'm goin' to Mexico, that's where the bulls are, that's where I'm goin to break into bullfighting."

We couldn't do anything but look at each other for a minute or so.

"So, what's gonna happen to me, to us?"

"You want to come with me?"

Once again she shook her head.

"What would I do in Mexico? And aside from that, who do you know down there? What will you do to earn a living? Where will you live?"

"Dondisha, I don't have the answer for any of those questions. I just know I'm goin', I got to do what I got to do."

She put on a brave face for a moment and then her whole thing collapsed. She fell into my arms and started crying.

"Chester, Chester, don't do this to yourself. Why do you want to make yourself suffer so much. When are you planning to go?"

"Next month."

"Why so soon? Couldn't it wait for awhile?"

"No, it can't wait. I have to do it now, as soon as possible."

Her tears soaked the left side of my shoulder. And I felt like crying too; but I had made my decision, this was my moment of truth.

I had about three weeks to go before my "get away" and the only other person, other than Dondisha, that I had spoken to about my departure was "Raul".

"Chester, looks like we've been reading each other's minds. You're saying you're gonna split the first week in June and I'm scheduling my get away for the last week in July."

We didn't bother to talk about money, place to live, anything that would've sounded too realistic.

"I'm goin' to California and from there I'll make my way down to Mexico City. What about yourself?"

"It's just a short hop to New York and I'll go on down to Buenos Aires from there."

I think we looked at each other like heroic figures. We were going to put our asses on the line in pursuit of our dreams. What we were planning to do may have sounded kind of crazy and outrageous to some people, but it seemed to be exactly the right thing for us to do.

"We need to have a way to stay in touch, 'Raul', you know, a way to keep each other updated?"

"I think the American Consulate would be the best place. From what I've read, you can go to the Consulate to receive e-mails and snail mails. And if we happen to miss that contact point, we can always check with our folks, they won't be going anywhere soon."

"Have you told your folks you're leavin'?"

I couldn't quite put my finger on what kind of relationship "Raul" had with his Mom and Dad.

"Well, my Momma and Daddy will know soon enough. My problem is gonna be with Stella."

"O wow! You haven't told her yet?"

"I'm goin' to wait 'til the first week in July to tell her because I'd like to keep the drippin drama to a minimum. What's with you and Dondisha?"

"I've already told her."

"No wonder her eyes were so bloodshot in the class on Wednesday."

The last week in May, I was hot to trot. Dondisha had decided to stop crying and face reality. I was going and that was that, there was nothing for her to do but accept that. We even got around to making love a couple times, you know, like she was giving me something to remember her for.

Mom left a message – "Chester, can you come over as soon as you get this message?" Thursday afternoon, about two p.m. Sounded kind of urgent. I jumped on the Express-Way for the fifteen minute trip to South Shore. Her car was in the driveway. Maybe I should've known that something was up from the way she opened the door and let me in.

She didn't give me the usual hug and kiss on the cheek. She simply turned her back on me and gestured for me to follow her into the dining room, the place where most of our family conferences took place.

"You want a cup of coffee?"

"Uh, no coffee for me. I'll be awake all night."

I was taking it all-in; her jaw muscles were clenching and unclenching and I could see that big vein on the side of her neck throbbing. Nobody in the pad but the two of us. She was glaring at me like she wanted to stab me or something.

"You know something, Chester", she started off real low and cold, "nobody would ever have made me believe that you would turn out to be the rotten bastard you are...."

Her words jolted me. Mom's profanity vocabulary was usually limited to an occasional "shit!" or "damn!".

"Woww, Mom, those are pretty strong words."

"You're damned right they are! I thought we had raised you to have some decency about yourself. Some respect for other people's feelings. How could you lead that po' girl along like that, making her think that you were gonna marry her?"

Uhh Ohhh. The cat was out of the bag.

"Mom, I didn't tell Dondisha I was going to marry her."

"Maybe you did and maybe you didn't, but one thing I know for certain is that you sat right up in here and lied to **me**. You told **me** that you were doin' a sort of trial thing and that your intention was to get married in June, this June, this Spring.

So, you decided not to do that, you decided to take your sorry ass down to Mexico. You oughta be ashamed of yourself."

I stood up to leave but she wasn't finished with me yet.

"Sit your ass down! Don't you dare get up to leave whilst I'm talking to you!"

I sank back down in my seat, no need to run the risk of having the center piece, cut glass fruit bowl thrown at my head. I don't know why I hadn't thought that Dondisha would cry on Mom's shoulder.

"I think it is very damned selfish and immature of you to be doin' what you're doin'. That girl took you in, gave you a place to live. Is this the way you show your gratitude?"

"Mom, I am grateful and I've told Dondisha that."

"So, is that why she's crying her eyes out, why she's so broken hearted?"

"I don't have an answer for that. . ."

"And what about us, what about your family? What were you gonna do, Chester, go down to Mexico and drop us a damn post card?!"

She was real angry, but she was beginning to piss me off a bit too.

"Mom, I haven't kept it a secret that I want to be a bullfighter. It's something you have to do when you're young; it's not an old man's game;…I'm going on 19. Some people might think I'm already too old to get into this."

She shook me up pounding both fists on the dining room table. She had a wild look in her eyes.

"Damn this bull fightin' shit! You hear me?! Me and your father were lookin' forward to having grandkids running around. . ."

"Louise is gonna have grandchildren. . ."

"So what's that got to do with you?! You're gonna take your ass down there and get all gored up and maybe even killed. And we won't even know anything about it.

Don't you understand, Chester? This is not just about you, it's about us too. We love you and we don't want to see you goin' off to some foreign country to waste your life."

She was crying and I was on the verge of tears. It was time to leave. I stood up, circled the table and planted a good solid kiss on her left cheek.

"I love you too, Momma."

She was wiping her eyes with the palms of her hands.

"When are you leavin'?"

"Next Saturday. I'm taking a cheap one way flight to San Diego, and from there I'll take a bus down to Mexico City."

The way she shook her head from side to side, as though she was trying to shake the words out of her ears, reminded me of Dondisha.

"Y'all want to come over here and have dinner on Friday, before you leave?"

"Uhh, the bullfight is on, on Friday night."

I had the feeling that she wanted to embrace me and strangle me at the same time.

"Well, how about Thursday night?"

"That'll work."

"About 6:30 p.m.?"

"6:30 p.m. – we'll be here."

I pecked her on the other cheek and headed for the door. A thought, an idea had popped into my head. José Mangual, "Cantinflas", the pastry chef down in the Drake Hotel kitchen, the dude who had set things in motion with his tickets to see "Manolete" at the World PlayHouse Theater, was from Mexico City. He could give me a little traction and a lot of advice.

❖

CHAPTER SEVEN

The Drake Hotel kitchen was as busy as usual. It was four o'clock, a couple of hours before the six p.m. dinner hour would turn the place into a madhouse. The kitchen would be preparing gourmet cuisine for the Drake Hotel dining room, as well as room service orders. It was busy, but it would get busier.

I nodded to a few familiar faces and they nodded back, the surly French-woman who made the exquisite little Japanesy salads, even smiled and waved. "Cantinflas" was at his station, breaking in a new helper, a Latino like himself. He stared at me for a second, as though he didn't recognize me. "Hey keed! How you doin', man? Look at you! You look like you added a couple inches to yourself."

"Maybe I have, I see you finally got some help."

"Ahh yesss, this ees Carlos Espinosa, he's from El Salvador. He's gonna be good when I finish wid heem. So, how come you're here? They told me you was fired."

"Yeah, I was fired, but I wanted to come back and talk with you about a couple things. You got a minute?"

"Sure, keed. I'm due for my break. You wanna go down to the cafeteria for a cuppa coffee?"

"Sure, good idea."

Jośe gave his helper specific instructions to do about ten different things while he was taking his break. I could tell it wasn't a nasty master-rebellious slave sort of relationship from the way the helper smiled and nodded.

"O.K. le's go I got twenty minutes."

———◆———

The employee's cafeteria was where the snooty waiters in their tight pants and bolero jackets came during their "down time"; where the Spanish speaking household/room cleaning staff, mostly women, came for their breaks.

"Cantinflas" was almost a celebrity in this setting. By the time we made it to a corner table, he had exchanged dirty jokes with half of the Spanish speaking men and flirted with all of the women.

"So, wassup, keed?"

"Jose, I'm going to Mexico, to Mexico City, to become a matador…"

"Hold on a sec, you wanna caffee?"

"Yeah, thanks."

He brought back two steaming cups of Kenya blend from the urn. And he had a serious expression on his comedian's face.

"So, Chester, you really gonna do it, huh?"

"Yes, I'm really gonna do it. And I think you can help me."

He smiled at me and stirred sugar into his coffee.

"Cheester, I'm a baker, man, I dunno nothin' about the inside of the bull world."

"You're from Mexico City, right?"

"Yesss, I'm a Chilongo."

"So, here's what I need. I'll need a place to live in the capital, and it can't be the big tourist hotel because I don't have that kind of money. I'll find out where the bullfight scene is, but I'll need a place to stay while I do that."

He took a sip of his coffee and made a production number happen with his big, expressive brown eyes as two heavy bottomed maids swiveled past our table. But when he turned back to me he was totally serious.

"You know, eets kinda fonny, all of the Mexicans is leavin' Mexico to come to el Norte and you wanna go there."

"Can you help me?"

He took another, longer sip of his coffee.

"Chester, you got a pen, some paper?"

I was prepared. I pulled out my ball point and five small flash cards (3" x 5").

"O.K., here's what I'm givin' you. I have some primos, som' couseens who live in a section of Mexico City called Tlaltelolco. Tlaltelolco is not beery good, you know what I mean?"

"I know what you mean."

"Also, my father's brother live in Xochimilco, a lil' bit outside the centro."

"I've read about Xochimilco, it's where they have the floating gardens and the decorated rowboats."

"Eggactly! My Uncle Pedro owns one of these boats; he make decent money in the tourist season. Now I give house numbers for both of these, my couseens and my Uncle Pedro. They don't have telephonos so you must go to them personal."

"So, which one of these do you think would be best for me?"

"Well, I do know that all of theem would like to make a few extra pesos. The primos in Tlaltelolco are young, like you self; but they don't really know the bullfight, they like futbol/soccer more. Not only that, they like to smoke mota a lot."

"Mota, Marijuana?"

"Si, Marijuana. You smoke?"

"Smoking anything is bad for the bullfighter, you need all the air in your lungs you can get."

José seemed to look at me with a little more respect.

"O.K., keed, maybe you do these. You go to Mexico City, do the hook up for a few daze wid my couseens, to get a feelin' for the city, huh?"

"That sounds like a good idea."

"I will teach you about the peso, how much you pay theem for each night. They won't feed you but no problem, food en the streets in Mexico is good and cheap, muy barato. You know som' Spanish, yes?"

"Lots of words, mostly about bullfighting."

"No problema. You know taco, burrito, machaca, stuff to eat?"

"O yes."

"So now you know the city and then you go to Uncle Pedro in Xochimilco. Hes a good person, he won't charge much dinero. But you know, in Mexico, many people still sleep on the mat, on the floor. Is a problema?"

"No, Jośe, no problema."

"Also, because Uncle Pedro is an aficionado, he will be able to tell you where the bull people go to eat and drink."

"GREAT! That's exactly what I want."

"I gotta go back up to my stacion, but let me tell you, Cheester… you most be berry careful of yourself. Theres a lot of criminals in Mexico City, bad people. Some people may keednap you for the ransom because you are a gringo and they theenk you hab money. You know what I mean? And many drogas, many drogas."

"I don't do drugs."

"Bueno. Now, here on thees card I write my name Jośe Tamayo Mangual and I poot my phon' number. If my couseens and my Uncle Pedro want to say who you are, they contact me and I weel tell them you are my freend and you want to become a matador".

"Jośe, thanks man. I really appreciate your help."

"No problema. I wish you mucho suerte."

"I'll walk out with you."

As we strolled out of the cafeteria, Jośe did his dirty talk to the men and his flirtation thing with the women. We shook hands on the pavilion level.

"Jośe, one last thing. You know when I was working here and I got you a lot of those onion skinned condoms, were you using all of them yourself?"

He looked embarrassed, gave me a shy smile.

"Well;, Cheester, I use som' but I'm not the Superman, you know? And then I sell the others. Sorry." So, Fox was right José had used us.

"No problema, Jośe. No problema."

I walked away from "Cantinflas" feeling all puffed up. I was on my way to Mexico City and I had some people to go to.

———◆———

Thursday evening I had to practically force Dondisha to go to my parent's house for dinner.

"Chester, don't you think this is going to make me look a lil' bit stupid? The deserted, fat, kindergarten teacher had her last meal with her beloved's family."

"Dondisha, you can choose to see it any kind of way you want to. All I'm saying to you is that Mom is a very good cook and she invited us to dinner.

Now you can read anything you want to into that, do you want to go or not?"

"What should I wear?"

Dad met us at the door with the Hennessey, my sister draped her arm around Dondisha's waist like they were ol' friends and Mom had us at the dining room table a half-hour later, surrounding a succulent leg of lamb, spiced with basil, garlic and green bell peppers. Basmati rice, creamed spinach and stir fried okra with cumin rounded things out.

"We got Key Lime Pie for desert"

It was close to an outer body experience for me. My focus was so cold. I saw Dondisha as a failed woman. Let me explain that. She might've been able to hold on to me, if her discipline hadn't failed. I'm not talking about getting chubby exactly, or anything like that.

In her case, it was like looking at somebody who had decided that she had her man, which was all that counted in her kindergarten life, and everything was supposed to be cool forever afterward. Obviously she hadn't thought about becoming involved with a potential matador.

It was good to look at Louise and see that she looked well, her career goals were being met; and that I could finally get away from sibling rivalry, no matter how petty it was, she almost looked happy.

Dad seemed to be enjoying himself. Maybe it was the cognac, I can't really say. Mom made damned certain that I was aware that she had done this leg of lamb for yours truly.

"No doubt in my mind Chester got into this lamb thing from workin' down at the Drake. 'Mom', he said to me, 'Why don't we have some leg of lamb?'

"We'll have leg of lamb, son, as soon as you bring me one.

He brought me two of 'em'. And I didn't flinch. I did a lot cook book research to figure out what to do with legs o' lamb."

"It's delicious, Mrs. Simmons."

"Girl!, I've told you to call me Lillian."

And so on. The food was really delicious which didn't require much beyond – "Please, pass me the spinach."

Gorgeously baked leg of lamb, beautifully steamed Basmati rice, creamed spinach, stir fried okra with cumin. It would have to be called a gourmet feast. Dondisha had seconds, with a look in my outer body face that said, "Fuck you! I may as well enjoy this, you're leaving."

Mom and Dad were my linchpin study figures. I could tell that they weren't completely down with my matador decision, but they had reconciled themselves to how I thought about that. That was one of the secrets of/for their survival and thriving. They knew how to make adjustments. Dondisha saw me as a brotha/brother who wanted to trip off into a "Twilight Zone" that she had never thought about. I could understand that. I could actually sympathize with her, up to a point. Louise didn't concern me a lot. She was my sister and I knew, come hell or high water, she would be there for me.

As I thought about it, in an outer body kind of way, I wasn't' too bad off. My closest family members were with me, my girlfriend was on the scene and I was getting ready to go out into the world and do my thing.

I came back to myself with the sweet tartness of the first fork full of Key Lime Pie.

"Mom, I gotta tell you – this tastes better than love."

"How would you know?" Dondisha sounded like a snake hissing when she asked the question. Mom, Dad and Louise tried to hide their amused expressions. Me and Dondisha could've gotten into something nasty; but I wouldn't take the bait. I smiled at her and took another thin slice of pie. The evening was winding down, we could feel that. So far so good. No one had jammed me about leaving; no one had tried to bust me with hard, cold questions and Dondisha was the only one who asked a sarcastic question.

It was very clever, the way they did it. Mom asked me to help her take the leftovers to the kitchen and slipped five crisp hundred dollar bills into my shirt pocket. I was wondering why she hadn't asked Louise to help her clear the table.

"Chester, you're doin' something real crazy, but you're still my son. Now, don't you go down there and suffer. You understand me?"

"I understand, Mom. And thanks."

Dad invited me to take a look at this new program in his computer-den, and slipped me an envelope with ten one-hundred dollar bills in it.

"No need to tell your Momma about this. And you've got my numbers -- work, home and cell phone. If you run into any kind of problems give me a jingle. O.K.?"

"I'll do that. And thanks, Dad. I really appreciate it."

I was leaving town with almost five grand in pocket. The exchange rate was pegged at fourteen pesos to the dollar. I was going to Mexico with seventy thousand pesos. I had no real idea how much things in Mexico would cost; but I felt pretty certain I'd be able to make it pretty well on seventy thousand for about six months.

The ending of the evening went real smooth. Louise gave me a big hug and a kiss.

"I love you, Chester. You ain't got good sense but I love you anyway."

Mom and Dad seemed to focus their attention on Dondisha.

"Dondisha, just because Chester won't be here shouldn't stop you from paying us a visit whenever you like."

"Yeah, don't make yourself a stranger."

"I'll remember that Mr. Simmons, Mzz Simmons. I really enjoyed dinner."

I had a real weird feeling grab me as I turned around to wave a final goodbye. Mom, Dad and Sis were standing in the doorway, waving, the light from the chantileer in the hallway formed a back drop.

I may never see them again. I drove away with that thought on my mind, I couldn't shake it. And I didn't know what to do about it.

Dondisha was folded into an angry knot in the passenger's seat, flinging me ugly glances from time to time.

"Dondisha, it's a nice night, you want to take a walk around Buckingham fountain?"

"Uhh, yes, that would be nice."

CHAPTER EIGHT

Strolling around the fountain, sort of a Chicago custom. I held Dondisha's hand as we strolled, surprising her a little I think. The light misty spray from the erupting fountain felt delicious. Lots of couples strolling around just like us.

I felt greedy about the whole scene; the Chicago skyscrapers on Michigan Avenue, the twinkling lights on the sail boats out in the marina, the smells, the distant sound of somebody blowing a trumpet. I couldn't ever remember feeling soft about Chicago. It was where I was born, but I had never thought of it as "home". It was where I was born, where I grew up, but it never claimed my heart. I think a bit of that changed on that warm June night.

"I'm really going to miss this…"

"That all you're gonna miss?" She said it with a little smile; so I could tell she wasn't being nasty. I led us to a park bench, I felt the urge to open my heart and guts to Dondisha.

"Dondisha, please let me explain something to you."

"I'm listening."

"I want you to understand that I have a very deep affection for you; I could call it love, but that wouldn't be the honest to God truth. What I really love is the bullfight."

"I know, you've told me that often enough."

"O.K., so I have. But what I think is important for you to know is that I'm not running away from you; I'm not leaving you because I don't have any feeling for you or anything like that."

I was out of words. What else could I say?

"Chester, let me explain something to you. I may be from the country, from Miss'ssippi and all that; but I have a pretty good mind and I've never been afraid to face the truth.

Yes, I would love to have you stay here with me in Chicago because I love you."

I felt like somebody had dropped load of bricks on my head.

"Yes, I love you. Is that wrong?"

I had to nod no, no, no, it's not wrong.

"You don't love me, you love bullfighting. I love you, that would make for a very unhappy situation in the long run. So, maybe I should be grateful that this is playing out the way it is.

I thought of a half dozen ways to try to keep you here, including not taking my birth control pills. But I didn't want to play games with you because you've never played games with me. I appreciated that."

I felt my heart drop down into my guts. Dondisha had never talked to me like this. Or maybe I had never listened to her before.

"You're going off on a great adventure and if I had the nerve to push everything aside, I would go with you. I might begin to love what you love and then maybe you would begin to love me. But I don't have that kind of nerve; I'm afraid to take those kinds of chances.

So far, in my life, the greatest risk I've ever taken was coming to Chicago from Miss'ssippi."

"I'm glad you came, I'm glad we got a chance to know each other, to be together."

"I am too, Chester, I am too."

We kissed. I don't know what the people passing by may have thought…that we were Spring time lovers maybe. But the kiss wasn't so much romantic as it was a contract. I felt the kiss said – well, there's no need for us to be angry with each other about anything, you're who you are and I'm who I am. Let's not spoil it by trying to put on phony masks.

I felt cleaner and lighter when we left the fountain, I only had a day and a half left before Mexico. Thank God, I wouldn't be leaving a woman behind who hated my guts.

Coming into San Diego. It was the palm trees that did it to me first as the plane taxied down from the sky. And after we landed, the bare flesh all around.

It seemed like everyone was dressed for the beach walking down the street…swim suits everywhere. Maybe they weren't really swim suits but they **looked** like swim suits.

The contrast with where I was from and this scene, well there was no comparison. In Chicago, some people didn't start taking off their winter stuff until they were absolutely sure that the summer had come.

My plan was simple: spend the weekend in San Diego and cross the border for a loonng bus ride to Mexico City. I should've been nervous or maybe a bit shaky, but I didn't feel any of that. I was completely calm.

I got in the first taxi I saw that was being driven by a brother. I figured the Black man would be more in tune with what I wanted.

"Where to?"

"I need a very cheap place to stay for a couple of days."

That was all I needed to say. The driver, one of those done-seen-it all types, with a toothpick in the corner of his mouth, glanced up at me and drove me straight to a run down, but clean, motel in the Black section of San Diego. I knew it would be there.

I took a cold water shower and sprawled on the camel backed bed. Just a few hours ago I was in a different place, a different world.

"Chester, make sure you have the serial numbers for all of your traveler's checks. Oh, and don't forget to take some aspirins, they're good for a whole bunch of things other than headaches."

Dear Dondisha, I can't begin to tell you how grateful I am that you didn't become a screamin' bitch during our last moments together.

"So Dondisha, what's going to happen. I mean, uhh, what…?"

"I know what you mean. I'm going to get married to some hard working brother, probably ten of fifteen years older than me, who wants somebody to feed his gut and pat his butt. And live happily ever after."

She had the saddest expression on her face when she said that. I don't think she realized that her expression reflected her sadness. O well, there was nothing I could do about it. I nodded off into a small piece of jet lagged sleep.

———◆◆———

I could tell that I was definitely in the fast section of town the minute I stepped out in the street bordering the motel. The usual suspects, the brothers who always seemed to be holding up a corner were clustered over there, chuggin' Forties and passing a finger sized joint around. A few sisters wearing skin tight everything blaséd down the street. A couple well polished vehicles rolled down opposite sides of the street, each one trying to shake the Earth harder than the other with their boom boxes.

I was one of them, after all, these were my peers. But I felt much older, more sophisticated than them. I could give the corrida, the bullfight, the biggest amount of credit for some of my feelings.

When I might've fallen into the usual, teenaged African-American hip hop-rap thing, the bullfight had steered me into Flamenco. And maybe "Raul's" tango class opened a few doors too. I heard the rap, shit, you couldn't help hearing it, it was all over the place. But it didn't grip my attention and imagination as strongly as this other music, music that I couldn't play, sing, or even understand unless I read the C.D. notes. I was beginning to feel a bit snackish. What did they have to eat in the 'hood?

From what I could smell, everything within walking distance was being fried in stale grease. I strolled along, weighing a bunch of options. I was a stranger, an outsider, everybody could see that. Which meant that I had to be double careful about how I approached people. If I stopped one of the skin tight sisters, somebody might think I was a trick. Or maybe a fool trying to hit on somebody's girlfriend.

If I approached the wrong set of dudes and they had some kind of negative vibes going on, well, no telling. I knew that I had to be on somebody's turf in gang country.

I spotted a brother loping along by himself. He would be a likely source of information.

"Uhh, my brother, where can I get something to eat?"

It only took a hard glance to see that I was talking to a dope fiend. Damn. He stared me up and down for a minute.

"You want somethin' to eat, huh?"

"Yeah, I want something to eat."

He scratched his head and went into a gentle nod. Heroin, I knew that kind of nod – Bowen Avenue and before that, the Almo Hotel had been my dope head observation points. He eased out of his stupor after a few seconds and pointed a dirty finger down the street.

"Stay on this street 'til you get to the light and then turn right."

"How far?"

"About two blocks. Uhh, look, my brother, could you let me have some of your spare change?"

I hated that spare change stuff. Why not just ask for some money? I handed him a dollar and kept walking in the direction he had pointed out.

The light and turn right, about two blocks. A Kentucky Fried Chicken outlet on one corner, a Taco Bell on the opposite corner, a Golden Bird on one corner and the double arches of the Almighty McDonalds on the other corner. O well….

Walking back to the Silverado Motel I got the awful impression of being on the fringes of an old fashioned chase'em'round'n 'round movie set. The police helicopter, better known as "the ghetto bird" across the ghettos of America, was circling and throwing down movie premiere lights on something suspicious. Police cars, some simply flashing the top lights, others howling and screaming around corners, were out in force. I couldn't see the thugs they were out for, but I had no doubt that they were there.

The sudden loud SQUAWK of the police car loud speaker caught me by surprise.

"Put your hands in the air and turn around slowly; do that NOW!"

I did exactly as told. I didn't come to San Diego to get killed by a couple trigger happy cowboy-cops. The light from the side of the squad car was blinding but I just blinked, I didn't try to shield my eyes from the glare. The headlines would say – "Suspect attempted to reach for a weapon in his waist band."

One of the cops got out on the passenger side with his piece drawn and held down beside his thigh. These babies were not playing around.

The driver approached me from an oblique angle with the light still blinding me.

"What're you doing out here?"

"I'm visiting San Diego overnight, I'm staying at the Silverado Motel. I just walked up to McDonalds for a couple 'burgers."

I knew it was important to be straight forward about things, not to make any attempt to be snappish. Dad had warned me about negative police behavior years ago.

"Don't do anything that's gonna be undignified, but don't be defiant for the sake of being defiant. You have to remember, a lot of these cops are racist to the core, 'specially when it comes to young African-American males."

"Where are you from?" He sounded like a gang banger.

"Chicago."

"So, what're you doing here?"

"I'm on my way to Mexico."

"What're you gonna do down there, buy dope?"

I didn't even make an effort to dignify that stupid question with an answer. I just stood there. I had a couple of the kind of cops in front of me that Dad had told me about. I had dealt with them in Chicago, now it was San Diego.

"Awright, get your black ass outta here, if we see you out here again, we're gonna run you in."

I hate to say it, but as I turned to walk away from them, I fully expected to be shot. I would've been an un-missable target. I didn't run, but I did walk quickly back to the Silverado Motel.

I took it in at a glance, somebody had been rummaging around in my room. I was traveling light with a rolling, medium sized valise, a shoulder strap carry on and a long, pool cue type bag with my muleta and capote.

The pool cue case was open, the contents disturbed. The shoulder carry and the valise had been "investigated", but nothing was taken.

My "investigator" or "investigators" were obviously not interested in clean underwear, deodorant or capes. They had come for money, no doubt, and when they couldn't find any they split.

I made a mental note to send Dondisha a thank you note for

encouraging me to write down the serial numbers of all my traveler's checks. I had the checks and serial numbers tucked into my "smugglers" waist belt. And if I happened to lose that, Dad had all of the stuff in a flash drive back-up guaranteed.

I had a wild impulse to go to the desk clerk and complain about the break in, but checked myself. There was no sign of anybody breaking in. It was quite likely that the desk clerk may have been the guilty one. Or the brother dope fiend that I had met, the one who had given me the directions to the golden arches. I braced a chair under the door knob before going to sleep, before **trying** to go to sleep. The random screams, weird yells, strange curses, boom box challenges and rough laughter made me think of the ol' Almo Hotel. I made a quick decision to leave for Tijuana, en route to Mexico City, the next day.

No need to hang around in the 'hood any longer than necessary, had been there, done that, had the T-shirt.

"Sorry, we can't refund your payment. You paid for two days and two nights…"

"I wasn't holding my breath, I just thought you might be willing to do the right thing."

"What's that 'sposed to mean?"

"Nothing, my brother, nothing at all."

———◆———

The La Estrella de Oro bus could've been a Greyhound leaving the terminal for Tijuana; but it soon developed a different kind of character a few miles down the road. Vendors popped on for a mile or so. I noticed the driver taking what he wanted without paying a centavo. Maybe that was part of the arrangement.

Farmers, male and female, struggled onto the buss with huge loads of all kinds of things; trussed up chickens, turkeys (?!), a couple medium sized pigs, birds in a large cage, baked goods, you could buy a sweet bread if you wanted, candy sellers. Like I said, all kinds of things.

People got on, rode for a few miles, got off. But I rode on and on and on. People glanced at me as they got on but nobody glared. Some of the more unsophisticated country types stared, but they didn't glare. It was like, nobody had an attitude. I took careful notice of that. I could easily imagine the shoe on the other foot – "Who is this Mesican among us?"

The country people smiled at me and I smiled back. The more sophisticated types read their newspapers, napped, stared at the moonscape we were passing through. I had no idea that there was so much desert in Mexico.

From time to time the driver stopped in some out of the way place to give us a chance to pee, grab a taco or whatever.

After a day and a half of watching each other fall asleep during our journey, he had gotten to know that I was "Chester", and he was "Octavio".

"I yam Octavio, the driver."

I would never be guilty of recommending Octavio for a bus driver's job anywhere but Mexico. There was no doubt that he knew every twist and turn of the road, every pothole and crack in the pavement. There <u>were</u> times when I thought we were lost. It had to do with these interesting detours he took.

Two days into our trip, he looked at me in his overhead rearview mirror and winked. What did that mean? Ten minutes later he steered his bus through the narrow back streets of a small town, double parked, left the motor running and disappeared behind a high stone wall surrounding a two storey building. I was probably the only one aboard the bus who didn't know what was happening. It he had to take a piss, why didn't he do what he usually did? Step to the blind spot behind the right rear wheel.

Fifteen minutes later he reappeared with a silly smile on his face, rubbing his stomach as though he had just had a really good burrito. It wasn't hard to guess why the hipsters on the bus were exchanging sly grins and double bladed remarks. Well, who could blame the dude for trying to give his sex urge a square deal?

I wasn't as much concerned about his sexual habits as I was about his driving. So far as I could tell he had only taken little cat naps whenever he stopped to give his passengers a chance to pee or grab or snack. During the course of one extended stop, a half hour/forty-five minutes, he draped a large hanky over his face, adjusted his seat back as far as possible and went to sleep. Like, really went to sleep, snoring.

I don't know why I grew to trust him. Let's face it, a guy driving a bus load of people who nods off from time to time doesn't inspire a lot of confidence, but there was something about the man that made me feel – well, he doesn't want to die, I could tell that from the way he ate, drank, and made his sex stop. So, I guess that made it possible for me to go into deep sleeps from time to time.

Traveling down through Central Mexico, through the great Sonoran desert gave me the feeling of having an outer body experience, of being in a spaceship – bubble. Maybe it had something to do with the people I was sharing this journey with. These weren't light beige skinned Mestizos/Mestizas, Spanish looking folks; these were Mexican Indians, straight up.

I looked across the aisle and saw profiles that could've come straight off of a temple wall. I looked around me and saw faces that looked mahogany colored Chinese people.

It was really a trip to see that my own walnut color was often the lightest shade of brown on the bus. The Indians glanced my way from time to time, but no one stared, re-enforcing my feeling of being in a bubble, of having this out of body experience. I could float up and down the aisle, checking out the scene. I could ask myself questions from "up there".

"Why do you want to do this?"

There were moments when I felt a tight feeling in my chest because I couldn't answer the questions I was asking myself. And then there were other times when I almost spoke aloud – *it's a challenge, I accept the challenge. I want to do it because the whole world says – I shouldn't do it, that I can't do it.*

"Who the hell are you anyway, to think that you can take your ass down into Mexico and make it?"

That was the question that caused me the most concern. It almost caused me to hop off the bus and go back the other way.

What right did I have, to think that I could go to where so many had failed, and I would succeed? I looked around at all the bronzed faces. What made me think that I could compete against so many?

Well, all of them didn't want to become bullfighters, so, I rationalized, the odds were in my favor.

"Where are you from?" The saggin' 'n baggin-hip hop gang banger's question before the Glocks spouted sparks.

"Where are you from?"

The question blew my confidence up. I was from the Almo Hotel – Bowen Avenue – Southside scene, places where rats stalked cats, where only the strong survived, where babies had babies. I made a mental note to find out what had happened to whatshername, the girl I got pregnant on the bathroom floor in the Almo Hotel. Wonder what she had, a boy or a girl? Too bad her dope fiend/wino parents moved away before the baby was born. I'll have to look into that someday. Where are you from? Hmmmm. . . .

———————◆◆———————

The mostly gentle swaying of the bus, the hypnotic humming of the tires on the highway caused him to have sexy catnaps, thinking about a few of the girls he had done it to in high school, and before, and after Dondisha.

"Chester, I love to make love to you, you know why?"

"Why?"

"'Cause you enjoy it so much."

"All men like to make love, Dondisha."

"That ain't what some of my girlfriends tell me. One of my girlfriends – you met Tamika?"

"Yeah, I remember her." O lawd h'mercy. Tamika Smith about 5'8", about 130, 38-22-38, or something like that. A cocoa colored sexual magnet, married.

"Tamika been married for five years now and she confided in me that she ain't never had an organism."

"But she has two kids, doesn't she?"

"Uh huh. But that don't mean that she has had an orgasm."

"Well, what's the problem…?"

"It's her husband, Jerome. She says he just jumps on her bones, has an orgasm and goes to sleep. He doesn't really seem to enjoy having sex with her. He just wants to do it and get it over with. That's what she told me."

I had to smile at the thought of so much pussy being wasted. I could just imagine my dick sliding slowly, in and out of Tamika's juicy cunt. Cum-cream coating my dick like butter-milk.

I came out of my sexual catnap, more than once to find a few bronzed faces, men and women, actually staring in my direction. Did I moan, remember how juicy and delicious Dondisha felt to me? How juicy and delicious Tamika would've felt to me?

Or had my fellow passengers watched this giant sausage erection swell up between my legs. I made it my business, whenever I nodded off, to have my cap in my lap. Or a bag of something to conceal my sexual dreams/arousals.

———◆———

"So, how do you fit into the picture?"

I had to adjust and re-adjust the lens in order to get a clear shot at that one. As a would be bullfighter I had to admit that most of the people in my community, my family, my friends, didn't think that there was a slot for me in the taurine world.

"Chester, my brother, who in the hell ever heard of a normal person, comin' off the Southside of Chicago, goin' into bullfightin?"

The person who might've been considered the most influential in my decision to take up the cape, Señor "Cantinflas", wasn't exactly hot on the idea of me becoming a matador either.

"Eh keed, you know these thing of the bulls is berry serious sheet, you know wot I'm sayin'? A man could get gored…in the cojones. You know wot I'm sayin'?"

The bus seemed to have the air conditioning system off a lot, leaving him to nod off in a stupor and wake up in a stupor, constantly thinking.

"Interesting. It seems like me and Dad grew closer after I split to Dondisha's pad. Maybe we needed to have that space."

And there were always the negative echoes, racial stuff.

"Black people got more sense than to be sky divin', mountain climbin, scuba divin', bungee jumpin', fightin' bulls. . ."

"Black people don't fight animals, we fight each other, or play against whoever. But we do not be fightin' wild animals 'n shit. That's White boy action."

"Mexicans ain't White. Peruvians ain't White. Venezuelans may or may not be White, depending on which tree they came out of, and quiet as it's kept, a whole lot of Spanish have a bunch of Moorish-Arab blood tucked away inside their DNA. . ."

⸻ ◆ ⸻

After all was said and all the dreams were done I was on my way to Mexico City, to find my way into the bullring. I tested my commitment many times by asking myself, "'ey you! 'ey you! Why do you want to do this?"

The answers varied – I want to do this because I **want** to do it, it has nothing to do with what somebody else wants me to do, this is what I **want** to do.

I had fallen in love with this incredible idea of a man facing Death in the afternoon. Did that make me a "death wish" freak? Well, I guess I could join a whole line of "death wish" freaks, starting with the Romero brothers, back in the 17th century. And before.

The deadly beauty of it, of the art of it. That grabbed me. I had never felt the urge to be a dancer or to go out into a public place to show off, but the bullfight seemed like an ideal place for a shy person to share private emotions. I wanted to confront this fear inside myself, and to show you how I'm going to do it. Can you dig it? –as "Raul" would've said.

I thought about the last fight I had seen before I left Chicago. The bullfighter, I'm not going to mention his name, was so scared that he had peed on himself. You could see the piss stain on the left thigh of his suit of lights. This bullfighter had a fairly good reputation; but he had chickened out in this fight. Maybe the bull's horns intimidated him. Maybe he had not prepared himself sufficiently, spiritually. Maybe he just felt not quite up to it on that particular day.

I would never be able to put a label on what happened in that man's head. I tried not to concern myself with what I thought about his actions, I was more interested in how I was going to deal with what I had to face.

What was I going to do when I face my test, my bull, my moment of truth?

I woke up, on the dog leg to Mexico City, to find a different driver behind the wheel of our bus. When did they change over? Where, what happened to Octavio? Well, what the hell, we were heading into the Mexican capital. Well, let's say – we were <u>almost</u> heading into Mexico City. It seemed to take us almost an hour to "negotiate" two blocks on the Paseo de la Reforma. The traffic was a beast-monster.

I had this incredible feeling that I was driving past an ant hill. I don't mean to be insulting by calling people ants or anything negative, but that was the impression I got. People were everywhere, doing every possible thing you could think of a human being doing. I knew that Mexico City had a population of 22 million or something close to that. And it was like they were all out in the streets at the same time. 22 million people, and I was jumping off right in the middle of all of them in the middle of the night.

It's one thing to hop off of a bus in the middle of the night and another thing to jump off into the middle of all of this in the middle of the afternoon. Midnight. All of the people I had traveled with hopped off the bus with people waiting to meet them, places to go. I hopped off of the bus and, for a few beats, I didn't know whether to shit or go blind, as some of the ol' hipsters used to say.

Midnight. I didn't think it would make a lot of sense to get out into the city to look for a room for a few hours. So, I decided to hug the bus station benches 'til dawn. Intuition, I found out, was a great way to go through life in Mexico City.

I think in many ways, it was only intuition that saved my ass in Mexico City, 'specially in the first few days I was in the capital.

By the time the sun came up I think I must've had every con game I could think of shot at me: people trying to sell me funny money at a discount, weasel types trying to sell me "precious gems". Precious gems?—in the bus station? Women with the faces of Madonnas offering me a shot of "paradise", cheap. I wanted to laugh at the games but I knew I had to take everything seriously or else I would be ripped off.

I remembered something an ol' hustler had told me one day, chillin' on the cool front steps of the Almo Hotel…

"It be like this, young blood – blink once in front of a bonafide hustler and he'll have a leg up on you. Blink twice and he'll be all over you, that's how fast the game can be."

I kept that right up in front of me as the games swarmed around me, plowed right into me. I was a gringo, un-Americano, and I had to assume that people were going to try to do it to me. All I could say is – "I'm ready". I had so many pickpockets come at me I actually started studying their methods.

The "frontal assault" types just came up in my face and while they pretended to be about something, or into something, or want something, or want me to do something with them, they would literally be digging through all of the pockets they could reach.

Gotta give it to 'em, the pickpockets became my favorites over the course of the night. Never met a bolder, more imaginative, more creative, hipper collection of artists. I just literally let them rummage through my outer pockets, to let them know that you ain't gittin nothing here. News travels fast. He must have it nestling against his nuts, no sense trying to pick that deep, he'll feel it.

Once they decided I was "un-pickable", they slithered away to other prey. I slumped in my seat and studied the various teams of artists "at work". Team #1; they used a gorgeous young, beige colored woman to open up "the prey". She slithered up to the "prey", flicked her split tongue at him/her designed some set of circumstances that would distract the prey so that the fellow members of her team could do their thing.

Whatshisname?; the ol' hustler was absolutely on the money. All you had to do was blink once in front of a bona fide hustler. I saw it in operation, in the raw. These people were not into bullshit, they were working for a living. Blink.

I knew something about Mexican bullfighting, about how people like Luis Procuna had graduated from selling tacos on San Juan de Letrán Street to becoming a better paid matador. I saw the same thing in operation in the bus station. As an example of one of the most hippest demos of the pickpocket profession, I saw three pros, a young man and a grandmother looking woman, give a novice pickpocket a beautiful lesson in how to do their art.

In a seeming random way, I thought, I saw these three "work" their way through a collection of foreign visitors to Mexico City. The first question I had in the back of my mind was – how did y'all wind up in the busstation? Well, why not? I was there, it was a transportation spot.

There were moments when I felt so down about what was happening in the busstation; but then I had to spray some reality on the scene. If I was struggling to survive in Mexico City I would probably be involved in some kind of busstation game myself.

Unreal...not just the pickpocket scene, but the way some foreigners, who might've been hip, savvy, intelligent individuals at home, suddenly behaved like ol' fashioned idiots in this setting. The Americans headed the list. Damn, we were just across the street from Mexico, in a manner of speaking. Shouldn't we know a little more about what was happening than other folks?

CHAPTER NINE

I focused on the African-Americans in the mix, easy to do, few to observe, definitely up tight, ill at ease. I watched the hustlers rip them off casually, without any malice aforethought, as the legal types say.

"Ahh, Senõr Heep Hop, please allow me to arrange your taxi transportation. Please give me the money for exchange to pesos. I can get the better rate than you."

"How much do I need to exchange."

"Feefty dolares."

"Fifty dollars?"

"Si."

So, he gives the con man fifty dollars to exchange for pesos. Huh? Why couldn't he walk over to the exchange booth and do the business himself? Well, he had been told that 'Mr. Feefty" could get a better exchange rate. Greed, the great motivator. "Mr. Feefty" submerged himself in the layers of people swarming around and, about ten minutes later, Senõr Heep Hop realized he had been taken.

I strolled out of the busstation-anthill, feeling fully capable of dealing with anything. If I could cope with all of the stuff in the busstation-anthill, then I could certainly cope with the street ant-hill.

Out on the street I felt the wildest impulse to run back inside the busstation-anthill, I was familiar with that. The streets were a **super** ant hill. Mexico City, in '09, had twenty-two million people. That's what the official figure was. I'm sure there were more than twenty-two million people swarming around. Hell, I felt like I was surrounded by at least eleven million alone. Well, I was where I wanted to be, nothing to do but get a tight grip on my balls and do what I came to do.

━━━━━◆━━━━━

It wasn't hard to figure out that the taxi driver who dropped me in the Tlaltelolco section, right at the address I gave him, was overcharging me by a hundred pesos, but what the hell. I knew I was going to have to pay for my early lessons. I vowed that I would learn fast and good.

The place the taxi driver took me to looked like the ol'fashioned Robert Taylor projects in Chicago. Maybe somebody had tripped to Chitown and ripped the design off. These weren't fifteen storey high rises, only five storeys. But the slabs of concrete looking like huge loaves of hard bread, with a large, triangular inner courtyard was the same. And if the people hadn't been mostly dark beige with straight dark hair, Mexicans, they might've been poverty entrenched African-Americans.

I knew I was in the right place based on the description José "Cantinflas" had given me.

"Cheester, I have to tell yu, my freend, the place where my primos, my cousins, live is not a nize place. Matter of fact, it's a dump, a garbage heap. And the people are not so nize either, so I have to warn you – be careful."

"Thanks, José, I appreciate that. And I will be careful. All I want to do is get a feel for things, find out where the bullfight scene is and all of that."

"My Uncle Pedro and his wife, Juanita, in Xochimilco, more nize."

"I'll get to them, but I think it'll serve my purpose better to start off in the city."

"Be careful."

I had José's warning uppermost in my mind as I carried my two bags and my long cape bag into the triangular courtyard. It seemed like the earth had stopped moving. The holler level of the place quieted down to the boom box level, every eye in the place had me in it.

104

The Black Matador, "Sugar"

Yeahhh, there they were, the homies lounging around a beat up wooden bench in the center of the triangle. Somehow I knew they would be there. Wherever the surroundings were like these, there were always going to be dudes like these hangin' out.

I walked toward them slowly and carefully. I didn't want to look threatening in any kind of way. They looked me over as I approached. What the hell was I? A lost tourist? A brother from the states who wanted to cop some of their weed? A trick looking for a puta? What?

"Anyone of you brothers speak Inglés?"

Six of them, raging in age from about sixteen to twenty, I guessed, hard core. The looked at each other with that universal expression that meant –what is this fool talking about?

[*A few words about the linguistic thing. I was determined to learn as much Spanish as I could, in order to help me a achieve my goal. But since I felt I would never become completely fluent, I decided to work at what I knew best, the bullfight.*

Now then, having said that, I want to also say that I didn't want to try to do this whole thing in some kind of pidgin Spanglish. I wanted to make this as clear as possible without dialectin' to death.

In a few places it became impossible not to use those Spanish words that are only meaningful in Spanish. Düende is a good example. The English translation might come down to something like – "deeply felt emotion", but that would only be skimming the surface. See what I mean? Meanwhile, back to the brothers in the Tlaltelolco/Mexican projects. Check out what Zola Salena, my Spanish to English translator did. HalleLuya!)

Two of the homies sort of half raised their hands. They were not the types to admit that they knew anything very well. I zoomed in on the one who had his hand up highest.

"A friend of mine in Chicago gave me the names of his relatives who live here…"

The one that I had focused on cocked his head to one side as though to ask' what are their names?

"Their names are 'China', 'Ernesto', 'Alberto', 'Carlos', 'Rudy', and 'Paula Mangual'." Of course it was my imagination but it seemed that the holler level went back up, the tension slackened, people blinked their eyes.

"The Manguals, there,'" my information guide pointed to #301, above us and to the left.

"Gracias…"

I trudged up the stairs, no sign of an elevator anywhere, and knocked on #301. A young woman peeked through the barely opened door to stare at me. She looked more Chinese than Mexican, which explained, later, why she was called "China".

A heavy grained male voice asked her, "Who is it, China?" She told him – "It's the matador from Chicago". Her announcement was my entry to the fuzzy wuzzy life of "China", "Ernesto", "Alberto", "Carlos", "Rudy", "Paula" and a dozen other folks who flitted in and out of #301 for the week I survived living there.

They welcomed me into their home, into their apartment with smiles and big handshakes. "China", "Ernesto" and "Carlos" were on the scene, with a couple young women sleeping on a mattress in one of the other rooms. "Rudy", "Alberto" and "Paula" made it in a couple of hours later.

The apartment had layers of marijuana smoke and incense in it, empty beer bottles on the kitchen table. I thought that they were having some sort of celebration at first, with the joint going 'round and 'round, and somebody bringing in another six-pack every couple of hours.

No celebration happening, just a bunch of lost folks doing that lost weekend thing day in and day out. From the first hour I knew I was not going to be on the scene for very long. I could turn the offer to smoke some of the weed down by explaining that smoking was bad for the potential matador. I took a sip of piss warm beer whenever necessary.

It may sound patronizing, but I felt sorry for them. This was their lifestyle, being bombed all the time. I fascinated them….

"You have come all the way from the land of plenty, down here, to where there is nothing, to fight bulls?"

We sat on the seldom mopped floor, trading ideas, notions, emotions, feelings. I couldn't disguise my reason for being there and they couldn't make themselves believe what they were hearing.

"Soccer is the big thing, man. This thing of the bulls...ahhh, it's nasty, vicious, dangerous. A man could lose his cojones. You know what I'm sayin'?"

I actually felt like a breath of fresh air because I was bringing in a bunch of ideas, knowledge, I guess you could say, about some stuff they hadn't thought about. I also got tired as hell and hungry. José "Cantinflas" knew what he was talking about. They smoked a lot of dope, and sold a lot of it too. But nobody cooked.

On the third day of my stay I found out about the drug dealing and that jarred me a bit. Damn, the last thing I wanted to do was go to jail in Mexico. "China" hipped me to what was happening – "Oh, Rudy and Alberto have gone to pick up the mota..."

"The marijuana?"

"How much are they getting?"

"Oh, about five kilos."

Five kilos. That was definitely more than was needed for home consumption, no matter how much weed they smoked on a daily basis. I made it my business to focus on my own business.

"Ey, Carlos, you were going to take me to this bull fight café tonight, remember?"

"You want to go to this place where these old men drink sherry, smoke cigars, talk about old bullfighters and brag about all of the young women they could've fucked?"

"That's where I want to go."

"We can go tonight, you have dinero for drinks?"

"I got a few pesos."

"Good, we go tonight."

———————•◆•———————

I would've paid just to get into El Canarios, just to see the bullfight pictures and posters on the walls. And the old men drinking sherry, smoking cigars, talking about old bullfighters and bragging about all the young women they could've had.

"You want a table or to sit at the bar?"

I chose a corner table, a spot that would give us a wide angle view of the scene. Carlos thought the whole thing was **old**, I could tell from the way he looked at the people, the way the place looked, all of it. I didn't give a shit what he thought about anything, I was in my world.

The bar was about fifty yards long, dark wood, the place where mostly single men sat, sipping their sherry, and sometimes knocking a few tequilas down. I popped for a couple of beers. I didn't want to get bleery eyed from tequila.

There was nothing dim and romantic about the atmosphere. There were fans slowly whirling in the high ceiling, the place was brightly lit, like a huge cafeteria with a black and white checkerboard tiled floor. But the bullfight posters and the pictures of the great matadores on the past filled me up. I had seen most of the modern people on television: Ordõnez, Procuna, Arruza, Capetillo, Leal, Litri, Chamaco, Eloy Cavasos, Ignacio Garibay, José Luis Angelino, José Maria Luevano and a bunch of others.

Carlos sat across from me, sipping his beer and talking on his cell phone. I caught the word "cocaine" a half dozen times. "Cocaina", cocaine. We weren't talking herbal stuff, marijuana, mota; this was the chemical stuff, addictive drugs.

A kind of mad idea started forming in my head. I started thinking about "espontanéos", those bull crazy young bloods who sometimes jumped down in the bull ring while a fight was going on. If they were lucky they could do a few passes and maybe a manager would come and bail them out of jail and into a career. A whole bunch of the best had started off that way. Eloy Cavasos, for example.

"Carlos, let's go, I need to get some sleep."

He looked surprised.

"You don't want to stay no more?"

No, I need some sleep."

My plan was almost fully formed by the time we got a taxi back to Tlaltelolco. We were into Monday night. I would get up early Tuesday morning, go up on the roof and do a couple hours of work with my capes, the capote and the muleta.

I had forgotten that I was living in a household where nobody seemed to sleep for more than an hour at a time, except for the two women, Anita and Teresa, who were out for most of the night and asleep on the mattress in one of the four rooms for most of the day. It wasn't hard to guess why they were so tired.

They had blocked off a corner for me with a couple sheets. I had more privacy than anyone in the house. I went behind the sheets and flopped down on my mat. I laced my hands behind my head and looked at the silhouettes flicking back and forth. Despite the noise I forced myself to go to sleep. I knew I would need to be as well rested as possible in order to do what I planned to do on Sunday at 4 o'clock in the afternoon.

CHAPTER TEN

I passed by Rudy, "China", Paula, Ernesto and a couple of other people leaning over the kitchen table snorting long lines of cocaine from the table top. I glanced at them and they glanced at me. What was there to say? They were doing their thing and I was going to do my thing.

A Mexico City tenement roof top at six a.m., Tlaltelolco. From the moment I unfurled my capote to do a dozen Media Vernonicas and Veronicas, I felt a sense of mystery, of magic, about what I was doing, about what was happening to me. I was on my way to becoming a bullfighter, no doubt about that, in my mind.

And when I switched to the smaller, half moon shaped cape draped across the sawed off broom stick to do an interwoven series of muleta pases, finished off by a quartet of left handed naturales, gently dragging the cloth in front of a crazed bull's horns as though I was opening a garden gate, I felt, I don't know what to call it – beautiful.

The sun was up and I was sweating when I finished. Word travels fast on ghetto-project rooftops, every where. Wednesday morning. The children of the 'hood, being the most open and honest, simply piled onto the surrounding roof tops and stared at every movement I made. I didn't hear their "Olés", I felt them. They knew enough about the bullfight to know that I was simply practicing. But I could sense when they approved or disapproved of a movement I made. I heard it loud and clear on Thursday morning when I was practicing Chicuelinas Antiguas, that truly magical, ballet type pase, when the bullfighter spins in toward the bull's horns and winds up with the swirling cape wrapped around his body.

Maybe it was because I had missed something, or a few days of serious practice, but when I performed the pase I heard a loud, very calm voice call out – "No, no Señor."

I looked around and this Mexican girl, fifteen maybe, pregnant, waddled away from her viewing place on the roof, took the capote from my hands and did six absolutely mind blowing chicuelinas antiguas. We, all of us, were stunned by her grace, her air of superiority, her sandunga; *another one of those Spanish words that have no English definition, but might be loosely translated as elegance, arrogance, a way of being.*

I didn't have to have more than her half dozen chicuelinas antiguas to be grooved. I would've been an idiot to **not** understand what she had demonstrated, shown me. From that point on I had her in mind whenever I did my roof top work. She didn't come out when I did the Chicuelinas Antiguas the next time, so I assumed that I was doing it right. Or maybe she had surrendered to her motherhood role.

My "family", my "household" had acquired a bit of ambivalent notoriety from having me on the scene. I think they really liked me personally. How do I know this? Well, because I had half understood enough conversations between the thugs about me to know what the deal was.

"Ey Carlos, about the Negro…why don't we hold him for ransom?"

"No, we will not do that, it wouldn't make any sense. Cousin José will continue to send us money for a long time. If we decide to hold this "Matador Negro" for ransom, no one will pay. And we will lose the income from Cousin José. Think, man, think."

So, basically, I was being given some slack because of realistic circumstances. Having put that in the proper perspective, there was nothing to do but get ready for Sunday. I would decide what to do about myself after that. I worked harder than ever, up there on the roof top.

My young wrists (Thank God!) hadn't frozen and I was jumping rope like mad. Good wrists and a good heart were my priorities.

The Plaza Monumental, one of the world's largest bullrings, main season – October to March. We were deep into July, the novilleros (minor league) bullfighters had the stage. They were on from June to October. Some of the gringo travel books mis-interpreted "novillero" to mean "amateur". The guys who had not been given the "alternativa" that godfather/iniation thing, were not "amateurs". Some of them had been fighting for years, and some of them had been elevated to full matador status; but if they didn't prove to have the magnetic thing, that something that one will have that the other one lacks, then they could step back down to the novillero ranks.

After a week in the city, tramping around with a couple of my "roommates", or by myself, I knew a little about how to go from place to place. I loved to walk up and down the Paseo de la Reforma, to Chapultepec Park, to the huge square called the Zocálo, to the Anthropological Museum and the neighborhoods in between.

I grew to associate Mexico with corn, corn with Mexico, because the aroma of it was always in the air. I passed places where women were grinding corn on a stone grinder, using a round stone to grind. The whole thing looked like something from Aztec times.

The swarms of people were not as overwhelming as they had been when I first arrived. There were times I just let myself get swept downstream just to see where I would wind up. I liked the people, they were warm, cold, cynical, trusting, deep shallow, laughing one minute, crying the next. I didn't like being hit on all the time. I complained to one of my "roommates"…

"Rudy, what can I do to keep these people off my ass?"

"What people?"

"All of these people who are constantly trying to sell me something."

He laughed.

"Shit! That's Mexico, man, people are always trying to sell me something too. Either you buy or keep moving."

The Black Matador, "Sugar"

I got up before dawn on Saturday to get in an extra hour of practice. I felt good, my wrists felt strong and flexible. I had to force myself to relax, to keep my nerves in check. I was going to fight a bull tomorrow. Well, correction, I was only going to jump into the bullring and do a pase or two if I could get away with it.

I hadn't mentioned anything to any of my hard smokin' "roomies". No reason to talk about anything to them; their only concern was for another joint or a beer. I had to ask around to find out who I should pay for the time I was staying in #301. Paula thought that Carlos was the one that I should pay. Carlos said that Ernesto was the one who took care of that. Ernesto pointed me to "China" who accepted my pesos, but let me know that she was going to give the money to Rudy.

"He's the one who pays the rent for this dump."

It was a free form household. Very free. It didn't really matter, I had already made up my mind to split after Sunday. I was going to get with the ol' folks in Xochimilco. No matter what they were like, they couldn't possibly be as out of the box as my "roomies" were.

The whole week had been filled with as much drippin' drama as I could imagine, and then it was Saturday night.

Saturday night in #301 was a few ticks up from what had been happening all week. There was always an argument going on about something. And if they weren't arguing it **seemed** like they were arguing. I had become almost numb, able to box out most of the madness and go into a twilight sleep. Nothing doing on this particular Saturday night. I was jarred out of my twilight sleep by the sound of glasses breaking, stuff being slammed around. An earthquake!?

I peeked through a slit in my hanging sheets. Ernesto, Alberto and somebody I had never seen before were having a three way fight (the Mexicans call them "pachangas") about something. And Carlos, Rudy, Paula, Anita and Teresa were egging it on. I pulled the slit closed and laid back down. There was nothing else I could do.

Once again I laced my hands behind my head and stared at the shadow show on the sheets. I thought of a bunch of funny things. One of them was to lean my head through the slit and ask; "Don't you guys have anything better to do?"

The very thought made me laugh out loud. I guess my laughter

113

must've sounded real weird to them because the pachanga died down for about thirty seconds. And then it was on again. I faded off into semi-sleep.

—◆◆◆—

I woke up early from my semi-sleep to peek out on a dysfunctional, battered household. Anita and Teresa were sprawled on their mattress. Carlos had the left side of his head flat on the kitchen table, snoring like a gorilla in heat. Rudy, Ernesto and Paula were draped across chairs, the dilapidated sofa, looking like surrealistic dollos.

Butt ends and roaches littered the ashtrays. A couple full grown rats prowled around, pausing to nibble on crumbs of one kind or another. I didn't bother them and they didn't pay me much attention.

I took it all in and ignored it, the whole crummy scene. This was going to be the day of my "espóntaneo", my spontaneous jump into the bull fight world. I felt I had to have a good grip on myself in order to do what I was going to do. I decided to take a walk, to get away from the Tlaltelolco world.

Mexico City, at five a.m. had a magic about it that couldn't be found anywhere else in the world. As always, there was the flavored aroma of roasted corn floating through the streets, and millions of characters calling it a night; or a day, depending on your perspective.

Ancient Indian hipsters winked wisely at me as though they knew what I was going to do on that particular Sunday. Little children roamed the boulevards, swarmed from place to place like schools of fish or birds fleeing a hawk.

Strange looking women who might have been men, or serpents, hissed at me from niches, suggesting that I slither into something with them. Vendors selling all kinds of rare stuff, performers spouting gasoline fueled flames out of their mouths at the intersections. Lovers strolling up and down the Paseo de la Reforma, holding onto each other. The men, with their arms shackled around the women's necks, made me think of the great Mexican feminista, Malinché… Malinche….

From the corners of my eyes I could see great art on the walls, the murals put there by Rivera, Orozco, Siquieros, Tamayo, people

I had only casually read about as I sopped up every drip of bullfight juice I could find.

The bullfight, always the bullfight. I wandered into the Zocálo, Mexico's heart. And when I got there, right in the middle of this gigantic square, I stopped and slowly turned to face the east, to watch the sun rise up like a giant gold lollipop.

The man who approached me from the east was dressed in a beautiful, feathered crown. He wore a kind of decorated apron around his hips and carried a smoking pot of incense. I could smell it twenty yards away. He walked toward me very slowly, like someone in a trance, or someone who was on his way to perform a serious ceremony.

When we stood face to face, he didn't have to tell me what to do and I didn't have to ask him to do anything. He spoke to me; gorgeous, liquid sounds that made me remember that I was standing where the Aztec pyramid-temples once stood; where devoted priests plucked the living hearts out of human sacrifices to please their gods.

I placed my palms together at chest level, closed my eyes and prayed. The priest, I'm sure he was a priest, he had to be a priest, continued speaking to me and gently touched my head, my shoulders, my hands, my stomach, my legs in front and in the back with his smoking pot of incense.

I prayed to be successful in what I was going to do. The incense aroma seemed to fade away before I opened my eyes. I didn't panic exactly, but I turned from one direction to another, looking for the priest who had blessed me. I wanted to thank him for what he had done, for the way he made me feel, offer him a few pesos. He was there, somewhere in the distance, but I couldn't see him. Nothing to do but stroll back to Tlaltelolco with the faint perfume of the incense pot on my clothes.

———◆◆———

If I heard it once I must've heard it a dozen times, "Only the corrida, the bullfight starts on time in Mexico." I had decided not to tell my "roomies" what I planned to do. I don't think it would've mattered to them one way or another.

By the time I returned from my walk, the household was revving up for a Sunday morning pachanga. I could feel it. Paula was up in Rudy's face about something. Carlos and Ernesto were shuffling a warm bottle of Carta Blanca back and forth between them on the kitchen table, trying to hold their hangovers down.

Anita was rolling a finger sized joint for "breakfast" and Teresa was brushing her hair and screaming curses at nobody in particular. Carlos, my guide to El Canarios, the bullfight café, lifted the Carta Blanca to salute me, or offer a toast. I took it as another blessing.

'Round about two thirty in the afternoon I came from behind the sheet/screen and waved to everybody on my way out.

"See you guys later."

I don't know who heard me, or who cared where I was going or what I was going to do. They were bogged down by their own stuff. I was totally focused on my mission.

I only ate two tacos all day so that I wouldn't have a gut full of food if I got gored. I hated the idea of even thinking about the possibility, but I had to be for real with myself. It took me almost an hour to decide which cape to sneak into the bullring with. Did I want to pop into the ring at the beginning of things with the big cape, the capote, and do a couple perfect veronicas? Or wait 'til the middle of the fight, when the bullfighter had switched to the small cape on the stick/sword, the muleta?

I decided on the muleta. I could wrap the muleta around my upper body and put the stick down into my pant's leg. I tied the stick at one end with a piece of cord and tied the cord onto my belt. I wore a black guayabera, that embroidered dress shirt that Mexicans like so much. It was the perfect cover for my muleta. The stick in my pants made me walk in a slightly stiff legged way, but in Mexico City, where there were so many cripples, who would give a shit about a young African-American man with a stiff legged walk?

————◆◆◆————

El Toreo is the second largest bullring in Mexico City, it can seat twenty-four thousand without being crowded. I bought an expensive sombra/shady side seat, four rows up from the wooden barrier that circled the ring. I didn't want to have to run down a bunch of steps before I jumped over the barrier into the ring.

As usual, people were selling things, pickpockets were at work, mothers were nursing babies, the whole scene had a holiday feel about it. I couldn't help thinking – I wonder if it was like this when the Aztec priests were doing their "sacred duty", long ago?

Maybe the pyramid had been inverted because of the Spanish conquest, instead of looking up at priests plucking the hearts out of sacrificed human beings, we were looking down at priests pushing their swords down through the hearts of bulls. It was easy for me to relate to the priestly thing because that seemed to be the most natural way to look at things; bullfighters were called to do what they did, it was not just a profession, it was a calling. That's the way I felt about it.

The arena was half full, about ten thousand people, half on the shady side, half on the sunny side. Ten minutes before the gate would open and this dude dressed in white lace and ruffles, riding this beautifully prancing horse, would ride across the arena to salute the president and be given permission to start the fight.

I had seen the whole thing so many times on television, I felt a part of it. It was easy to see the class difference in the arena. The poor folks, all dressed up, rowdy, drinking beer, sat in the sun. In my section, in the shade, people were much more reserved, cool. This was not the first time they had been to a bullfight.

It was the first time I had ever been to a live bullfight and it knocked me out, all of it, the crowd, the smells, the music, the expectations.

The man on the beautiful horse doffed his King Charles feathered hat, received permission from the president of the arena to begin the event, and backed his prancing horse back across the arena to the gate where the bullfighters and their helpers, their cuadrillas, were waiting to do their stiff legged struts across the ring.

Manolo Marquez, Carlos Mayano "Suaves" and Pablo Verano "Macho". I had seen Mayano and Verano a couple times on television. Marquez was the new guy to me. In the fights I had seen with Carlos Mayano "Suaves" and Pablo Verano "Macho" I hadn't been too overwhelmed by the stuff they did.

They were competent, no doubt about that, but they didn't make people scream or faint, the way Carlos Arruza had done in his time. I had the memory of a Carlos Arruza performance with a huge bull, the kind they call toros banderas; that made it seem as though he had actually charmed the bull. Even while the bull was charging him again and again, he stood his ground, like his feet were planted in cement, and directed the bull with his muleta. Once you've seen the very best, the others have a tough row to hoe.

I took it all in, analyzed everything as hard as possible, waited for my chance to become an "espontáneo". I decided that it would be best to wait for the last bull of the day, that would belong to Marquez. That was the rotational order of things.

Each man would fight two bulls, starting with Mayano and ending with Marquez. The bulls were from Pastejé, the finca/bullranch owned by the Carlos Arruza family, and they were incredible looking animals. The first one to charge into the arena ran right out into the center of the ring and stood there for a moment, as though to say, I am the king here, who challenges me?

Large, sheeny black, well muscled, well armed with a set of horns that looked too wide for any bullfighter to escape. I felt the fear and excitement that Carlos Mayano "Suaves" must've felt. What the hell would I do with something that big, that mean and evil?

Well, the first thing was to bring that huge head down a bit. Otherwise the matador wouldn't have a possible way to go in over the right horn for the kill. It would've been a crazy joke to think that any man would've been able to handle a completely healthy, uninjured animal. In comes the picadores. A few seats away from me I heard someone say in English; "Uhh oh, here come the bad guys." Picadores, bad guys? The men who were going to shoot the tips of their lances into that huge roll of muscle above the bull's shoulders weren't bad guys, they were on the scene to make certain that the rest of the ritual would be possible.

The Pastejé bull went at the first picador to make it around the circle into his range of vision. It was an uninterrupted thirty hard charge and when he hit the padded side of the blindfolded horse he lifted the horse and the man up a few feet in the air and dropped them.

Capes came out from everywhere to distract the bull, and the arena attendants, dressed in white pants and red shirts and caps, nicknamed "monos sabios"/wise monkeys, helped the picador escape being crushed by the squirming, struggling horse and the bull trying to get at him.

I leaned forward to check out the reactions of the American tourists, a man and a woman. The woman held her hands over her eyes and peeked at the scene through her splayed fingers. The man was half sitting, half standing, and looked horrified. What were they doing at the bullfights?

One picador (bad guy?) down and rescued, one bony pony led away by one of the monos sabios. I couldn't help but think of the bad ol' times when the horses were blindfolded and not padded, and how often the bullfight critics of that time described how often the horse's guts were ripped out by the bull's nasty horns. Hemingway. Conrad.

Mayano didn't give the bull a chance to slam headlong into the second picador's horse; he knew that this bull, the name above the entrance tunnel said "El Brujo"/the Witch, had to be piced before he could fight him. What could a hundred and fifty pound man do against the undiminished strength of the twelve hundred pound animal with horns?

The matador did a quick series of media veronicas that placed the bull in exactly the right spot to see the picador and his horse. From the fourth row I could see the sweat dripping off of the side of the picador's face. The absolute fear in his eyes. Bad guys?

"El Brujo" stabbed the earth once with his right hoof and charged. It didn't take a lot of imagination to take myself into what the picador must've felt. He had already seen what this bull's power could do, so when he leveled his pic into the muscled hump behind the bull's head, he was really trying to stave off the bull's attack as well as punish him. It was a survival technique.

Three well placed pics. The bull was prepared to take more, but the sunny side people were screaming insults at the picador – "Assassin!" "Leave some fight in him!" "Matador stop this now!"

The matador lured the bull away from the horse with a series of chicuelinas antiguas, the pase that my pregnant neighbor girl had done so beautifully on the rooftop. I thought that she had done them better, more sexy. Was it because she was pregnant; or, in spite of her pregnancy?

The banderillas came next and Carlos Mayano placed them himself. The Mexicans have an awesome reputation for doing the sticks – Armillita, Arruza, Procuna. One night I saw an old grainy film of Joselito Huerta placing the sticks while he was standing on the strip that circled the inside of the bullring. I still don't understand why or how he didn't get nailed against the barrera, the fence circling the bullring.

Mayanós first two pairs were done well, but not extraordinarily well. He did that quartering run up to the bull that the banderilleros do and at the correct intersection he plunged the sticks in. The bull went one way and he went the other way. I guess, to show off the Mexican power with the palos, he broke the last pair in half on the top of the barrera, came out almost to the center of the ring and just stood there.

One of his helpers caped the bull around to face the matador. Once again, "El Brujo" dug his right hoof into the earth and charged. A fighting bull can out run a race horse over a short distance, and from fifty yards away "El Brujo" proved it. Carlos Mayano "Suaves" stood like a stone statue dressed in his sparkling suit of lights, slowly raising his arms, with the half length banderillas in his hands.

He was going to place these barbed, half sticks in the bull's hump by leaning to his left, by suddenly faking with his left leg, and as the bull swooshed past his open body, he jammed the sticks in. It was olé-olé-olé from that point on He took the muleta and did a short series of interwoven patterns, but nothing spectacular. It was obvious that he wanted to get rid of "El Brujo" and it was obvious that "El Brujo" felt the same way about him. The bull had suddenly become more difficult to deal with; he started a charge and then stopped midway through it. It was as though he was saying – "I know someone is waving this cloth in front of me, where is he?"

Mayano positioned the bull's front hooves in a paralled position so that he could slip the sword down between the shoulder blades, cutting the bull's heart muscle. I held my breath and felt sweat trickle down from under my armpit. This is what I'm going to have to do one day.

Almost as though it were in slow motion, the bull charged the cape just as Mayano crossed over the right horn to push the sword down and in. No good, the sword must've hit a shoulder blade and flew into the air as though the bull had thrown it into the air. The matador's helper retrieved the sword and handed it to him.

The situation was critical now. The bull had a pretty good idea of what the man was trying to do and he had become totally defensive. If you want to kill me, c'mon and try...I am not going to cooperate.

Carlos Mayano made two more bad thrusts. The sunny side folks were cat calling – "You bum!" "here, you need this!" Someone threw a little plastic pistol into the ring, a classic joke that I had seen on T.V. from time to time.

Even some of our sedate shady side folks had started whistling. I checked the bullfighter's face. He was crying. I knew, I felt his shame and frustration. He had fought well, had placed a pair of extraordinary banderillas. But he was having a terrible time trying to end the whole thing the way it was supposed to end, with the bull killed by a clean thrust through the heart muscle.

The first aviso was blown, the trumpet signaled to the matador that you are getting a failing grade. Who wants to come see a killer of bulls who can't kill? Mercifully, "El Brujo" suddenly collapsed as though all of the air had been pumped out of his body. Mayano's helper, the puntillero, the guy who delivers the coup d'grace by slicing the bull's spinal cord, sneaked up behind the bull and did his dirty work. No one wanted to see "El Brujo" up and walking again.

CHAPTER ELEVEN

Next up, Pablo Verano "Macho" fighting "Alegre I". The bull was up to snuff but Pablo obviously wasn't He didn't place his own banderillas and his work with the muleta was jerky and uneven. I had seen him a few times on T.V. and I knew he could do better. I turned to the two middle aged Mexican men on my left and asked in my best Spanish, "What is the problem with the matador?"

They exchanged coded looks before the one nearest me said, "Senõr Verano got gored in the Tijuana ring three weeks ago, in the balls. He is still healing; I think that is the problem, I think." His friend nodded in agreement.

Gored in the testicles three weeks ago and he's back in the ring already? Well, I had found out enough about how the bull business operated to know that the matador couldn't afford to be off the scene for longer than necessary. The public was fickle and they were always ready to accept a new phenomenon and forget the ol' phenomenon.

Gored in the balls. God, what a gruesome thought. I looked at the bullfighter doing everything he could possibly do to earn our olés; but all I could do was wish that he would disappear from the ring, he was too great a reminder of what could happen in a bull ring. I was more than happy to see him plunge his sword into the bull's vital section, up to the hilt. He made the kill as though he was angry at the bull. I could understand why.

Manolo Marquez was the third man on the bill and he had "Huachinango" to deal with. It didn't take very long to figure out why they had named the bull "Huachinango", a fish, the succulent red snapper in Mexican seafood cuisine that was called "Huachinango a la Vera Cruzana".

"Huachinango" was slick, difficult to lure into the fight. Maybe he had been fought before by some "espontáneo" in the pastures one night and clearly remembered the difference between the cape and the man. As a potential "espontáno" myself I felt something about that possibility, but I wasn't guilty of anything that crazy.

Marquez did a couple beautiful veronicas, playing the human statue with his capote acting as a seductive fan in front of the bull's hooking horns. And after the picador had done his work and a member of his cuadrilla had done a good job of punching the banderillas into the bull's muscular hump, Marquez requested permission for the beginning of the third act, the faena, the kill or be killed part. The president nodded yes. He came to the center of the ring, took off his montera, that black, low cut, double edged bullfighter's hat and slowly pivoted to dedicate the bull to us, to the aficion. I thought it was a nut brain gesture. Why dedicate the bull like "Huachinango" to us? The bull was giving him all kinds of problems. He would charge straight ahead one time and then charge again, hooking from right to left, the next time.

I caught a hold of what Manolo Marquez was doing with "Huachinango" after his second pase de pecho. He was giving the bull his opportunity to be bullish, while he took advantage of the bull's irregular behavior to channel him into a flowing pattern he controlled. I joined the gentlemen next to me shouting "Olé!"; when I realized what was happening.

Marquez could've taken the easy way out and done a few regulation pases with "Huachinango" and the hipper bull fight fans, the serious aficion would've forgiven him; -- "Ey! Why spend your whole life trying to solve one problem?" But he took another route, he chose to show us what a bullfighter, a matador, is about.

He worked the shit out of "Huachinango". When the bull didn't want to leave his querencia, the place he had chosen to defend, the matador violated that space and lined the bull into a beautiful series of left handed naturales. Manolo Marquez, with his fight with

"Huachinango" helped me to understand what is meant to be a matador. It clearly meant "bull psychologist".

It took two thrusts of the sword for Manolo to kill "Huachinango" but the fans, us, the aficion, were so impressed by what he had done with this beautiful, crazy beast, we waved our white hankies, asking that he should be given an ear or two, at least.

The Mexico City El Toreo plazas pres. would only approve of one ear. One ear for doing what Manolo Marquez just did?

The aficionados next to me nodded…this is Mexico City, not Tijuana. An ear is a great thing. The brave bull "Huachinango" was dragged out of the ring by the mono sabios and, a few minutes later "Tecalote' rushed out to become Carlos Mayano "Suaves'"s second challenge of the afternoon. I took note of that, it was becoming very chilly in the shady section.

"Tecalote" was a good bull for Mayano "Suaves". He charged the horses honestly, he charged after the banderilleros honestly and when the moment came for the sword to go in it slipped between his shoulder blades like a knife going into a mound of soft butter. Pablo Verano "Macho", struggling to control his pain, didn't have the same kind of luck with his second bull of the afternoon, "El Mozo", the waiter. "El Mozo" was huge, had wide spread horns and seemed to be very calculating, if you could say that about an animal.

After a few minutes of watching the matador's pain filled expression, and his awkward movements I almost felt compelled to jump into the ring and help him out. But I maintained control of myself. This man was having his struggle and I would have my struggle, no need to mess things up with a lot of excess sentimentality.

I think we all sighed with relief when "El Mozo" was finally put down and Pablo Verano took his tortured balls out of the arena. Manolo Marquez studied "Yambu" as the bull chased his helpers around the ring. And I studied "Yambu" and Manolo Marquez. This was the bull I was going to do my first live passes with.

"Yambu" was a roan/reddish colored bull with the kind of horns that most bullfighters liked; they curved inward and had a nice "cradle". During the picador part and the banderillas I was so nervous my knees started trembling, but when Marquez went over to exchange his capote for the muleta and his sword, I felt extremely calm.

The Black Matador, "Sugar"

I could've been alone inside an invisible bubble as I stood to pull the broomstick out of my pant's leg; to uncurl the muleta from around my waist, take the quick walk down the arena steps and hop over the double fences into the bullring. I heard two words – "Mira! Mira! Espontaneo!"

"Yambu" was about ten or fifteen yards from me. And for one solid moment I felt the urge to hop back over the fence and forget about the whole thing. But that urge was over whelmed by a kind of high, an intoxication. I was in a real bull ring with a real bull and there was no one close enough to stop me from doing a pase or two. If the audience was shouting I couldn't hear them. I wasn't aware of anything but the bull and my own fears.

Down there on the blood soaked sand of the arena, my fears flashed me back to the night I woke up in the Almo Hotel to find a giant rat scurrying back and forth across my chest. Fear kept me from moving. If I moved, this ugly thing would bite me in the face. I felt that. So, I pretended to be asleep and kept my body from trembling or doing anything that would betray me. I controlled myself. The rat scurried away to play elsewhere.

Was it a nightmare, or something that really happened? The crazy summer night that made me feel that I could get on my just stolen ten speed and race through the Bridgeport section of Chicago, an Irish neighborhood that was "off limits" to African-Americans. It took the young Irishmen a full minute to realize that I was dissin' them by ten speedin' through their turf. And the chase was on. Fuck y'all.

It only took a full block of ten speeding for me to realize that the bike was not going to be my vehicle of salvation. I hopped off the bike wheels still spinning, and lit into my shot gun sprint. I glanced back at the pursuing, racist, red faced Irishmen, and smiled – I got fifty yards on you motherfuckers you'll never be able to catch me.

And then my head lit up by flashing stars, flashing beams of light, flashes of pleasure maybe. And pain. A great deal of pain. I had glanced behind me, at the slow footed White boys, and ran full speed into an unfamiliar fire hydrant.

Despte their racist feelings, a couple of the Irish guys knelt close to me. One of them asked, (never will forget it); "Hey, niggerboy, you o.k.?"

I was in so much pain I didn't have a reasonable answer for this unreasonable question. I managed to pull enough strength together to whisper ---"Fuck you, man.". I can't say why but that nudged a button in them. They laughed, prodded me a few times with their steel toed boots and strolled off, making jokes about the "nigger boy" who had enough sense to run into a fire hydrant when he tried to "invade" their neighborhood.

I don't know how many hours I laid there next to the fire hydrant, trying not to cry from the pain of the injury to my right knee. It was an Irish neighborhood I was suffering in, and I think that most of the people who paused to stare at me felt that I had received what I deserved.

I had invaded their neighborhood and God had inflicted punishment on me for my sin. My knee hurt so bad I couldn't even scream. I didn't do that til a week later. It was 'round about twilight when some of the racists who had chased me into the fire hydrant came back. I was folded into a fetal knot, trying to figure out who/what/how I should scream.

"Nigger boy, you still here, are ya? Well, we're gonna have t' give ya a little help t' git otta the neighbohood, we can't have ya hangin' 'round here after dark."

I crawled home, the six-eight blocks from where they had dumped me. And because I was such an unusual character, even then, it took my relatives – Aunt Mary, Uncle Percy, the gamblin' house regulars – a week to realize that there was something wrong with me, there was probably a reason why I was dragging myself around and moanin.

Once I got past the screaming. And my reason for the screaming. To an explaination of what caused the whole thing – "You should'nt've had you' black ass over there in Bridgepo't anyhow, you know how them honkies is. Maybe this'll be a lesson to ya."

That's what I imagined coming at me, the non-racist feeling of a bull that didn't recognize racial circumstances. He would gore anybody on his turf. The value of having my experience with the Irish was that it had taught me the value of "aguantar" /to stick it out. If the bull was going to gore me. Well, that might not happen. I prayed. But I had put my ass on his turf and I had to survive on his terms, in a manner of speaking.

The Black Matador, "Sugar"

It was all right there in front of him. My fears: Will they think I'm a coward? Will they think I'm too brave/suicidal? Will they diss' me because I'm a hip hop Black and I don't know the traditions of the art? Will they laugh at me? Laughter was the divining rod for a matador. That was the reason why "Cantinflas" didn't make it, people thought he was funny. People can't think that bullfighters are funny – that's a no no.

"The crowd is the real monster in the arena", some well known person once said. Chester glanced around the arena. The crowd in the bullring is the real monster is pure bullshit. The real monster is the bull, that huge, slavering, threatening creature over there.

It was too late to pray. The first Arrucina was the result of a reaction, a serendipity. He didn't have any time to think about it, he found his right arm holding the muleta on the broom stick behind his back, with his left hand offering—pulling at a tiny section of cloth for the bull to charge.

And he charged. Four times, he charged. Chester, felt the rat prancing across his chest, he felt his knee thrubbing. And, because he had sucked his stomack into his backbone he hadn't been gored. His imagination, which embraced the possibility of what it felt like to be dead, helped him to remain in place, as though his feet were cemented to the earth.

Odd thoughts danced through my mind as I waited for the bull to turn and attack me again. See a Black man doing this? How do I see myself? Suddenly for the first time in my life, race was not the real issue, survival was the real issue.

This motherfucker would gore me, if he could, no matter what my skin color or eye color happened to be. The thought caused me to smile as I cited the bull for one more pase. The aficion saw it as a demonstration of confidnece and applauded my smile. The bull, an equal opportunity menance charged again.

It felt like a living freight train as he swooshed past my body. He turned around to make another attack as I switched the muleta to my left hand. He went for the trick again. The pase is called the Arrucina and it was invented by Carlos Arruza. I did it four times, two times from my left side and two times from my right side before Manolo Marquez's helpers caped the bull away from me. I think they did me a favor because I had no idea what I was going to do next. The next thing I knew, three of the redshirted monos sabios had penned my arms and were dragging me out of the bull ring.

"Stop!" Manolo Marquez called out to them before they pulled me out of the arena. As he did his athletic, light-footed run over to where I was being held, I suddenly became aware of olés from the crowd, music being played, flash bulbs from cameras to my left and right. I also became aware that Manolo had his sword and muleta in his hand. Was he going to run me through with his sword?

He gave me a huge hug and said – "You fuckin' crazy, man". Maybe he was very pissed because I had stolen his bull for a few pases but it wouldn't've been good P.R. for him to trot over and run his sword through my chest. What could I say?

"Suerte, luck", that was the only word I could think of before the monos sabios hustled me into the callejon, the circular alley between the fence surrounding the bull ring and the first row of seats. Six burly Mexican police pulled me out of the gentle hands of the monos sabios and hustled me into the cool darkness underneath the stadium seats. Uhh ooh, this is where they're going to beat the shit out of me. I was grateful to be disappointed about my expected ass kicking when they pushed me into an office.

"Thank you", this large, walnut colored man spoke to the policia and gave one of them, the man with the most stripes on his arm, a fat bundle of peso notes. The cops bowed out and left me alone with Don Luis Miguel Flores. Of course I didn't know that Senõr Flores was one of the major figures in Mexican bullfighting. He was a promoter, had an interest in several bull rings, owned three or four outright, had a small stable of bullfighters under his wing, his pudgy/jeweled fingers in a lot of pies. I didn't know any of that, then.

Senõr Flores looked like a Mexican version of Jackie Gleason, the ol' comedian I used to sometimes see on a late night comedy show called "The Honeymooners". He wore dark tinted glasses, a pearl grey Stetson and smelled like he had just taken a baby powder bath.

He gestured for me to sit in a chair on the other side of his desk. He kicked his cowboy boots up on the side of the desk, lit a flowery smelling Cuban cigar, blew a few smoke rings to the ceiling. He was obviously someone who enjoyed the good life. And was used to taking his time about things. I just sat there on the edge of my seat, coming back to reality. I could've gone straight to jail for what I did.

"You speak Spanish?"

"Uhh, not well, mostly words about the bullfight."

He was quiet for a few beats. I found that that was a habit he had, a way to digest and analyze.

"What's your name?"

"Chester Simmons."

"Chester Simmons?"

"Yes. Chester Simmons, Jr."

"Where are you from, Chester?"

"Chicago."

"Chicago?"

"Yes."

It was almost funny, the way he repeated what I said, as though he couldn't believe what he was hearing.

"There are no bulls in Chicago, I've been there; where did you learn the arrucina?"

"From watching the bullfights on television."

"From watching the bullfights on television?"

"Yes."

He smiled and took off his dark glasses. His eyes were bloodshot and piercing. He polished his glasses with a designer cloth.

"Bullfights on television, huh?"

"Yes."

"So, you want to be a matador, huh?"

"Yes."

His questions didn't need a lot of extra words to answer and I got the impression he liked that. He also had a very interesting accent, like some of his words sounded Jewish.

"O.K., I will be your manager."

I felt like jumping across the desk to hug him. I was going to be a full fledged matador, I had a manager.

"You living in Mexico?"

"Yes, I have a visitor's...."

"We'll have to get you a permanent resident's card. We will take care of that. Here is my deal, take it or leave it."

I didn't like the tone of that – "take it or leave it" – but what the hell, what did I have to lose?

"I'm going to put you under my personal care, my contract will explain what that means. Do you smoke dope? Drink a lot? Run after the putas?"

I nodded no, no, no.

"Good. How old are you?"

This was a crucial question. I wanted to say seventeen, but I didn't think he would buy it.

"I'm nineteen."

"Nineteen, huh? You're getting a late start. Well, you have the heart and we can improve the skills if you're willing to work hard."

"I am, I am."

"Where are you staying?"

"Uhh, I am renting a space from some friends in Tlaltelolco."

"Tlaltelolco? We will have to take you away from there."

"Good, I'm ready to go."

"I have some properties in the Polanco section. Are you familiar with this section?"

"Only from reading the travel books."

"I have three other young men, boxers, who are sharing this house I own in Polanco. It is near Chapultepec so that you can do your roadwork with them. And we have a complete gymnasium where you can exercise. You must be in excellent condition, have very strong legs to fight the bulls or other people."

Once again, that silent smile and an indulgent puff on his cigar.

"I will grant you a weekly allowance in pesos until you have your first fight, and then I will deduct the allowance from that. One last thing, my contract will show that I am to receive 65% of your earnings from the bulls, as well as endorsements, etc., etc., etc."

What could I say? It was a "take it or leave it" situation. I had no choice but to shake his pudgy hand.

"Also, we will have to find you another name. Chester Simmons sounds like a bookkeeper, not a matador."

We both smiled this time.

"When can I go to the house in Polanco?"

"Any time, there are people there who will make you welcome and comfortable – here, show them my card."

He scribbled on the back of the card – "*This is my Matador Negro, take good care of him, Flores*."

I **floated** out of this under the arena office. I was about to become a made man, a matador.

———◆—◆——

Mexico City is a large city with millions of people but news travels in a small town kind of fashion. By the time I got back to the dope den my "roomies" knew all about my escapade in the bullring.

"Ey man, you should have told us!"

"Yeah, Chester, why didn't you tell us? We would've gone with you, to give you support." Yeah right.

It all boiled down to me funding an all night beer bash. I didn't give a shit, I was going to be on my way in the morning to a decent neighborhood, to be around some people who cared about something other than the next joint or the next beer.

I thought about José "Cantinflas"'s uncle and aunt in Xochimilco. Well, I wouldn't be staying with them, but I made a mental note to pay them a visit in the near future. 'Round about three a.m. during a temporary lull in the "festivities", I crawled into my little sheet covered space, determined to get a couple hours sleep before dawn. A few minutes later, Anita crawled in beside me, reeking of reefer and beer. Uhh ohh…

"Chester, are you asleep?"

"Well, not yet, but I'm <u>trying</u> to go to sleep."

"Wake up, I wanna give you a lil' goin away present."

I sat up on my mat, thinking of the best way to handle this. I thought of telling her that I was gay, but that would definitely operate against me in Mexico. "El Gay Matador" – I could just see Senõr Flores tearing my would be contract in half, turning his back on me.

Anita was pulling her loose fitting dress up over her head.

"Chester", she whispered in a fake, sexy sounding voice, "please, unbuckle my bra."

"No, Anita, no, we can't do this…"

"It's o.k.", she assured me, "this is a present, one on the house."

Strangely enough, I took notice of her body for the first time. She had that clear, cocoa colored skin of the Indian, with a Western woman's big boobs. I was tempted, no doubt about it, but I was also paranoid knowing what I knew about her made me think of disease first. I didn't come all the way to Mexico City for a shot of the claps or a case of AIDs.

In addition to that, there was a possibility that Carlos, Ernesto, Rudy, or one of the others might be waiting for us on the other side of the sheet with a handy little instamatic camera, just waiting for me to get into the bacon-with-two backs-position-to snap a nice little blackmail photo. Or maybe just one to laugh at in the middle of one of their smoke outs.

"Anita, no…"

"You can use the condom if you are afraid…"

"Anita, no. Just no, o.k.? Put your dress back on."

"Hey Chester, I don't understand, you are a young guy, you don't like me?"

"Anita, I like you, now put your clothes on."

Well, now I would be damned if I did and damned if I didn't. She was definitely going to spread the rumor that I was gay. When does a real man turn down a free piece of panocha? O well.

It must've taken her five minutes to slip her dress back over her head. She was clearly puzzled.

"Chester, you like women, no?"

"I like women very much, yes. But this is not for me."

She eased through the slit in the sheet/curtain, even more puzzled. She would've been surprised to see what she had aroused on me, the feeling she had inspired. How long had it been?

———◆———

I left my "roomies" a nice little note, picked up my two pieces of baggage and cape bag and eased through the beer bottles and the funky mota smoke. Time to move on. Anita stared at me from the mattress in the other room and made a shy wave my way. I felt the urge to go and kiss her goodbye, but I resisted the urge. This was not the time to become sentimental.

Outside of #301 I looked around at the courtyard, at the people, some good, some bad, going about their daily stuff. The young pregnant girl caught me as I was about to escape from her world. The chicuelina antigua teacher.

"Senõr! Senõr!" She waddled toward me holding something behind her back. Now What? Don't tell me she has a present for me too. She held the sports page from La Tiempo, the big daily newspaper, up in front of my face. "Un Espontanéo Negro". That was the headline. And two great photos of me doing my thing, from the left and the right.

"Arrucinas", she said, "very difficult."

I took a hard look at what I had done. NO trick photography here, there were two photos shot by two different photographers, showing "Yambu" slicing past me so closely that it seemed impossible for the bull not to have gored me.

"Can you sell me your newspaper?"

"The Kiosk is just there, at the corner."

"I want your paper."

Poor bunny, she looked down at the ten dollars worth of peso notes I placed in her hand as though I had just given her a fortune. Well, I guess I had. I tucked the paper into my cape bag and strutted out to the streets. I wasn't rich yet, but I **was** famous. I was in La Tiempo.

CHAPTER TWELVE

The house that Senõr Flores sent me to was a mansion. The Polanco section was full of mansions, estates with high walls, with an armed guard at the ten foot high front gate. They didn't smile or act friendly.

"Senõr Flores told us you would be coming – go to the front door."

It was at least a fifty yard walk to the front door, up a winding cobble stoned path. The grounds around the house looked like they had been manicured, carefully groomed. Tall, dripping shady trees, rose bushes, spacious. The short, slender man standing in the open door stared at me as I approached.

"Aha! El espontáneo", he greeted me with a sarcastic smile and a warm handshake." I am Ricardo Ortega, but most people call me. "Nacho".

I shook his hand and introduced myself. He took my bags and gestured with his chin for me to follow him. There was a sofa over there, a couple big stuffed chairs over here, a long table in the entrance, but basically we were in a huge empty mansion.

'Nacho" led me up to the second floor.

"Here, we have the bedrooms. This is your room."

A huge, well lit bedroom with a big bed, a table and a chair, no luxurious items anywhere. It was like a section of paradise after my week with the druggies. No sheets for a room divider, no mat on the floor, no rats.

"Uhh, where is Senõr Flores?"

"Nacho" curled his lip corners down and shrugged.

"Who knows? He is here, he is there. He may be in the United States, Europe, China, Guadalajara…. We will begin our training tomorrow at six a.m." I blinked at him, what else could I do? Training?

"Training?"

It was his turn to blink back at me.

"Si, yes, the season for the novilleros will be past in September but Senõr Flores would like to have you as an added attraction during the professional season. You must be ready, I will train you. We don't have much time."

Ah ha, so I was going to be the novelty act, the lil' colored boy from Chicago. O well, what the hell, I had to start somewhere.

"I'll be ready."

"Good. We will have food at four o'clock, you can meet the others then. Meanwhile, check the place out, it is now your home. Welcome."

And then he limped away. Interesting dude I thought, a kind of bi-polar, hot and cold at the same time. Two o'clock, nothing to do 'til dinner time.

I took a shower. Two bath towels, two smaller cloths, a couple of small wedges of soap. Like I said, no luxurious items anywhere. I changed into jeans, T-shirt and sandals to check the place out.

The place could've been an empty train station, a place full of nothing.. No need to focus on that. I strolled down the winding staircase to the first floor, through the long corridor that led to a kitchen that was as huge as a small auditorium.

A long table ran down the center of the kitchen, long wooden benches on each side of the table, a large pot of something bubbling on the restaurant sized stove. I took it all in.

A winding veranda outside the back exit, tables scattered here and there, an acre of "back yard". I strolled on the grounds. Two guards carrying automatic weapons suddenly popped up from nowhere. What was that about?

Here and there on the grounds were places to do chin-ups, weights to lift, benches to lay down on for sit ups. The place was just one big ol' gymnasium. And right over there, in a grove of shady trees, they had a full sized boxing ring.

The place was a full-fledged, beautifully landscaped training camp, fully equipped and well guarded. The guards puzzled me, we crossed paths as I strolled around the grounds. I nodded at them and they nodded back, but no one smiled, and the automatic weapons they carried were not on safety.

4 P.M. Dinner time. Whoever said Mexicans are not organized? Senõr Flores's operation was on time. I was introduced to the trio of boxers and their trainer: Jesús, Paco, Fidel and their trainer, Fernando. "Nacho", my trainer, explained… "These are the boxers. Senõr Flores has others in Tijuana. The guys in Tijuana fight in the border towns – Rosarita, Nogales, places like that. These guys here mostly fight in Mexico."

It would've been pretty easy to tell that they were boxers from the broken noses, cuts above their eyes, the grape bunched muscles on their bodies. They were obviously country boys, real Indians from the interior. No one had to tell me that they were tough, I had seen enough Mexican fighters on TV to know that they would fight until they couldn't stand up; or got knocked out. We used to say, "Be careful, he fights like a Mexican."

They looked like thugs but they were strangely shy. Their trainer, Fernando did most of the talking.

"Senõr Flores picks the cream of the crop and I train them. I can tell you right now that you are looking at three future world champions."

Fernando looked like and talked like Muhammad Ali's old trainer, Angelo Dundee. All I could think was if he's as good as Dundee was, then the championships are in the bag. Did I mention Senõra Chavez cooked two meals a day for us, one at 11 a.m. and the dinner at 4 p.m.? It was a style of Mexican cooking that I didn't know anything about. My experience with Mexican food had been tacos, burritos, refried beans and rice, basically.

She prepared one type of food for the boxers and a slightly different thing for me. My diet was mostly fish, different kinds of fish fixed different ways, with rice or pasta. "Nacho" hipped me to what the deal was.

"These boxers need more meat for stamina; you don't need that as much. You will never be as strong as a bull, no matter what you eat. And you can never allow yourself to have a big belly like me."

"Big belly"? The guy was about 5'8" and weighed about a hundred and fifty pounds, looked almost fragile, with a neat little waist line. He looked to be almost 40 or so, I didn't ask. But I was very curious about his limp. I planned to ask him about the limp at the first available opportunity.

"We will go into our training mode tomorrow morning at 6 a.m., so I would suggest you get plenty of sleep. Oh, also we have freshwater in the dispenser over there, drink a lot of it, it is good for you."

---

6 A.M., jogging through Chapultepec Park with the boxers. They left me a mile behind after the first mile. "Nacho" frowned.

"Hmmm…you are not in very good condition, young man."

That was all he said, but it was the beginning of bullfight boot camp.

"The matador must have very strong legs to take him out of danger, to keep him safe. Remember, the bull has four legs, you only have two."

The first week was hell. I developed blisters on my heels from running and blisters on my hands from handling the muleta and the sword.

"Some use the stick with the muleta in training. I don't like that, I think you should be familiar with the weight of the blade, from the beginning."

Jogging from 6 A.M. to 7 A.M.; "breakfast", a cup of tea and honey, a Mexican pastry called churro and into the weight room in the basement (another surprise) for two hours – "the matador must be thin, but very strong."

Take a lil' rest for an hour and then a few bullfight basics before brunch, starting with the placement of the banderillas. "Nacho" was almost academic – scientific in his approach to the bullfight. He used a blackboard to show where the man and the bull should meet in the arena.

"It is like arriving at an intersection in the streets. The bull is coming from that direction and you are coming from this direction – the sticks go in at the intersection, the bull exits in this direction and the banderillero exits in that direction."

What might've been drudgery to some was a pure joy for me. I was training to become a professional bullfighter, a matador, and I was willing to work as hard as necessary to make it happen.

"Nacho" was critical, but fair. "I don't think the banderillas will ever be your strong suit."

Brunch was always interesting but never too much. It was at brunch that I usually saw the boxers, Jeśus, Paco and Fidel. We exchanged small talk and they were back to doing their thing. A half hour rest after brunch and then work with the capote, the big yellow work cape, magenta on the outside, yellow on the inside.

We were only into our second week of training, but I felt like we had been at it for a month. The work with the capote was astounding. I had no idea that there were so many pases you could do with the capote. "Nacho" took me from one to the other.

"You may not be as good with some as you are with others, but they will be in your repertoire."

These are just a few he taught me…Pase de Adorno, Ambulante, Aragonesa, Bel Montino, Brionesa, Caleserina, Chicuelina, Chicuelina Antigua (thank you, lil' pregnant girl), Farol, Fregolina de Frente por Detras, Gaonera, Larga Afarolada, Larga Cambiada, Larga Cordobesa, Larga por Alto, Larga por Bajo, Media Veronica, Navarra, Quite de Oro Rafaelina, Rebolera, Recorte, Remate, Derodillas, Serpentine, Suerte de Frente, Tapatia, Valencia, Veronica. Like I said, I was astounded to discover that there were so many pases with the capote before we got to the muleta.

Most of the pases have really interesting histories, like the Ambulante Aragonesa, the Brionesa, the Caleserina, the Chicuelina, the Gaonera, all named after bullfighters who had invented these pases.

"The Veronica, a basic pase with the Capote, is said to be named after the woman who wiped the sweat from Jesus Christ's face when he was on his way to be crucified. The pase should be done with great elegance and feeling.

The remate is your signature, the swirling flourish many of us use when we write our names. Here, it's done at the end of a series of pases with the capote. Carlos Arruza could actually spell his name with his capote or so some thought.

Pases de Rodillas are pases done on your knees. One must be very careful and agile to do de Rodillas, no artharitis people can do these – hah, hah, hah."

I'll just list ten to give some idea of how many pases come out of the muleta: Afarolada, Arrucina (the one I performed as an espontáneo), Celeste Imperio, Chicarrina, Pase de la Firma, Manoletina, Pase de Pecho, Sanjuanera, Trincherazo and so on.

The Pase de la Firma was like the linchpin/foundation for most of the muleta pases.

"This is a pase invented by one of the old great ones, a matador named Granero. It is a variation of the basic natural, the muleta is snatched down from in front of the bull's face as it goes by. Granero was killed by a bull called 'Pocapena' in Madrid, May 7, 1922. "Popapena" tossed Granero under the estribo against the barrera and gored him through the head, killing him instantly.

Fighting the bulls always offers the possibility of the unexpected.

Pay close attention, young man. The Manoletina, the Pase de Pecho, the Sanjuanera and several other pases may look alike, but the placement of the hands on the muleta is different. One must know the difference because different effects will result. In any case, the aficion, the people who really know bullfighting, will know the difference. And that's why you are in the arena, for the aficion."

You have good strong wrists…good."

"Nacho" would do the pase and then have me imitate him. When I did it right, he would only have me repeat it twenty or thirty times. If I did it wrong, he would "request" that I do it until I got it right. Some of the simplest pases took the longest.

"You cannot just wave your muleta in front of the bull, you must bankrupt yourself with your muleta, this is what the afición is coming to see."

That's what he always called bullfight fans, "La afición". 4 P.M. Dinner. Senõra Chavez treated us like her sons. She called us "mihijos" and fed us these delicious soups and dishes from all over Mexico.

"Senõra Chavez, this is a delicious sauce, what is it called?"

"This is a mole from Oaxaca." Or, "This is the way the huachinango is prepared in Vera Cruz." Or, "This is the way the Jalapeño is stuffed in Jalisco." She was also big into the food that was in Mexico before the Spanish came – roasted grasshoppers, for example.

And a kind of ant that tasted exactly like mint chewing gum. I had my first taste of a certain kind of grub, never did find out what it was, that tasted like walnuts. "Nacho" was pleased that I didn't reject real Mexican food.

"You know, young man, I think we would've had some problems if you had not been able to eat our Mexican food."

"I love it."

"Good. Now, let's go back to work. The left handed naturale should look like a man opening a garden gate, very slowly, with calmness and deep passion."

No need to b.s. about it, by the time we got into the end of our second week, "Nacho" had converted me, had made me his disciple.

"Nacho", I look at the way you handle these capes, all the stuff you know about the corrida and I have to ask – why aren't you in the bullring? What kind of career did you have? You're a master…"

I didn't have to blow smoke up his butt, he didn't need that. I was honest with him because I could see that he was being honest with me.

"You are correct, young man, I am a master. I **was** a master from the beginning because the bulls came naturally to me. I feel that it is this way for you also, despite the fact that you come from the North Pole."

That's what he called Chicago, "the North Pole". And I was definitely puffed up by the compliment he laid on me, about the bulls coming naturally to me.

"I became a novillero when I was fourteen, but I had already been going to the fields and caping bulls since I was about twelve. I've often had nightmares about how stupid I was to go out into the fields in the middle of the night with just a capote or a muleta. Fortunately, because God looks out for fools and drunks, I was never gored, not even scratched.

As you can well imagine, if I had been gored out there in the fields

I would've died. As a novillero and as a full-fledged matador I was phenomenal".

He spoke without a trace of ego, just the truth.

"Yes, I was a phenomenon. I could sculpture movements with the capote and many say that only Manuel Capetillo was my equal with the muleta. I was not blood thirsty, like some, so I didn't kill very well in the beginning. Later, as I got a better feel for it, I became much better."

I didn't know where this was heading so I had to be patient.

"Yes, I was a phenomenon for about ten years. I could do any pase in the book and many that are not in the book. The bulls nicked me here and there but I was never gored, not until I was gored by a bull from the San Diego de Los Padres ranch called "Gallito', the little rooster".

We were taking a break, sitting on one of the stone benches on the grounds of the estate. He stopped talking and looked down at the ground for a full minute. I thought he was finished talking.

"Gallito" ran his right horn through my upper thigh and the curve of it came out just below my navel…just as I was crossing in over the horn to make the kill."

"Did you make the kill?"

He gave me a sudden frown and a smile.

"The aficion gave me two ears and the tail, but nothing could take away the pain. A month later I was back in the Plaza Mexico".

The thought made me shiver, a goring that bad, back in the bullring a month later?

"I wasn't completely healed. It was the kind of goring that would never heal, mentally. Do you understand what I'm saying, young man?"

"Uhh, I think so."

"Some matadores are gored, the wound is cleansed and sewn up and the matador goes out to fight just as bravely as before. For others it is a different thing. It was a different thing for me. I couldn't work as closely to the bull as before, I couldn't stop my feet from dancing. And the aficion took notice.

They didn't whistle or throw things at me. They became silent, they sat on their hands. No 'Olés' any more. Silence is something that a bullfighter does not want to hear in the bullring." He smiled at his own "In" joke.

"Enough of that, it's history. Let's go back to the capote. This pase, the Veronica, is said to be the name of the woman who used her apron to wipe the sweat from the brow of our Lord, Jesus Christ, when he was on his way to be crucified. One must show compassion and tenderness when you wipe the bull's face with the pase."

I could see it—I could see it. I could see the big difference between the computer generated pase that Dad had programmed for me and this. This was the real deal.

◆

On Friday of the second week "Nacho" took me to a slaughter house somewhere between Mexico City and the end of the world. I don't know where we went and I would never be able to find it again, but he thought it was important that I should know what the inside of a bull, in this case, a cow, looked like.

"You see how the cow is like the bull but without the muscle. Come, my friend Juan will allow us to kill a few for him."

"Nacho" gave the guy in charge a bundle of pesos and we took our swords and capes over into the small pasture.

"I gave Juan money for ten animals. I will kill the first two and you will kill the others."

One of the workers let one cow at a time into the pasture. "Nacho" warned me – "Be careful, these are not fighting bulls but in this small space they sometimes become quite brave."

He approached the cow as cautiously as he would have approached a fighting bull. The cow gave him that dumb look that cows have, but when he unfurled the muleta to attract her attention she suddenly changed from a dumb cow to an animal with horns.

He lined her up by focusing her attention on the muleta and when her hooves were parallel he crossed perfectly and buried his sword in the space between her shoulder blades. She dropped like someone had turned the lights off in her body.

The second cow was not quite as calm, maybe she smelled the scent of death. He got the sword in well, but it took a few minutes for her to settle to her knees, hemorrhaging. One of the slaughter house workers snuck up behind her with his puntilla and sliced behind her head, severing the spinal cord.

"Your turn, young man."

It suddenly dawned on me as I watched my cow come into the pasture – I've never killed anything in my whole life. Face-to-face, the cow was enormous. Her horns seemed huge and the way she eyed my approach to her didn't fill me with confidence.

'Remember who you are and what you're supposed to do in the ring", "Nacho" said to me in a calm voice.

She wouldn't let me line her up properly. She was beginning to piss me off. Hold still! Shit! They're gonna kill you in there, why not die out here?

Maybe my mental message reached her because she suddenly stopped fidgeting and I went/crossed right into the space between her shoulder blades. She dropped, dead by the time she hit the ground. A few of the slaughter house employees checking out the action applauded, a few shouted good natured "Olés". I was on top of the world.

"Nacho" didn't give me a chance to get puffed about myself; he signaled for the next one and the next one and the next one. I did well with six out of eight, two of them put up a strong resistance to being killed, a strong resistance. The sword hit bone, it hit a rough spot. I really felt bad about the pinchazos, bad sword thrusts, because I wanted to put the poor beasts out of their misery as soon as possible.

"Nacho' was pleased with my work, I could tell that from the way he clapped his right hand on my shoulder and said, "Not bad, young man, not bad", after it was over.

———◆———

Leaving the slaughter house and the animals I had killed, I felt a strange vibe going through me. It wasn't guilt, or sin or anything that depressing. It was something else. My mentor noticed it.

"So, what is it?"

"I was just wondering – why should the bullfight end with the bull being killed?"

He nodded as though he had expected the question. And it took him almost two days to supply the answer. This is what he told me.

"Many people, much wiser than myself, have written and spoke about this, about why the bull should be killed. Some of what they have written and said is pure bullshit. Here is my opinion, what I think.

Number one: Spiritually, I think most of the afición would agree that the bull, this great symbol of strength and vitality, is a sacrifice to forces that are deeper and darker than anything we will ever be able to understand.

Understand me well, young man, I can't speak about the bullfight to those who just see it as a savage spectacle. On one level I can understand what they feel but I do not agree with their views. Animals, including human kind, have been sacrificed for one reason or another down through time. Is it wrong? Is it right? Who can say?

I cannot say because we are talking about something that we are called to do, something like priests."

I paid close attention to what he said as our taxi waded through the swarms of people who filled up the streets buying, selling, surviving.

"Culturally, I think, here in Mexico, the bull dies at the end because our culture sees it as the natural consequence of life. We have a Dia de la Muerta, a Day of the Dead, when we actually celebrate Death. I don't think you would find such a thing in Switzerland or the United States."

He paused, to give me one of his tricky little smiles.

"In Portugal they have these bloodless bullfights where the bulls horns are shaved. I have been there, it is wonderful to see, but I don't think it would wash well in Mexico.

The Mexican wants to see blood, the most precious liquid on Earth, released. I think we feel that we are cleansed by the killing of the bull. And because, sometimes the bull may kill the man, or injure him, the corrida forces us to remember that we are not invincible."

I felt like he was talking a kind of poetry, that he was opening up another door for me.

"Psychologically, the killing of the bull brings a sort of closure... something we all want. Well, I am not the Pope and I think I have done enough preaching for the day. I would suggest that we do a little work on this business of crossing, the double movement we must make when we are making the kill."

My wrists were beginning to feel like steel whips, it had to do with twisting the muleta in the right hand, the left hand, making various pases while guiding the cloth with a sword.

"Bulls are not killed with sticks, so we do not train with sticks, we train with swords."

My arms and shoulders ached too, but I didn't complain. I couldn't complain. I could see that "Nacho" was judging me, cataloguing my strengths and weaknesses.

That evening, long after dark, we had done a half dozen pases with the muleta – Arrucina; "This is your signature, but it can only be done with certain bulls, with good eyesight. You were very lucky...."

"Pase por Alto", "Par Alto con la izquierda", "Molinete", "Manoletina", Pase de la Muerte", "Pendulo", Pase en Redondo", "Sanjuanera", and "Remate" – I felt really ready to fight a bull.

"Nacho" cooled me out with a back handed compliment.

"Young man, I think you have the making of a very good muletero, someone who works well with the muleta, but you must bring more alma, more soul into your work."

Ouch! Imagine somebody, anybody telling a young blood from Chicago that he should bring more "soul" into his work?

Yeahhh, I was pissed off for a few minutes, but I understood where he was coming from, what he meant.

I was out there for a long hour after he left me, slowly dragging the muleta-naturale in front of a viciously dangerous bull. Nothing else mattered, other than doing this movement correctly.

I don't know if I had done it perfectly, or if "Nacho" had gotten tired of watching me work on it.

"Young man, there is tomorrow, knock it off!", he called from the first floor window.

I stood in place for a few minutes, staring up at a full moon. I wanted to scream back at him – "Who told you when to stop when you went out into the bull pastures after dark?" But I chilled, folded my capes and got ready for tomorrow.

Sunday morning, after my long jog with the boxers (I could almost keep up with them now), we worked on the proper killing technique while he continued talking about why the bull should die at the end.

"No matter how we try to get away from it, the corrida, the fighting of bulls is a play, theatre. There is a first act, a second act, a third and final act, if everything has been done correctly.

Finally for practical reasons, the bull must be killed because it can never be fought again, should never be fought again. Bulls are smarter than most men and if they were fought more than once they would remember that experience and some would-be matador would be in serious trouble."

"Do you think that you may have caused some would-be matador a serious problem because you caped bulls out in the pastures?"

I felt like biting my tongue the second after I asked the question. "Nacho" frowned and stared down at the ground for a few seconds.

"Perhaps. Now, going back to the business of killing the bull. The sword does not always have to be hasta la bola, all the way in up to the hilt, to have a clean kill. It is the angle of the sword that matters, it must slice the heart muscle, that's what counts most."

He surprised me at two o'clock by announcing – "Make yourself presentable, we are going to see what the matadores are doing today."

A very interesting thing happens when you get behind the scenes of a Scene. I had lost track of the number of fights I had seen on T.V. in Chicago, 'the North Pole', but I had no real idea of what the scene was behind the Scene.

I didn't know everything, of course, but I had a much stronger idea of what the Scene was about after a very brief period of study with "Nacho". He force fed me info about the bulls and the men fighting them.

"This is the first bull, what do you see?"

On the honest to God level, all I could see was a huge black beast with huge horns. "Nacho" pressed me to look more critically.

"He doesn't see well out of his left eye, you see how he jerks his head around to try to see everything with his right eye. You must be able to see these things, they will be very important for your survival."

I swallowed hard and looked harder. He was just as critical about the men in the ring.

"What do you think of this one?"

I really didn't know what to say. The matador seemed to be doing a good job.

"Uhh, looks like he's doing a good job to me."

"Nacho" gave me his sarcastic little smile.

"Yes, you are correct, he's doing a good job, that's the problem."

"Uhh, I don't think I understand…"

"If I wanted to see someone do a 'good job', I would go to the seashore and watch fishermen. Why should we spend our dinero to watch someone do a 'good job'?"

"So, what should he do?"

"He should be exposing himself, doing all of the things that the average person would be terrified to attempt."

"'Nacho', are you saying that the bullfighter should be suicidal?"

"Never, I'm saying that the bullfighter should be willing to do the things that the average person would be terrified to attempt to do." And his jaws clamped shut.

Later, during the course of the sixth bull, the last fight, he pointed out one more thing that hadn't even come close to my mindset.

"You see how ignorant this man is. He is trying to force the bull to accept his style, his point-of-view. He should be altering his style, his point-of-view, to accommodate the bull. We have to always keep in mind that the bull has a mind, a certain way of looking at the world."

The last fight was over, after a long series of mis-moves and a clumsy attempt at killing. "Nacho" clapped his had on my shoulder as we started to shuffle out of the arena.

"Now, young man, you see what should be done. Come, we must visit Senõr Flores."

"Senõr Flores, where is he?"

"In his office", he answered.

And there he was, tinted shades, the baby powder scented cologne, the pearl grey Stetson, the cowboy boots, the Cuban cigar, in his office under the stadium.

"Please, sit."

"Nacho" leaned against the wall near me, taking it all in. A bodyguard guy stood off to one side.

"'Nacho' has given me very good news about you, -- that you will be capable of fighting in September."

I swallowed hard. Was I ready?

"If he thinks I'm ready, then I guess I'm ready."

"Nacho" exchanged smiles with Senõr Flores.

"Good. I had to knock a few heads together to get them to make you the third man for the fight in Tijuana, first Sunday in September."

"September? In Tijuana?"

"Yes. I thought it would be a good idea to start you off at the border. A lot of Americans come to the corrida there, and they are not as critical as the Mexican aficionados. From Tijuana, to Ensenada, Acapulco, Vera Cruz, Guanajuato, Guadalajara, back to Tijuana. Don't worry, you will have the schedule before the end of the month.

We are calling you "Juan Negro 'Azucar'"."

I couldn't do anything but blink; this guy was laying my life out in front of me – Juan/John "Sugar" Black, or John Black "Sugar". That didn't sound so bad.

He pulled a fat wallet out of the breast pocket of his expensive suit and counted out $200.00 in pesos.

"This is your allowance for the past two weeks. Also, I have messages, e-mail from your people in Chicago; they have been in touch with the Embassy. Your mother and father seem to think that you have been kidnapped by bandidos down here in Mexico."

I couldn't do anything but stare at him for a moment.

Mom, Dad, my sister, Dondisha, all of the people up there. I had practically blotted them out. I had pushed myself so deeply into my dream that they seemed like ghosts, almost.

"I'll e-mail them tonight, to let them know that I'm o.k."

"Also, I have an e-mail from your friend in Argentina, 'Raul'."

"Raul", in Argentina – he made it. I glanced at the pages that Senõr Flores held out to me. How did he manage to get a hold of my e-mails?

"Senõr Flores, hope you don't mind me asking but how did you get these?"

He smiled, took off his glasses to clean them. The same sharp, blood shot eyes. Obviously he didn't do a lot of sleeping.

"I have friends in the Embassy, they make certain that I'm made aware of communications that might affect my interests. If you need to use the computer, use 'Nacho's' computer."

I simply nodded. I didn't know 'Nacho' had a computer. As a matter of fact I had never been inside 'Nacho's' space.

"So, there it is. Any questions? -- things we need to talk about?"

I nodded no, no questions, nothing to talk about. He had laid it out for me. "Juan Negro 'Azucar', matador.

"Good, I'm going to Europe day after tomorrow. I'll be gone 'til the last week in August; but I will definitely be back for your debut in Tijuana."

We shook hands and "Nacho" led me out. That was it, that was the program. The whole thing made me feel a little bit unsatisfied. Hard to say why exactly. Maybe it had something to do with how impersonally Senõr Flores treated me. The man was giving me the chance to do what I had been dreaming about and paying me for it. But there was something cold about the whole set up; about our relationship. Well, what the hell, I had a father already, I didn't need a father figure as well, but I did feel the need for a warmer relationship.

"'Nacho', let's go shopping, I need to send a few presents to my folks at the 'North Pole'. He smiled at my joke and clapped his hand on my shoulder. Maybe that's what I wanted, a little more companionship, a friend.

———◆———

We had been pushing it prior to our visit with Senõr Flores, we went into a heavy pushing mode after our meeting underneath the stadium. "Nacho" had me doing one hundred yard sprints backwards – "Your legs will take you out of danger when your work with the capote and the muleta fail."

And more trips to the slaughterhouse. "Remember, 'Azucar', beautiful work with the capes alone will not make you a matador, a killer of bulls."

I liked the "Azucar" thing. Up to the point he had only called me "young man", as though I didn't really have a name.

"'Azuca', you are not putting enough of yourself into the pase..."

"But I'm only practicing."

"Practise is reality in the corrida, if you do it in a sloppy way here, you will do it a sloppy way there. Be aware!"

——◆◆◆——

The telephone calls that I made to my parents were filled with humor.

"Chester, are you eatin' right?"

"Yes, Mom, we have a lady named Mrs. Chavez who cooks beautiful meals for us, healthy, delicious."

"You met anybody down there?"

"You mean, like...?"

"You know what I mean."

"No, I haven't met anybody. I haven't had time to meet anybody, I have been pretty busy."

"Dondisha stopped over the other day, she wanted to know if it was o.k. to contact you."

Dondisha? O yeahhh, the girl I left behind. What harm would it do to stay in touch?

"Yeah, it's cool. I'd like to hear from her."

What harm would it do? Dad's stuff was a lot more to the point.

"Chester, I'm glad to hear that things are working out well for you; call if you need anything. And be sure to use condoms, o.k.?"

"Don't worry, Dad, everything is cool What's happenin' with Sis?"

"I think she's trying to convince herself that she's in love with this knucklehead she just met. Anything you need?"

"No, I have everything I need, things are going well."

"Well, you stay in touch, o.k.? We were beginning to get a little concerned about you."

"Don't worry, I'll stay in touch."

It seemed almost unreal that they would be so close and so far away at the same time. What was the Mexican saying about America? "So close to America and so far from God."

"Raul".

"'Nacho', I need to send an e-mail to a friend in Argentina."

"Any time. When you finish, we need to work on the pattern of the corrida, the pases that seem to feel best for you. And the kill, we must return to the slaughter house."

"I'm ready."

"Brother 'Raul', I was glad to get your e-mail, to hear that you're a part of the Argentine Tango Group. It looks like both of us are having the doors to our dreams opened. It would take along time to run the whole scene, my scene, down to you. I know you have a similar story to tell, so we'll just have to wait until we get together again to exchange notes.

Interesting, huh? We both opted for South America and we're doing our thing. Let's stay in touch.

Later, Chester

P.S. I'm in serious training for my first fight in Tijuana this coming September."

August was a blur, that's the best description I can give. Aside from training sessions, the visits to the slaughterhouse, I had to get fitted for my suits of lights, the trajes de luces, four of them.

"You will need changes because, if you work closely to the bull there will be blood on your clothes."

And "Nacho" hand picked the men who were going to be my helpers, members of my cuadrilla.

"Later, you may want to hire your own banderilleros, but for now I have chosen this guy I know. He is not spectacular, but he is dependable, he will get the job done.

And, I have also chosen three others to work with us; all good men. You must have people around you who would be willing to risk their cojones for you."

I met the members of my cuadrilla and I could tell that they were all seasoned veterans. They were respectful, but I could sense that they were thinking – o.k., Mr. Juan "Azucar" Negro, let's see what you can do.

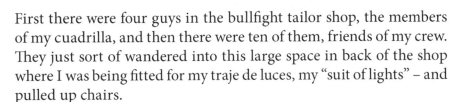

First there were four guys in the bullfight tailor shop, the members of my cuadrilla, and then there were ten of them, friends of my crew. They just sort of wandered into this large space in back of the shop where I was being fitted for my traje de luces, my "suit of lights" – and pulled up chairs.

Somebody came in with a six pak of cold Coronas and that's when the signifyin' started. It got to me a little bit at first, having these dudes drink beer and talk about me as I posed in front of a large mirror, in my undershirt and briefs. It wasn't 'til "Nacho" gave me a big wink that I realized they were pulling my leg, putting me on.

The ones who spoke English definitely let me know what they were sayin, in sly, almost Black barbershop tones – "Got a nice ass on him, the kind the bulls love to touch".

"Nacho" gave me whispered translations of what the pure Spanish speakers were saying.

"Ahh, this one says that you may not be able to find pants large enough to hold your cojones. It's like a compliment, 'Azuca', like a compliment."

I smiled at the beery jokes often enough to let them know that I could take a little ribbing. I even got off a zinger or two myself.

"Well, a least I won't have to pad my crotch with hankies to fill out the empty space." That was a little gem I had come across in one of the bullfight trivia books, about some bullfighters who were not "well endowed", pushing hankies into their crotches to macho up their stuff.

I had a lot more trouble with the traje de luces than I had with the jokesters. The panty hose tight pants with the "machos"/drawstrings at the knees. The tight waist line…

" 'Azuca', you must loose a kilo for this to fit properly".

"A kilo? Two pounds?"

"Si, it will make a big difference".

And the jacket. It felt like somebody had stuffed my upper body into an American football player's shoulder pads; or an upper body bullet proof vest. The jacket was **heavy**.

"Damn! How much does this thing weigh?"

"It **is** heavy", "Nacho" agreed.

"How come they couldn't design a lighter one, something made out of silk?"

"This is traditional, 'Azuca', traditional, you understand?"

"Nacho" smiled at the idea. A thin, lightweight silk jacket? Absurd.

I had four outfits, a yellow, a blue, a white and a red.

"It is good to have a red one because it doesn't show the blood stains so much, the bull's blood or your own blood".

I stood in the front of the full sized mirror, looking at someone who didn't look like Chester Simmons, Jr. Or somebody named Juan Negro "Azucar". It was as though I had been transformed into somebody else. I was no longer the person I had been, and I wasn't sure what kind of matador I would become. That would be decided by the bulls.

I started having nightmares and doubts during the last few days in August. Strange dreams that came from nowhere and seemed to mean everything. In one of them I was in the middle of the bull ring, naked, no cape, nothing. What was I doing there? How did I get there? I ran around the ring, praying that the bull wouldn't suddenly charge through the gate. A huge crowd, quiet as a tomb, not a sound. I woke up bathed in sweat.

In another one, like an out of body experience, I saw myself sailing through the air as a huge, white bull waited for me to land on his horns. They were nightmares, no doubt about it, but the one that left me trembling was the picture of me having an attack of cowardice come down on me. The bull was charging so slowly, giving me plenty of time to run and hide. The problem had to do with me being so scared I couldn't even run.

I decided to talk with "Nacho" about the last dream. I just couldn't hold it in. He smiled when he spoke, but his words were totally serious.

"Azucá, all bullfighters, past, present and future are scared in the ring. A man would be crazy not to be scared of the wild bull. If we pray hard enough we are able to master this fear, to channel it into the ability to do unusual, maybe even great things in the ring.

But don't worry because you are having bad dreams, all of us have had them. Do you pray?"

"I'm going to start…."

<hr />

September popped up on the calendar much too quickly. I was amazed to see the days come and go so fast. One day it was September the first and then it was September the third. Unbelievable.

I was on the card, with Manuel Rodriguez and Pablo Gonzalez "El-Encanto", to fight two bulls each from Pastejé, the Carlos Arruza ranch. I stared at the poster, at my name, like a man in a dream. Come Sunday I was going to go into the Tijuana bullring and fight two bulls.

I hadn't talked to my folks about the up coming event because I feared that they would try to fly in to see me. That was the last thing I needed; Mom screaming and crying, Dad trying not to scream.

Interesting thing about my Dad. So far as I was concerned he had been the dickhead of the day when he first got back on the scene after his ten year bit. But after I got together with Dondisha, he warmed up to me. Maybe it had something to do with me having the nerve, the balls to get out on my own.

Now that I was in Mexico, really far away from home, we had bonded in a way that never existed before. In the last phone conversation we had he had actually said, "I love you, son".

"I love you, son". That really played well on my head.

I think every boy wants his father's approval, in one way or another, and I was being given that approval.

I had come up the ladder from being a crazy young asshole, waving capes around, to someone who was being given his props and love. I couldn't ask for any more than that.

"Nacho" was what they called my "peon de confianza". I don't really know what that translates into, in English, my right hand man, maybe…

All I can say is that he took care of business. Traveling with a cuadrilla is like traveling with a small army. They have to be housed, fed, stroked. "Nacho" did all of that plus.

We were going to fly to Tijuana on the morning of the fight. Our station wagon was being driven down two days before to meet us and we would travel by vehicle from that point onward.

The night before the fight, at our four o'clock dinner table, my boxing roomies wished great success. Paco made a great water toast.

"I pray and hope that our friend, Juan Negro "Azucar" has the great success that he truly deserves."

We drank our glasses of water down with gusto. I was pleased and impressed by these tough guys. For weeks we had sweated, ran, then sweated some more. And now we were about to part. I was off to fight bulls and they were off to fight other men.

"Suerte, hombre". I would hear that – "Luck, man" – a whole bunch of times, but it never carried the same weight as it had when Jesús, Paco, Fidel and their trainer, Fernando, said it.

I couldn't sleep that night. I seemed to dream most of the night. No nightmares, just strange dreams: #1) I had scored a profound triumph with two huge, wide horned, dangerous bulls and made two great kills, the bulls dropped by my correct sword thrusts into their bodies. But there were no people there, no audience; #2) I had done every pase that I could think of with the capote and the muleta, but there was no reaction from this huge audience in the Plaza Mexico, one of the biggest bullrings in the world. Feeling crazy as hell, I pulled one of the aficionados, who didn't want to appreciate my art, from his first row seat and ran my sword straight through his chest. I didn't need an interpretation for this dream. I think it was saying, "Don't take it out on the aficion."

When "Nacho" knocked gently on my door and announced "It's time to go, 'Azucá'…" – I was already dressed and ready to go.

———◆◆◆———

"Tijuana can be tough on a bullfighter. Because the city has a reputation for having a mean streaked past, concerning drugs and murders, a lot of people don't respect the bullfighting tradition. But there are those who think that the standards of the bullfight community should be held high, no matter where we find ourselves."

That was something that I read in La Opinion a couple years before I made my trip to Mexico. Senõr Flores said that a lot of Americans came to the bullfight in Tijuana and that they weren't as critical as the Mexicans. So, where did that leave me? Were the Mexicans going to be more critical of me because I was an American? Or, were the Americans going to be less critical?

I didn't lose a lot of sleep about the matter because I was determined to do my best.

———◆◆◆———

The bullfight suit, the suit of lights, is tight, kinda strange, with the double stockings, the strings tied at the knees the cumberband around the waist, the heavy jacket.

"Nacho" helped me get dressed as the members of my cuadrilla lounged around, chatting softly. I was in a daze. I hoped that no one could read my thoughts, could tell that I was in a daze. My body felt good, I was in excellent condition but my mind was having trouble processing the scene I was part of. I was on my way to the Tijuana bullring to fight two bulls. I had to keep telling myself that, just to stay focused.

"Well, gentlemen, it's time for us to go", "Nacho" announced, and then whispered to me – "Would you like a few minutes alone before we go to the arena?"

"Yes."

I think I was supposed to get down on my knees in front of the white and blue candles that someone had set up on my hotel room writing desk. I didn't do that, I went to the bathroom and vomited my guts out. Afterwards while I was wiping my mouth, I stared at myself in the mirror above the wash basin and smiled at the handsome brown skinned matador I saw. Well, here I go.

--------◆◆◆--------

I didn't know what kind of reception I would get from Manuel Rodriguez and Pablo Gonzalez "El Encanto", my fellow bullfighters. I didn't have to give it a second thought when we assembled in the passage way that would open into the bullring. Both of them came over to shake my hand and give me a hug.

"Suerte, hombre", good luck, man.

"Suerte."

They made me feel like I was a member of a unique fraternity. How many men in civilian life ran the risk of being gored to death every time they went to work? I looked around at the men around me. Nothing extraordinary looking about them. They could've been shoe salesmen, professors of one thing or another, parking attendants, priests.

Except that they weren't any of those, they were in the bullfighting business and I was certain that most of them had the scars to prove it.

We could hear the sounds of the crowd, a kind of dull roar, and then the sound of a beautiful trumpet solo announcing – the beginning of the event.

Antonio, one of the members of my cuadrilla, whispered to me – "Some of us call this 'the pants wetting time.'"

I could pull ancient photos out of my album that show me and the others strutting across the arena, the others looking grim and determined, me with a smile on my face. Truthfully, I felt afraid but I was still smiling from Antonio's comment – "Some of us call this 'the pants wetting….'"

A Tijuana bull fight crowd at it's raunchy peak is a helluva experience. Señor Flores was right about the American vibe. I got the feeling that a lot of the young Americans thought this bullfight thing as a contest between a man and a bull; but more like a football game than an ancient ritual.

The arena was like a wash basin, held everything; the cigarette/cigar smoke, stale beer smell, outrageous behavior. I saw, walking toward them across the arena, three beautiful young blondes raise their colorful peasant skirts up to their faces – they didn't have any panties on. "Nacho" came to my side in the callejon, the circular alley framing the bullring, the area between the first row of seats and the stout fence that enclosed the arena.

"You must dismiss all the madness around you and focus on your reason for being here or else you may be killed."

He didn't say it in a – I'm-trying-to-frighten-you-way, but rather as a matter of fact. I took him seriously.

Manuel Rodriguez had the first bull, "Machete", and he ended his struggle to survive the honest charges of a good bull by going in for the kill much too soon. I could see a whole bunch of things he could've done with this beautiful reddish colored bull; but I was not Manuel Rodriguez and I didn't feel the need to be his personal bullfighting critic.

Pablo Gonzalez "El Encanto" had drawn a large, well armed bull named "Azteca", who was the exact opposite of the bull that Manuel Rodriguez had half fought. "Azteca" was tricky, devious, cunning. Maybe he had been fought before. I really sympathized with Pablo. What the hell could you do with a really hip bull, one who **almost** understood that there was a man, a stationary something waving something before his eyes?

The bull was veering in, more and more toward the man; but "El Encanto" wouldn't surrender his superior knowledge to the bull's instincts. In one of his most dangerous moment, "Azteca" paused in the middle of a charge, parallel to "El Encanto's" face, seeming to debate about whether or not he wanted to complete his charge, or just to hook to his left and impale the stationary something that was waving this distraction at him.

"El Encanto", reading the bulls ambivalent thoughts, stood his ground and gently waved his muleta, enticing the bull to continue his charge, and not to impale his groin, or chin.

It was pretty easy to see that most of what just happened was lost on the "touristas" and a lot on the Mexicans who had come to drink some beer, flirt with the panty-less blondes and forget a few moments of the misery of their daily lives.

I was still a half step into where "El Encanto" had taken us with his mastery of "Azteca", complete with a media estocada kill – meaning that he had not plunged his sword all the way into the bull, but just far enough to cause him to drop dead. "Nacho" had told me –

"Don't focus on this up-to-the-hilt business. Focus on the feeling of severing the heart muscle. Don't worry you will feel it."

"Bongo" was my first bull. He was large, well muscled and had beautiful curved horns, that is to say, they formed a kind of cradle, rather than antler-like branches. I felt that I could work with him. "Nacho" stood next to me, whispering his observations.

"This is a good one, one of the kind we call nuns. See how straight he runs, like a train on the tracks, doesn't hook with his right horn. Go to work!"

I felt, with the opening Veronica, that I was doing something dream-like. "Nacho" was right, the bull ran straight, which made it easy to do chicuelinas, to do statuesque pases.

I heard the crowd screaming from a distance – "Ole!" and "Azucar!" – as I worked the bull into the picador's lance. After two good pics I requested a change from the president, I didn't want the bull to be worn out when I went to him with the muleta. The banderillero, the man in my cuadrilla who is responsible for placing the sticks, pranced through his routine – leaving four well placed sticks, two didn't go in deeply enough and dropped to the ground. It was my turn again.

I stepped from behind the barrera, took my hat off and dedicated the death of "Bongo" to my friend, my trainer, my mentor Ricardo Ortega, "Nacho".

"I dedicate this brave bull to my friend, Ricardo Ortega, "Nacho". Many thanks for everything."

"Nacho" looked like he was going to give up a tear or two for a second before he accepted my dedication and gestured for me to "go to work".

I opened up my faena, my fight with four chest high passes, the ayudado por alto. I stood as stiff as a brick and simply lifted the muleta as "Bongo" swooshed past underneath. I did right handed naturales and left handed naturales dragging the cloth inches in front of the bull's snout, as slowly as I could.

I ended the first series of pases with a simple Arrucina, my signature pase. When I made a suave step away from "Bongo", to give him a chance to take a breather, I suddenly became aware of the sounds of the raucous crowd. The Mexicans were calling out "Ole!" and applauding, the Americans were screaming all kinds of things. Stuff like – "kick his ass, Azuka!: and "You're the greatest!"

The greatest? I glanced up into the stands to see if I could spot the one who called out such a ridiculous thing. The greatest? My hands were sweating and trembling, my legs suddenly felt rubbery. The greatest? Half way into my first real bull fight....

I think that stupid statement was responsible for me making such a lousy kill. I shouldn't blame an anonymous voice for me being forced to go in for the kill four times. After my third attempt, someone threw the little plastic pistol into the ring.

Here, if you can't kill it with your sword, use my pistola.

"Bongo" finally dropped to his knees and Antonio came up behind him to slice the spinal cord. It was over, I had fought my first bull and survived. I had done a lousy job at the end, but my cape work was respectable enough for the aficion to give me a victory lap around the ring and one ear. I was high.

I barely paid any attention to Manuel Rodriguez's second bull or to Pablo Gonzalez "El Encanto's" second bull. I was focused on what might be coming out of the gate for me.

Without giving it a lot of thought, I knelt in front of the gate where "Gordito" was going to enter the bullring. The pase is called Farol de Rodillas and it's done by swirling the cape around behind your head just as the bull is racing to the attack.

If it works it looks flashing and graceful; if it doesn't work the bull's horn can go right through your head. I felt I had to do something to make up for the lousy job I had done of killing "Bongo". I got away with the Farol de Rodillas twice, once when the bull charged through the gate and the second time after the bull had raced around the arena, forcing two people to jump over the barrera.

If "Bongo" ran on track, like a "nun", "Gordito", the little fat one, was way off the track. I didn't really need "Nacho's" critique to tell me that this one was dangerous.

"As you can see, he hooks with his right horn. But he also hooks with his left." The greatest, huh? So, now, what would the greatest do?

CHAPTER THIRTEEN

"Gordito" was huge. Bulls are large when fully grown at four or five years old, but some seem to have a more intense, bullish look about them. "Gordito" was one of the brutish, bullish looking types.

It took a bit of effort to lure him to the picador but when he spotted the padded horse with the blindfold he crashed into it. The picador shot his lance straight into the morillo, the huge donut of muscle at the back of the bull's neck.

I tried to lure him away from the horse but he returned three times. On his third charge he knocked the horse and the picador down. We all ran out, waving our capes to distract him from his attack. He came for me and I had the presence of mind to lead him away with a series of Veronicas and one wrenching media veronica, half way across the arena.

The monos sabios/"wise monkeys" had pulled the horse up and were leading him away. The picador was being supported by one of the helpers to get behind the barrera. The picador wears an iron boot on the side that he turns to face the charging bull. The boot weighs about fifty pounds and is designed to prevent the man's foot from being crushed when the bulls attack the horse. I took careful notice of where the bull was and where the picador was. If the bull had charged past me and **at** the picador, the picador would've been nailed against the barrera unless he could jump over the barrera with a fifty pound weight on his foot. Fortunately, for him, the bull didn't charge. He stood in place, blood trickling down from the lance wound in his neck, mad as hell.

I came out of the arena to give Miguelito time to place the banderillas. He managed to get three of them in before he was chased back behind the burladero, the shield in front of the fence openings.

"This one is smart enough to read Latin", Miguelito announced to all of us. An old saying – if the bull seems to be **too** smart, they say he can read Latin. It was my turn with the muleta. I went as far as I could to the center of the ring, took my hat off and did a slow turn around, indicating that I was dedicating this bull to the aficion, to them, to the people who paid to come see me.

A large group in the sunny side seats started chanting – "Azucar! Azucar! Azucar!" And then it was on, just me and "Gordito" in the arena. He came at me and I deflected his charge by leading him into a circular pattern, en Redondo. I wanted to wear him down a bit before I tried to do anything fancy. Nothing was working well with this monster. I couldn't get off on him, couldn't set up a rhythmic series of passes. When I provoked him to charge he would pause in the middle of the charge and look from me to the muleta.

I was never certain which he was going to go for. I had to remain completely still and entice him to go for the cloth and not my body. He was a weird, erratic animal, probably the result of bad breeding. He knocked me down three times, brushing past me to get at something in the distance. Was he seeing ghosts?

I rolled a couple times when he bumped me to the ground and jumped up before any members of my cuadrilla had to rescue me. "Gordito" really pissed me off. It was kind of an unusual feeling. I wasn't feeling afraid anymore, I was feeling angry. The asshole was spoiling my show, I felt like punishing him in some way.

The greatest punishment I could lay on him was death; I did a series of pases with him, lined him up perfectly and went straight in over the right horn. He was dead before he collapsed to the ground. Antonio snuck up behind him for that coup d' grace/knife slash to the back of the neck. It wasn't really necessary. "Gordito" was already on his way to bull heaven, or wherever bulls go when they are killed.

The crowd was screaming their heads off as I stared at the face of "Gordito". He made me think of the story of an old time bullfighter who had had such a hard time with a bull that he had his head mounted and, from time to time, when he got drunk, he would pull out his pistol and fire at his dead enemy. I could understand the old timer's feelings, that's the feeling that "Gordito" brought up in me.

"Gordito" was dead and I was alive, time for me to take a victory lap around the ring with two ears in my hands. My cape work with the capote had been shitty, ditto for my work with the muleta, but I had made a beautiful kill. That's what the aficion was rewarding me for, for making a quick, hot sacrifice.

"Nacho" draped his right arm around my shoulders as we shuffled through the crowd outside of the arena.

"You see how it is, Azucá…fancy capework is wonderful, but a great kill is the icing on the cake. Let's see if you can do as well in Ensenada next week"

———————◆◆◆———————

Ensenada was a weird re-play of Tijuana. I had one bull, a tough customer called "Gaucho", that I could do anything with. He seemed to love everything I did with the cape. He was especially turned on by my left handed naturales. Timing, I was beginning to find out, was everything; the thing that reveals the matador's control of the bull by the speed he uses to pass the bull. The slower the action, the greater the man's control.

I did a whole bunch of spontaneous things with "Gaucho", including kissing him on the forehead, after I made damned sure that he was temporarily out of gas. The problem came with killing him.

When it came time for me to make the kill I felt like my sword was trying to pierce an armored car. After three attempts I managed to put him down, but Antonio had to sneak up behind with his puntilla and put his lights out just before he was about to get up and make another charge. I came away from that one with a sprained wrist.

"Nacho" reassured me, "It's no big thing, Azucá, sometimes your wrist will be hurt trying to kill the bull, it's one of those things that happen to a bullfighter." I noticed these green eyes in this goregeous Indian face for the first time. How could I not notice her? Right there in the first row, shady side.

From Ensenada to Guadalajara. Senõr Flores had booked me into the regional bullfights, places that wanted to see this "Azucar" Negro. I didn't realize I had a rep going for me 'til I heard another large group in the sunny side seats chant "A-zu-car! A-zu-car! A-zu-car!" They had done it in the Tijuana bullring too.

What did it mean? I couldn't really put my finger on the vibe. Were they cheering me on? Were they asking me to do more? What?

Miguelito, the man who placed the banderillas, explained it in a very matter of fact way.

"These aficionados may have seen when you jumped into the ring in Mexico City, or they may simply have heard about what you did. Or read about it in 'La Opinion'. They are saying that they are with you, that they support you. If you continue to do well and to do better they will be able to say that their support carried you forward into greatness.

The aficion of Mexico is very complex. Sometimes there will be a superb matador that they do not like. Why? Maybe it is because he seems too arrogant, or he is stingy with his talent, or maybe his neck is too long, or his butt is too big.

And then there is this other one who is not so great in ring, but there is something they see in him that they like.

Very complicated. Sometimes the aficionados in the shady section will like a matador that the aficion in the sunny section does not like.

I'm not an educated man, Azucar, I can only speak of my experiences."

"Thank you, Miguelito."

Well, I had some place to go now, a frame of reference. It seemed that my fan base was on the sunny side. There were also some other things I began to notice too. The ways that the young women and some not so young were beginning to come onto me. The green eyes were beginning to intrigue me. She was there and then she was gone, like a beautiful brown ghost.

I had a pretty good afternoon with two La Punta bulls in Guadalajara. "Nacho" gave me some info and a double clap on the back after I had decent kills of "Pastueño" and "Alegre I".

"The La Punta bulls come from Lagos de Moreno, Jalisco, the world's largest fighting bull ranch. The owners have blended the bloodlines of Saltillo, Vistahermosa and San Mateo bulls to make the La Puntas some of the best in Mexico." "Nacho" could talk about fighting bull bloodlines and what went into the making of a great bull ranch in the same way some people can talk about wine and vineyards.

"The modern bull is a descendant of five 18th century herds: Cabrera, Gallardo, Jijóna, Vázquez and Vistahermosa. The Spanish have been the best breeders of fighting bulls for many years, but I must say that we Mexicans are not doing too badly."

"Which bulls are the most dangerous?"

"The Miuras", he answered without hesitation. "The Miura breed comes from a ganaderia, a ranch near Seville, and the Vistahermosa, Cabrera, Gallardo, Vázquez mix gives them a look of nobility, but their great nervio and casta make them very dangerous.

Think of it – four great matadors, 'Espartero', "Dominguin", "Pepete I' and 'Manolete" have been killed by Miuras. Don Eduardo Miura was not proud of the deaths that his bulls have caused, but he was proud of his bulls.

Here, in Mexico, the Pasteje ganaderia, started by Carlos Arruza when he retired from the corrida in 1953, has Vistahermosa and Murbe stock but I think it has gone down a bit because of too much inbreeding.

Some people say that a great bullfighter is made by fighting great bulls. I think you had a good afternoon with the La Punta bulls, no?"

We were sitting in the cool, dim barroom of our hotel. The members of my cuadrilla had scattered to do what they did, "Nacho" was sipping a frosted bottle of Carta Blanca and I had a coke with a cherry in it. "Nacho" glanced over my left shoulder a couple times while he was talking, but I didn't pay it much mind.

Suddenly he cut himself short, chugalugged his beer and stood up to leave. All I could think was – the beer must've hit his bladder awfully hard all of a sudden.

"We are going to take Monday and Tuesday off and then we will have a three day training session before next Sunday in Acapulco."

"Whatever you say, Nacho."

A two day rest in Guadalajara – great! I wasn't feeling exactly worn out but the tension of fighting an animal that could stab a horn through your head, your chest or your groin, amongst other places, had worn me down just a tad.

"Oh, before I forget – Senõr Flores asked me to give you this." He pulled a hundred dollars worth of pesos out of his wallet and placed it beside my coke. A hundred dollars worth of pesos didn't strike me as a lot of money.

"Where is Senõr Flores?"

"Nacho" performed his usual shrug – who knows?

"He will see you in Acapulco, he loves Acapulco."

"My last payment was $200.00, now it's $100.00, I don't understand that."

"Talk with Senõr Flores about it when you see him in Acapulco."

I stuffed the bills into my sports coat pocket. I wasn't hard up for money at all, I still had four grand in traveler's checks, but a $100.00 for a very dangerous afternoon's work struck me as kind of shitty.

"I **will** talk with him when I see him."

"Good. I will see you later."

"I'm not going with you?"

"No, stay here and finish your coke."

The abrupt way he limped away left me feeling, well, a bit pissed. And the tone of voice, like I was a kid or something. I was Juan "Azucar" Negro, matador, he couldn't talk to me in that tone of voice. I debated the question of how I should let him know that his tone of voice had pissed me off. I stared up into the jade green eyes.

"Now that your friend has left you, may I share your table with you?"

An Indian woman, for sure, with jet black hair and walnut colored skin; but taller than most Indian women, with a trim, hour-glass figure and wrapped up in black and yellow silk. A world class lady, by anybody's standard. The one I had seen in the arena.

"I would be honored to have you join me."

I had to smile. Ahhh "Nacho", you ol' fox you.

A beautiful woman, not according to any Hollywood kind of standard; I'm sure they would've thought that her nose was a trifle too wide, that her cheekbones were too high, -- a beautiful woman, by my standards.

"May I offer you something?"

"Yes, I would like that. What're you having?"

"I'm having a small coke with a cherry in it."

"That sounds delightful, I'll have the same."

I liked that, I really liked that. She could've made some kinda funny remark about the big bad matador sipping a soft drink; but she didn't go there. She was so cool. And those greenish colored eyes looking at me. She took a couple sips of her coke and leaned in close to me. She was wearing Chanel No. 5; I knew the fragrance from my delivery boy days in the Carnegie Drugstore.

"I saw you fight this afternoon," she said in a soft voice.

"Do you think I did well?"

"I thought you were beautiful. Beautiful and very creative."

Beautiful and creative. First time I had ever heard anybody link those words together to describe a bullfighter.

"Thank you for the compliment, it makes my hard work worthwhile."

There was a very pregnant pause. We felt relaxed, at ease with each other, no need to try to jam a bunch of words into the empty spaces. People were coming and going at the tables around us, but I hardly noticed them. The waiter must've stood by my side for five minutes before I paid him any mind.

"Ahhem, will you and the lady be having dinner, sir?"

"Are we having dinner?" I re-directed the question to her. She reached over to place her hand on my arm.

"We don't have to have dinner here…"

Nothing else need be said. I paid the check and strutted out behind her dragging a whole bunch of envious male eyes with me. The doorman rushed over to us –

"Taxi, sir?"

She waved him away – "I'm parked in the lot."

The subtle perfume, her beautiful skin, her way of talking, her green eyes. I felt a kind of rush go all up in me. I was 19 years old and I hadn't had any pussy in four months -- since Dondisha.

She was driving one of those expensive little German Karman

Ghias. Or is it Italian? It didn't matter. We eased into the car and when she turned to look at me her green eyes were glittering like marbles. It wasn't one of those head swiveling, head bobbling Hollywood/T.V. kisses, we just held the sides of each other's face and melted our lips together. That's the only description I can give.

How long? Two minutes? Ten minutes? I don't know. But I do know that the kiss stirred up my urge for more kisses from her.

"I don't live far from here."

Guadalajara had less traffic than Mexico City, a less frantic sense of pace, a flowery kind of smell to it. I took it all in as I studied her profile. An Indian woman with green eyes. I can't honestly say what I expected, I was just drifting along on hormones.

"You know something. I don't even know your name."

"My name is Maya."

A gated community with armed guards patrolling. It wasn't a community of big estates like Senõr Flores's place in Mexico City, but it was plush. I wanted to know all I could about Maya, she made me feel that way.

We shared another kiss the minute we pulled into her garage. And then a longer, more intimate one the minute she let us into the front door. I held her around the waist and stared into her face.

"Are you starving?" she asked me.

"Yes, I am" and kissed her again.

She unwrapped her egg yolk yellow rebozo from her shoulders and gently gripped my fingers to lead me up a carpeted, curving staircase.

Maya knew how to give me everything I wanted; she was "beautiful and creative". By the time we collapsed into a sexual slag heap I felt absolutely drained and satisfied. We went to sleep kissing.

And when I woke up there was no one to kiss. Gorgeous room to wake up in, full of filtered sunlight, dark blonde furniture, clean cut lines. There was a canary colored terry-cloth robe draped across the bottom of the bed and a note for me on the bedside table.

"Juan, 'Azucar', I have gone to do market for the food we didn't have

last night. I have given my people the day off, so you will have to fend for yourself. Be back soon, Love Maya."

I took a shower and then a long hot bath. My muscles were still tight from yesterday's bullfight. I made a mental note to get a good massage.

8:30 a.m. Nothing to do but roam around this fabulously furnished, two story, four bedroom pad, I counted, with two bathrooms. The place made me think of an Aztec Temple. I can't really say why. Maybe it had to do with the art she had on the walls, the sculptures.

I had to smile to myself for thinking, when she first asked to join me at my table, that she was a puta, a whore. How many putas owned four bedroom pads stuffed full of pre-Columbian art?

I raided the 'fridge for a tall glass of orange juice. Maya re-entered my life ten minutes later. She got as far as putting the huachinango/ red snapper fish in the 'fridge.

"Are you hungry?"

"yes, yes, as a matter of fact I **am** hungry."

We melted into each other and, minutes later, we were back upstairs. Who was it that said, "You can always eat, when can you make love?"

Actually, I really was starving by the time we came up out of our sexual catnap, 'round about noon. Maya looked glamorous at night and gorgeous after our midmorning love feast.

"Come down to the kitchen with me, I want you to be near me while I prepare our food."

I stared at her body as she slipped on a lemon colored, gauzy see through gown. She had what someone once called "a divine body". She was full up front and ample behind; but not too much in either place. She was exciting just to look at.

"Well, are you coming or are you just going to lay there and smile at me?" she teased me.

I felt tempted to pull her back in bed with me; but I **was** hungry.

I hadn't had anything to eat since the previous afternoon. I pulled on the yellow terry-cloth robe; evidently she had a strong thing for yellow.

On the ground floor she pointed out her library – "This is my workshop, where I keep my computers, files, stuff like that."

I strolled into the library. What was it Dad once said? "'Show me a house without books and I'll show you a poor person, no matter how much money they have.'"

Three shelves of books on the bullfight: "La Fiesta Brava", "The Life of Carlos Arruza", "Manolete", "Belmonte", "Luis Procuna", "La Corrida", and hundreds of other books about damned near everything else you could think of. I pulled a huge picture book about "The Aztecs" off of the shelf.

"Once you read that one you'll know a great deal about me."

"Oh, are you an Aztec?"

"All the way back to Moctezuma on my mother's side."

"What about the other side?"

"I've never taken the time to find out who those gold crazed, blood thirsty rapists were."

Well, no need to dig too deeply into that wound.

"I assume that's where your eyes come from."

"You're very observant", she said with just a hint of sarcasm.

She had four high-stools at a kitchen bar set up. I laid "The Aztecs" on the bar and plunked down in just the right spot to grab her for a little kiss or a gentle touch as she glided from place to place in the kitchen.

"Do you like huachinango?"

"I love huachinango", I told her as I ran my hands down her hip line.

"Juan, maybe you should go back into the library so that I can devote my full attention to this fish."

"O.K., I'll behave myself," I told her and kept on doing what I was doing. We were enjoying each other's company.

"Maya, you just called me "Juan". You know my real name is Chester, Chester Simmons."

She had a wonderful laugh, it sounded like a old man coffing or something.

"What're you laughing about?"

"I was just thinking how funny it is that I would be making love with a man with two identities. Are you a split personality?"

"No, I'm not bi-polar, if that's what you mean. Can you say the same? And is Maya the only name you have?"

She was slicing this, cutting that, gutting the big, firm red snappers. She paused to answer my question.

"Maya is my professional name, my complete name is Maya Xochitl de las Reyes. And yes, I must confess that I am different people at different times. I feel that the Aztec in me wants bloody sacrifices from time to time. But then there is another side that hates the sight of blood. I feel that conflict in me very strongly at times."

It seemed so natural, our relationship. I felt like we could talk about anything.

"Now, the salad is made, the fish is baking – it will take a half-hour. Would you like some tequila? Oh, sorry, I forgot you don't drink. Would you mind if I took a little something?"

"No, of course not."

I don't know what I expected when she reached into the 'fridge and pulled out a two ounce vial, sprinkled some of the contents on the counter/bar and efficiently parted the powder into four thick lines. Coke, cocaine. She rolled a crisp thousand peso note into a tube and snorted up two lines, one for each nostril. When she gave me the tube, I felt she was making me an offer I couldn't refuse. I had never snorted cocaine before.

"It's from Bolivia, almost pure."

———◆———

CHAPTER FOURTEEN

The fish was firm fleshed, succulent, delicious. The cocaine was cold, cold, cold. The chill that started in my nostrils made my face feel like a frozen mask. I couldn't really say whether I liked the feeling or not. We sat in the dining room at a table designed to seat eight, just the two of us, surrounded by all of this great art, sculptures, talking about anything that came into our heads. She was amazed by the story of how I came into bullfighting.

"That would make a great book some day…"

"So, now what about you? I've told you my story, what's yours? You say your professional name is Maya, what's your profession?"

"I'm a sculptress, primarily. If you look closely at the base of some of the pieces around the house you will see my name. I am also into painting and ceramics. Right now I'm working on a special kind of glaze that will enhance the colors used on pottery."

A sculptress, an artist…

"I don't want to get up into your business or anything like that, but your art must be selling pretty well to afford all of this…"

It seemed like a little shadow drifted across her brow, a sadness.

"I do o.k. with the art, but I earned the money to do all this the hard way."

What else could I do but look puzzled. What the hell was she talking about?

"Uhh, you want to break that down for me – the hard way?"

"Yes. Maybe I should explain…"

"That's what I'm asking you."

"I'm from a family that once had great wealth, silver mines, a couple bull fighting ranches, land…"

I loved the way she paused to smile at me. I smiled back and sipped my orange juice.

"The great wealth went down the drain when the silver market fell in the '50's, 60's. We were still rich, but not too rich anymore. I was twenty-two years old, becoming almost an ol' maid by our standards.

My parents, God bless them, made an arranged marriage for me. Don't look so shocked, it's old fashioned, but it's still done. I suppose you could say they made a political trade off.

The man was twice my age, a widower, with tremendous wealth. He wanted a young bride and the prestige of our family name. So, the deed was done. But before we got married, my mother, bless her soul, insisted that we have a pre-nuptial agreement. He resisted at first, but she insisted and my mother could be **very** persistent. We had a pre-nuptial agreement that was guaranteed to make my life a richer one if he died or got a divorce."

Once again that little shadow of sadness crossed her expression.

"I was young, I had been a free spirit, doing anything I wanted to do, going wherever I wanted to go. He stopped all of that. He didn't even want me to attend the bullfights – "It's a savage spectacle! I forbid you to go!"

I had beautiful clothes, jewelry, three homes, including this one, everything but happiness. And sometimes, when he came home late from being with his other women we would fight. I say – we would fight because I would not submit to a beating, like a common Mexican wife."

"How long were you married?"

"For six long unhappy years. He was driving, drunk, on the Paseo de la Reforma, two years ago and smashed into a tree. He was killed instantly and the woman with him died two days later of head injuries.

So, now you see why I can say I earned the money for all this the hard way."

She studied my face for a full minute before she came around to sit on my lap.

"Stop. I can see your brain going like a calculator. I was twenty-two when I got married. I was married for six years. My husband got killed two years ago and I'm now thirty, an ol' lady."

It was my turn.

"Maya, stop. You may be thirty in years, but in some ways, you're like a teenager."

"You make me feel that way," she whispered in my ear. I'm sure she must have felt that I was about to punch a hole in her gauzy lemon yellow gown. I still had a couple more questions.

"You're a beautiful woman. I'm sure that a few men must've noticed that you weren't married any more and…"

"And they wanted to sleep with me. In Mexico, many men think of widows as "used goods'. I was a virgin when I got married. I was faithful to him, even though he was unfaithful to me. You know why we didn't have any children?"

"No, why?"

"Because he always used a condom when he came to me. I didn't understand the reason at first, but later I thanked God that I had been prevented from getting a disease. I was a virgin before I got married and I've been celibate since his death."

Maybe it was the Bolivian cocaine, but my head suddenly felt swollen. She was leading me back upstairs.

"Mind telling me how I managed to be the 'Man of the Year'?"

"I saw you in Mexico City, when you jumped into the ring, espontáneo…"

"You were there, you saw me?!"

"Yes, you were very brave and I felt I had to get to know you. I didn't know how or when; but when I read that Don Luis Miguel Flores had become your manager I knew you would be coming to Guadalajara, sooner or later."

"If you wanted to get acquainted, why didn't you come to Tijuana or Ensenada?"

She wrinkled her brow and pulled the corners of her mouth down. "I don't like those places very much, they have become too commercial. As you can see, here in Guadalajara, we have given up a lot to Americanisimo; but we have retained a lot."

We sat on the bed and just stared into each other's face for a long time. "Azucar", she whispered, "would you mind if I did something?"

"Do what you want to do", I whispered back. What else could we do that we hadn't done? She parted my robe and gripped my 'Jones' very gently as she sprinkled a little of the cocaine on the urethral opening. And then she blew softly on it.

A half-hour later I was beginning to feel like I was on some kind of cosmic voyage. I didn't know that men could have multiple orgasms 'til then. A few minutes later, we snuggled beside each other, deliciously exhausted, our thighs smeared with each other's juices.

"Maya, how did you know about this, about the coke on the tip thing?"

I can still visualize the sly, mischievous smile she gave me.

"I'm an Indian woman, Indian women know a lot of things and besides', she added, "I've read the Kama Sutra a half dozen times. I just needed somebody to work with."

"To practice on, you mean."

"You may be righ", she said with a smile.

———◆———

Later that day...

Guadalajara is a beautiful old city with lovely little plazas and churches. We spent three or four hours walking around. It really helps to be with somebody who knows the neighborhood. We walked through a huge flower market, flowers of all kinds, especially the lilies that Diego Rivera painted.

Maya seemed to know everybody and they all knew her.

"They recognize me because I have paid some of them to pose for me, either for my sculptures or my paintings."

I was also pleasantly surprised to discover that there were people who recognized me. They didn't do any kind of paparazzi thing on us; they just nodded, smiled or spoke, "Buenos tardes, matador."

Matador. I was a matador. In the brief period I had spent with this beautiful, incredible woman, I had almost forgotten that part of my world. The bulls seemed very far away.

We paused for bowls of soup in some out of the way, hole in the wall restaurant.

"The men say this soup is like a Viagra. You don't need any for that reason, enjoy the shrimps in the soup."

We sat on a bench in one of the lovely little plazas and talked about cocaine.

"Maya, you know coke is addicting…"

"I know, I've always heard that."

"So, aren't you a bit afraid of becoming an addict?"

"No. Let me explain why. The cocaine that we shared has been in that vial for almost a year. A Bolivian girlfriend I have gave it to me about seven-eight months ago, a little present. The first time I used it, I was working on a project late at night, getting sleepy, and sniffed a couple thin lines.

The effect was like having a couple of cups of strong coffee. I talked to Silvia, my girlfriend, about it. She said that this was good cocaine, no addictive additives in it or anything."

A red flag went up in the back of my brain. I didn't want to come off with a "moral attitude" or anything; but all I could think of was the crackheads I had grown up around.

"Maya, I'm sure you must know that I definitely enjoyed doing what we did, with the coke, but I would've enjoyed doing what we did, no matter what. Coke, even the so called non-addictive kind, can sneak up on you and when it does you can lose your soul.

I've had friends who just did a lil' toot every now 'n then. And then one day they slipped and did more than a lil' toot and they went downhill so fast it would make your head swim."

"So, what do you think I should do?"

"How much do you have left?"

"Just a tiny bit."

"I would suggest that we go back to your place, use it up and record the beautiful memory of it."

She reached over and shook my hand.

"Azucar, you are wise beyond your years. Thank you for your

advice. And don't worry about me, I have a strong discipline, like yourself."

"I know you do, sweet thing, I know you do."

"What did you just call me?"

"Sweet thing…"

"Ohh I just love that, come on, let's go home."

By the time Tuesday rolled around we had worked our through so many things it was unreal.

"I want to see you fight but I don't want to follow you around, I don't want you to become distressed to look and say – ahh, there she is again. So, I may be there or I may not be there, and you won't see me because I will camouflage myself in the sunny side seats, with the peasants."

"Chester, "Azucar," there are many beautiful women in Mexico and some of them will come to you because you are a handsome man, because you are a matador, because you are Black,"

"Because I'm Black?"

"Don't play games with me, Senõr; you know the Black man's reputation."

"O yeah, right, that we're the great studs of the planet."

"Well, it's true, isn't it?"

She had a great sense of humor. And this ol' man's coffing laughter.

"If you find that one of these women is irresistible, please use a condom." We hadn't used one, so what was that about?

"Maya, to be honest with you, right now I can't imagine any other woman, Mexican or otherwise, who could do anything for me."

"Use the condom anyway."

"Well, what about you? What if one of these Casanovas manages to catch you on a weak night?"

"It didn't happen for two years after my husband's death, 'til this moment, it won't happen again 'til we are back together."

"Use the condom anyway."

We had another beautiful meal, lit by those candles that she stuck in a quartet of stone candle holders that she had designed. And more down to earth talking.

"In the hotel bar, on Sunday, I made a signal to the man you were talking with."

" 'Nacho,' Ricardo Ortega, he's my trainer, my mentor."

"Ah hah, I see. I gestured to him that I wanted to talk with you."

"So that's why he jumped up and left so suddenly."

"Well, what would you expect? He's a Mexican man, they know when to hold and when to fold."

I was really impressed by her knowledge of her own culture and the American culture.

"I grew up speaking Spanish, English and French. My mother, blessed be her memory, didn't think you were truly civilized unless you spoke French. So, that meant I went to live with somebody, a family in France every summer, from the time I was twelve until I was about nineteen. At that point Mama thought it would be better for me not to be surrounded by a bunch of hippie French boys. Papa spoke English very well, even though he called it "un idiõma de Los perros," a dog language, because it sounded so guttural to him.

I always had an English speaking nanny, either from the U.S. or the U.K. I recall one of my nannies, a girl named Abigail was fired for teaching me to say things like "bloody," "ye Gods!" and "blimey!"

Despite the fact that Papa didn't Love America, he took me there very often, to business meetings in New York, Chicago, where you're from, New Orleans, Seattle, everywhere.

"These people don't have to understand us very well because they are rich and powerful, but it behooves us to understand them so that we can survive, so that this powerful baby in the North won't accidentally crush us."

Tuesday night, we sprawled in bed beside each other, reading. I was trying to pronounce some of these tongue twisting names in the "The Aztecs," while Maya was re-reading Machiavelli's masterpiece, "The Prince." There was such a groovy vibe about the scene. Tomorrow morning, I was going to return to my hotel and go back into mode, but now we were in a different moment. We felt so close we could lay propped in bed, reading, like a couple who had been married for years.

At one point she sighed deeply and placed her book on her stomach.

"Just think of how different things would've been, how things would've turned out if the Emperor Moctezuma had had the advice of a Machiavelli."

"What do you think he would've told him."

"Don't let'em in here, Sir---- start fighting them on the coast, don't let them get a foothold anywhere! He also would probably have told the Emperor to straighten out his relations with the Toltecs and the other people that Cortez enlisted to help him conquer the Aztec empire.

He might've told him also, check Malinché out, she's a girl with a lot on the ball. But as you know, Moctezuma was quite a chauvinistic guy and he would've found it hard to take advice from a female."

"Yeahh, lots of guys have tripped on their own dicks because they wouldn't listen to a female."

My comment provoked a laughing fit from both of us. We got caught up in a contagious fit of laughter, squeezing each other for the fun of it. And then we just got caught up period.

━━◆◆◆━━

CHAPTER FIFTEEN

Wednesday morning, she insisted on driving me back to the hotel.

"I drove you away, I'll drive you back."

"Nacho" was leading the members away from the hotel on a ten speed, starting a two mile morning run. It was 6:30 a.m, time to go to work. He gave both of us a big, warm smile.

"Azuca', change into your sweats-------follow us!"

Well, here we go again.

"Maya, I'll call you"

"I'll look forward to hearing from you."

A quick, hot kiss and she was gone. Time for me to go back to the bulls.

------◆◆◆------

Acapulco, The small, fancy bullring seemed to be filled with drunk celebrities and their entourages, obviously more focused on being seen then anything having to do with a bullfight. The sunny side audience was small, this was an expensive arena to get into. I looked hard but I didn't see Maya anywhere. But I did see my first goring. It happened to Francisco Torres "Minuto" the second man on the card, a small, fearless Venezuelan.

The bulls were not outrageously large but they showed what bad breeding will do. "Nacho" was clearly disgusted with how treacherous and uneven the bulls were.

"These bastards are assassins, don't try to do anything spectacular with your bulls, give them a little show, line them up, make your kill and let's get the hell out of here."

"Minuto" was attempting to do the fancy spinning pase called the molinete with his muleta when the bull, a viciously hooking animal named "Bigote" suddenly veered into the man and ripped his left horn into his right leg, slicing his leg open from the knee to the thigh.

It happened too suddenly for anyone to help the man. I was looking at the action from behind the barrera, studying "Minuto's" moves. And suddenly, as though a surgeon had sliced through his leg – it was split open. I heard "Minuto" scream at the bull – "you motherfucker!" before he tried to stumble away from the bull on his sliced open leg. By that time we were all in the ring trying to distract the bull with our capes. The bull stabbed him once more in the shoulder while he was on the ground before we managed to distract the bull and carry "Minuto" out of the arena.

My turn next but first I would have to kill "Minuto's" bull. I found out later that "Minuto" lost a lot of blood and almost died because they didn't have a first rate infirmary in the arena, just a first aid station. A lot of time and blood was lost before an ambulance came to rush "Minuto" to a hospital many blocks away.

Antonio, my banderillero, was mad as hell-----"that's how it was when I got my first cornada in the Plaza Mexico. They had an infirmary but no doctor."

My turn next. The drunken celebrities seemed to be a bit more interested in what was happening now, now that they had seen a man's leg slit open from knee to thigh.

"Nacho" cautioned me – "Azuca, remember just a little show, line him up and make the kill. Don't go in over the horn if he doesn't cooperate, go in over to the side. He has just gored 'Minuto' and he has a 'memory'." He was suggesting, telling me to cheat on the "moment of truth." I did a few pases with "Bigote" and lined him up as quickly as I could for the kill. I felt that I was taking revenge on the bull for goring "Minuto". And I didn't do it by slipping over to one side, I did it the right way.

One bull's eye plunge into the space between his shoulder blades and he staggered like a drunk man. I felt blessed, I had hit exactly the right spot. I glanced up into the elite boxes in the shady section. Senõr Flores was there, checking out the action. I was glad that I had ignored "Nacho's" advice, this time, my manager was on the scene, no time to play cute and safe.

As the third man in the rotation, I had fulfilled my responsibility to kill "Minuto's" bull, now I was going to face my own first bull and then my second. Three bulls, I had a chance to shine or blow it. My first bull was called "Rojo" because of it's dull, reddish color. I took careful note of the way he hooked as Antonio went out and dragged his capote in a quick zig zag in front of him.

When I stepped from behind the buladero to do my first veronicas I felt as calm and serene as a Buddhist priest.

I lured "Rojo" to the nearest picador for two hard pics and then caped him away from his attack on the padded horse with chicuelinas antiguas. I could feel the crowd settling down, beginning to go with me.

Some of the crowd called out "Olés," others just simply called out. Miguelito managed to plunge two sets of banderillas out of three into "Rojo's" lump of neck muscle and gave me some good advice as he ran back behind the barrera.

"Kill him as soon as possible, he looks like he's been fought before."

I heard him, but I didn't hear him. I heard "Nacho" mumbling curses under his breath and giving me the same advice, "these rotten bastards, giving us bulls like this----kill him as soon as you can."

When I requested the change to the muleta section, to my faena with "Rojo." I felt a lot of things going through me, I was terrified of being split open, like Francisco Torres "Minuto". But I also felt like a superior being, I was Juan Negro "Azucar", the matador from Chicago. I had to put my ass on the line to prove a point.

Subconsciously, I rationalized that "Rojo" was a crazy ass bull running around, and that I was human being, a rational, intelligent, thinking animal. In some ways the battle seemed unequal; I had my human intelligence going for me and he only had his horns and animal instincts. But then I had to remember that he was bigger and had horns.

I started to work with him by taking calculated chances; if he wanted to charge fast, I delayed him with slow capework – naturales with the right and left hands. When he wanted to hook, I gave him in-the-face derechazos and ki-kiri-ki, movements to wrench his bull body spinal column, to wear his ass out.

When I finally got a complete grip on the situation, having worn "Rojo's" ass down to where I wanted him, I leaned forward and gently, gently, placed my forehead so close to his that it looked as though I was placing my head against his head. The crowd went nuts. What they didn't understand is that the bull is wall eyed, like a fish and doesn't see very well directly in front of him. If he is temporarily "aplomado," out of gas, there are a number of stunts like that you can do with him.

I killed him well, after a few more passes, but he managed to dig a bit of his right horn into my right thigh as I went in over the right horn to make the kill. It was a small snag in my suit of lights, a small slash into my flesh that would take fifteen stitches. But I had killed him well.

I have to say, a lot of romantic, idealistic stuff died with me that afternoon in Acapulco. Maybe I had over romanticized the idea of bullfighting. Maybe I hadn't thought hard enough about the role of the audience. Maybe I wasn't meant to be a bullfighter.

But I couldn't allow those kinds of doubtful thoughts to grab hold of my mind because I still had another bull to deal with.

Carlos Navarra, the first man in the rotation, "the first sword," did badly with his second bull, a cowardly animal who had picked out a section of the arena, after the pics and the banderillas, and seemed to dare the matador to come for him. **His querencia.**

My sympathy was with Navarra, who showed clear signs of being afraid. Number one, he couldn't stop his feet from doing a little dance. I remembered "Nacho" talking about his problems with remaining stock still while making his passes, the reason why he retired. Maybe Navarra was focusing on "Minutos" gored leg, maybe this particular bull had intimidated him.

When the "Moment of Truth" came it seemed to last for an hour. As usual, some wise guy tossed the toy pistol out into the arena. "If you can't kill it with the sword, shoot it!" It was a cruel joke, which of them would be willing to trade places with the matador?

Finally, the bull hemorrhaged and dropped to the sand. Navarra's puntillero eased up behind the bull and made the fatal neck slash.

I had the last bull of the afternoon. I glanced up at Senõr Flores. He gave a cool wave---- "I'm here, what're you going to do?"

"Cachuco" was the name of the bull that trotted out of the torilles gate. "Nacho," standing next to me, took that as a bad sign.

"He's too calculating, too deliberate in his movements." So what was I supposed to do about that? I was there to kill the bull, that was my job, I couldn't put him on the shrink's couch and analyze him. I watched Antonio closely as he did his one handed zig zag dragging of capote in front of the bull, running backward. He tripped and fell and the bull was stabbing the ground with his horns, trying to get to him. Antonio, a seasoned pro, started rolling away from the bull's attack the second he hit the ground. We flashed our capes in front of the bull and prevented Antonio from getting a serious goring. I was taking a real hard look at the members of my cuadrilla, they were a cracker jack, Johnny on the spot crew, quick and ready to do whatever is necessary.

When someone goes down under a bull's attack in the arena everybody, the other cuadrillas, the mono sabios/wise monkeys/the custodians of the bullring, come to the rescue. They know it's a matter of life or death.

My turn, I lured "Cachuco" into the picador's lance with a sculptured series of veronicas and one cool media veronica.

The first bullfighter, Navarra, lured the bull away from the picador with a couple serpentina/serpent pases. The man had recovered a bit of his nerves. That was fine, but he was caping my bull and I let him know, with one long, dirty look, that I wasn't pleased with him. He backed off.

Miguelito shot the banderillas in, one, two, three. Evidently he had decided to do his bit as quickly as possible. I petitioned the president of the arena for a change of the muleta part of the fight, the faena, the part that ends in the kill. I took off my montera and dedicated the bull to the crowd. They liked that.

Now it was between me and "Cachuco." Why did I do it, I don't know, but I decided to face him on my knees with a series of passes. I started off with a couple pase de rodillas. He came at me hot and heavy. Then I met him again with a series of molinete de rodillas, rodillas literally means – on your knees.

By the time I stood up for my next series of passes, naturales with left and right hands, the crowd were doing the "olés" in a rhythmic pattern. It gave me a rhythm to work with, like an Afro-Cuban drummer with the clave.

"Cachuco" was mine, that was my feeling. I had read something an old time bullfighter, a guy named Antonio Ordónéz, once said about a particular fight, about being drunk, bull drunk, intoxicated by what he had done.

I felt that craziness with "Cachuco." It seemed that I could dredge up the memory of many hours of swirling a cape in the vacant lot behind the place we lived in on Bowen Avenue, Chicago, the Southside. I could dredge up memories of bone chilling days on the Lakefront, swirling my capote, or pretending that I was doing close muleta work with "un cathedral", a cathedral of a bull. I always liked that, a cathedral.

Weirdly, I could also pull up the graphic effects of Dad's computer generated bulls, the one's that I killed expertly with my cursor/mouse.

But then was then. "Cachuco" was crowding me, I could sense, as I did a series of passes that were going to lead us to having a real thing happen-------your death or mine?--- that he knew I was going to try to kill him. And that he was trying to get to that place first.

It's very important not to cape a bull too long because they are so intelligent. "Cachuco" had been pic-ed, he had been struck by the pin pricks of the banderillas and lured into charging a flowing curtain. He was on the cusp of understanding too much, maybe he was a Scorpio. It was the right time for "the moment". But since we were doing so well together, I decided to extend the life of our relationship with a few more passes.

I did a classic pase de pecho, the chest pass, the one where the matador raises the muleta to chest height as the bull passes underneath, it's the logical finishing pass for a series of naturales. "Cachuco" missed plunging his horns into my chest, but he did catch me in that natural cradle between his horns. I was lucky, I hadn't been gored, I had simply had the ribs on my right side cracked by his misjudged charge.

I was so off into our thing that I hardly noticed. O.K., you bastard, you just cracked my ribs----wait til you find out what I'm going to do to you. I jumped right back into position.

My cuadrilla took note of the rib cracking bust and tried to interfere – I wouldn't have it, this was between me and "Cachuco". I waved them off the point, this was between me and Senõr "Cachuco". Dejelé! /Leave us!

What else I did after my ribs had been cracked may always be a mystery, until I look at the videos again. But I do recall the great still moment that happened, just as I profiled to plunge into "Cachuco's" body.

Ever heard of "instant prayers"? Beyond prayers before dinner and stuff like that?

"Nacho" had spoken to me about praying, in matters concerning the bullfight: O Lord, please give me a good bull, one who is willing to die easily, etc, etc, etc.

But my mentor hadn't prepared me for the prayers that may happen between the bull and the man. "Cachuco" had given me all he could give as a bull and I owed him a debt to give back as much as I could give him as a man.

The shit became real deep on my mind. This is not really a thing between a man and an animal, it's about the sophisticated ways that a man has invented to ask for, request consideration from spirits we haven't even thought about. Crazy, huh? But the thing that provoked that thought was the notion/idea of what would've happened if the Bull Civilization had decided, at the end of each Human fight, a Human Being would be sacrificed.

I plunged my sword "hasta La bola", up to the hilt in "Cachuco's" body. He stared up at me with his wall eyes then sank to the sand of the arena, as though to say, "You're killing me for these people, Why?"

The Black Matador, "Sugar"

When I paraded around the ring with two of "Cachuco's" ears, I felt slightly nauseous. Maybe a little bit neurotic.

———◆◆◆———

My meeting with Senōr Flores didn't take place under the arena this time. After a visit to the local hospital and an X-ray that confirmed I had six ribs cracked on my right side.

"Don't worry, young man, we will have you properly bandaged and you will be doing your hip hop at the local bodega this evening."

Well, I had no plans to go dancing, but I did have a meeting to go to with Senōr Flores. The round the body bandage was tight and forced me to take shallow breaths but I hadn't been sliced open. I paid "Minuto" a visit in the intensive section.

The little Venezuelan looked pale as a ghost, but he was alert and talking on his cell when I came into his room. He looked surprised and pleased to see me. His people made a discreet move to the corridor to give us a chance to rap.

"Azuca', many thanks for killing that evil beast that gave me this." He pointed to his thigh.

"I can assure you it was my pleasure. So how's it going with you?"

He gave me a little macho shrug of the shoulder laying flat on his back – "I've had bigger scratches before." He pulled the sheet aside to show me horn wounds/scars on both thighs, his right side, his stomach, his chest. This handsome little dude laying in the hospital bed had a body that looked like a Frankenstein movie. I felt like puking.

"Well, take it easy, see you later."

"I'm scheduled to fight in Mexico City next month, I have to be ready for that." I waved goodbye, what else could I do?

———◆◆◆———

Senōr Flores was staying in the penthouse of our hotel. He welcomed me with a limp handshake.

"Azucar! C'mon in, please, would you like a soft drink?"

"A glass of water would be fine."

I glanced at the two buffed up guys standing behind Senõr Flore's big black leather chair. Obviously bodyguards.

A very curvy blonde woman slunk through the room, smiling at me as she went through the door at the other side of the room. Hmmmm....

One of the bodyguards bought me a pint of bottled water as I eased into leather chair opposite Senõr Flores. My ribs hurt, felt like they were on fire. Senõr Flores seemed to be truly concerned.

"So, how's it going with your ribs?"

"I'll live."

He thought that was very funny and actually laughed out loud for the first time, maybe he wasn't the cold fish he seemed to be.

"Hahhah hah...well, it's good to know that you'll live. Now then, "Nacho" tells me that you're concerned about the money you're receiving..."

"Well, I don't want to sound like whiner, or anything like that, but I thought the money that I would be receiving would be, you know, becoming more, not less."

"So, you are not satisfied?" He sounded real hard when he spoke. I felt a little shaky about having an argument with him about money, about anything. I was so naive I didn't really know how much money I was supposed to be getting anyway. I had signed a contract that said he would receive 65% of my earnings, endorse-ments, all of that kind of stuff. And, of course, without a lawyer there was a bunch of fine print I hadn't even thought about. In Spanish yet.

"Senõr Flores, I don't want to sound dissatisfied, but I have to say – receiving $100 after I was previously paid $200 just doesn't seem right."

He took off his tinted glasses to clean them and gave me his bloodshot, piercing stare.

"Azucar, listen to me closely because I am not going to repeat myself. I took a chance on you, as a foreigner, as an espõntanéo. I put you in the hands of an excellent trainer, you will agree that "Nacho" has helped you a great deal?..."

What else could I do but give him a dumb nod...yes, yes, yes.

"I put you in my house in Mexico City. I have paid for your meals, for your bullfight clothes, I have given some people in high places big money to make certain that you had the necessary papers to work in Mexico, I have..."

"Mr. Senõr Flores, I can appreciate everything you've done, I really can, but it seems to me..."

"Let me finish. I stuck my neck out, as you say in America, to arrange for you to be on programs in Tijuana, Ensenada, Guadalajara, now Acapulco, next week Vera Cruz, then Guanajuato, then back to Tijuana, and possibly a turn in Mexico City. In addition, I'm sorry I have to tell you this, but I'm getting a lot of heat from the Bullfighter's Association, they are somewhat pissed off, to put it mildly, that I am promoting you as a full fledged matador when you haven't even been a novillero. Do you understand what I'm saying?"

Once again I had to nod yes yes yes.

"I want to make it quite clear that the Bullfighter's Association is not against you because of your race, they just simply don't like the idea of a stranger getting a slice of their pie.

You must not concern yourself about this matter. I am betting that the weight of public opinion, la aficion, will weigh heavily on any decisions that they choose to make concerning you. As you must already know, you have developed a tremendous following in a very brief time. Some writers are calling you the Pele of the Mexican bullfighting scene."

I had to smile. It was cool to be placed alongside Pele, whoever that was, but I was pretty damned certain that he got more than a hundred dollars for work.

I spotted the curvy blonde peeking through the door she had went through. Senõr Flores took off his glasses and pretended to clean them as he gave me a lascivious left eye wink.

"Now, it we have no other matters to discuss, I have other matters to attend to." He stood to signal that our meeting was over. He didn't reach out to give me his limp handshake as he escorted me to the door.

"I understand that you have acquired a girlfriend in Guadalajara. That's good, a good thing, but I must warn you, "he said with a sly smile," be careful of these Mexican women, they can be quite treacherous."

I stood outside the door for a minute after he had dismissed me, feeling vaguely frustrated, like I used to feel with my Dad during his post prison authoritarian period.

We hadn't talked about a larger share of the gate for me; if I was the "Pelé of the Mexican bullfight scene" and I had "developed a tremendous following in a brief time," where was the money from all that? O.K., so he had funded me out of his own pocket, it was time for me to take a look at the above the line and below the line costs. Did he have an accountant I could check with?

I felt really stupid at that point. If he had opened up every book in the house I wouldn't have been able to tell a nick from a scratch.

I walked away from his penthouse door feeling disgusted with my ignorance, his arrogance, and pain from my healing ribs. I tried to take a deep breath – I have to be ready for Vera Cruz this Sunday.

⬥

Because of my ribs, which wouldn't allow me to do anything strenuous, I took the time to re-connect with a bunch of folks, Maya.

"Azuca, I'm so glad you called I was worried."

"Why?" I was just teasing her, I felt the need for her, for somebody to be concerned about me.

"Because I thought you had been gored, when you jumped up after the bull butted into you I was afraid that you had a cornada. Bullfighters are very strong, I've seen them continue to fight after they had received serious injuries."

"How do you know the bull had butted me?"

"I, uhh, I saw the fight on television."

"The fight wasn't televised."

"Uhh, I heard it on the radio."

"You're lying, Maya."

There was a long pause.

"I was there, I saw the fight."

"I didn't see you."

"Azuca, you can't see every face in the arena..."

"Why didn't you let me know you were there?"

"I thought it would be best not to distract you with my concerns."

"Well, next time – please distract me. O.K.?"

"Yes, where to next?"

"Vera Cruz this Sunday and Guanajuato, back to Tijuana, San Luis Potosi, Guadalajara again, a couple other places in between. My manager tells me that I may have an opportunity to appear in Mexico City before the season is over."

"Sounds like you're hot and getting hotter. You say you'll be in Guanajuato after Vera Cruz?"

"Yes..."

"It's a beautiful little place, next to Guadalajara I love it the best."

"Would you like to meet me there, show me around?"

"It would be my pleasure, I look forward to it."

"So, you'll come to see me fight?"

"If you don't mind?"

Another long pause.

"Azuca, I've been doing a lot of thinking about you, about us."

"I have too, we'll talk about it when we get together in Guanajuato."

"Azuca, be careful."

"I will, see you in Guanajuato."

"Adios."

Next, phone calls to Mom and Dad, Mom sounded slightly pissed with me.

"We thought you had broke you finger or something, that you had forgotten how to use the phone. And I know you're computer literate; so what's happening' with you?"

"Not a whole lot, I'm doing a Mexican tour, fighting bulls in different places..."

"Chester, are you happy doing' what you're doin'?"

The question caught me a little bit off balance. What did "Happy" have to do with it? I was definitely doing what I always wanted to do, no doubt about it, but happy"? I couldn't imagine what a "happy" bullfighter would look like.

"Yeahh, Mom, I guess I could say I <u>am</u> happy. It's hard work but I've developed a pretty nice fan base and I'm getting better all the time."

"That's good – here's your Daddy, he's tryin' to snatch the phone out of my hand."

I think my chest must've blown up a couple inches---my Dad was talking to me man to man, mano a mano.

"It's looking good, Dad, it's looking good. I have a manager whose getting me fights all over the place and I don't think I'd be bragging to say that I'm getting better all the time."

"How's the money?" It was a casual question but I knew, coming from a stone businessman, that it was a serious question.

"Uhh, I'm being paid in pesos you know."

"I checked the exchange rate recently, what is it? About twelve-fifteen pesos to the dollar?"

"Something like that. I don't really have any money worries, I haven't even had to get into the stash that I brought down here with me."

"Good, I'm glad to hear that. What about the people, you met anybody...uhh,..."

"Oh, I've met a lot of people since I got here."

"Hah hahhah, front me off if you want to. Oh,' incidentally, Dondisha comes by pretty often. She's lost a lotta weight."

The code was on. Dondisha was carrying the torch for me and I should get in touch with her because she had gotten herself half way together.

"I have to get in touch with her, I promised myself I would do that. How's Sis?"

"Doing pretty well. Still dealing with this knucklehead but she hasn't let him get her pregnant and she'll be getting out of nursing school in another year, if she sticks with it."

"That's good, glad to hear it..."

"Here's your mother."

"Chester, when are we gonna see you again? It ain't like you're on the other side of the planet, you know. People are always askin' me, 'When have you heard from Chester? Where is he now?'"

Yeahhh, right.

"Uhhh, I was thinking about coming for Christmas for a few days." The words just bubbled up out of me.

"That's fine, we'll look forward to it. Did your Dad tell you that Dondisha comes by pretty often? She's lost a lotta weight."

"That's good, I look forward to seeing her. Well, that's it, Mom, gotta go now – I love you."

"I love you too, baby. And you be careful, don't take any chances with those bulls, O.K.?"

"Don't worry, Mom, I'll be careful."

"Love ya"

"Love you too, Mom."

CHAPTER SIXTEEN

I hung up the phone and laughed as hard as my cracked ribs would allow me to laugh. Her advice – "Don't take any chance with those bulls" – was the funniest thing I'd heard in weeks. Didn't she know that that was all the bullfighters did, take chances with the bulls?

I delayed trying to contact Dondisha that day because I couldn't really figure out what I could say to her.

Hey, Dondisha, my mother and father tell me that you come by a lot, that you ain't fat no mo'.

A short parade of people went through my mind. My ol' work mate, Johnny Fox, from the Carnegie Drugstore delivery boy days, Bobo...well, BoBo had become a dope fiend before I left the States, so I was pretty certain I knew he was probably in jail.

José "Cantinflas" Mangual, the pastry chef in the Drake Hotel Kitchen. I sat at my writing desk to scribble him a note. This was the dude who jump started me into this whole thing with two tickets to see Manuel Rodriguez Sanchez, "Manolete," at the old World Theatre Play House.

"Dear "Cantinflas," José,

I'm here and I'm doing it, I'm fighting the bulls and since I have killed a few of them now I can call myself a matador. You were right about your cousins in Mexico City, they are really into the drug scene. I don't have any complaints, they treated me well, while I was in their space. But it's a shame that they've decided to go for the low side of life, instead of the upside.

The Black Matador, "Sugar"

I'm embarrassed to admit that I still haven't had the time to visit your uncle and aunt in Xochimilco yet. I promise that I will pay them a visit when I get back to Mexico City. Right now I'm in Acapulco, then Vera Cruz, etc, etc.

The Mexican people are giving me a good reception and I'm having a good time, what more could a man ask for? Hope all is well with you,

Sincerely yours,
Chester Simmons aka Juan "Azuca" Negro

I had to go to "Nacho's" room to ask for the use of his lap top. He was "busy." I caught the rear view of a brown skinned naked female body through the five inch slit he opened to slip the computer through.

"I just want to check my e-mail, I'll return it when I finish."

"No problem, Azuca, no problem. Take your time, I have no need for it right now." A lascivious wink with his left eye.

I had to smile at the wink, I was beginning to discover that the bullfighter's cuadrilla, people who were into the bullfighting business, were a little like a bunch of drunk sailors on two days of shore leave. I could easily understand their attitudes. Live fast, live hard, because tomorrow you may not be alive.

"Raul" had a long e-mail for me.

"What's up, my brother?

I'm reading a lot about you in the papers these days. I wouldn't like to suggest that I'm having the same kind of acceptance/success that you're having in Mexico, but I'm doing pretty well, if I have say so myself. The thing that you have to remember is Mexico is Indian and Argentina is "Italian." I don't mean totally, but there is a majority of people of Italian descent here. I think what I'm trying to say is that I think it would be easier to find a broader level of acceptance in a "colored country", then it would be to find acceptance in a non-colored country.

Argentina once had Indians, but no one seems to know what happened to them. Yeahhh right. The truth is that they were slaughtered. They didn't even herd them off onto reservations, like in the States, they just genocided the shit out of them.

I don't want to get off into that, let me stay with our stuff for the time being. Maybe it's my fate, but I've lucked into these two middle aged sisters--------no, they're not African-Americans, sisters. These are actually two middle aged sisters bio-logically speaking. They've providing the cushion I need to help me cope with the physical and financial problems I might have.

My place in the tango group is pretty solid and it looks as if we might be doing a little tour of the States in the coming year. Won't that be a kick in the head? Well, that's it for now, from Buenos Aires, Your friend, "Raul."

———— ◆ ◆ ————

I e-mailed him back, congratulating him and telling him a little about what it was like to be "Azucar" in Mexico but I didn't mention Maya. I was still trying to put that together in my own mind.

———— ◆ ◆ ————

Vera Cruz, I was puzzled, and I have to admit, a bit surprised to see so many African faces in the bull ring. I tried to be cool but my curiosity overwhelmed my cool. Just before the first bull was released into the arena, I edged up to "Nacho."

"'Ey 'Nacho', where did all the African-Americans come from? Did they bus in a lot of tourists today or what?"

"These are Mexicans," he said with a slight smile.

"These are Mexicans?" I must've sounded like a complete dummy.

"Yes, Azucar, these are Mexicans of African descent. There are many here. This is Vera Cruz, it was a slave buying and selling center back in the old days. So, as you can see, there are many "Azucars" here."

It's true, travel is broadening. I had never thought about Black people in Mexico, and when they started chanting my name, I felt a strange sense of pride. "A-zu-car!" "A-zu-car!" "A-zu-car!" I was once again "the third sword," the third man on the bill. A big time egotist who called himself "EL Ciclōne," the cyclone, Vicente Mendes, was first. Jaime "Chamaco" Ostos was second and Juan Negro "Azucar", yours truly was third.

The Black Matador, "Sugar"

The bulls were not too awfully large, they didn't seem to be "dishonest", and "EL Ciclone" and "Chamaco" weren't spectacular, but they did do good work, I have to give them that.

I was terrible. I couldn't find the rhythm for a good faena. It had to do with my ribs. The first time I made a full fledged pasé with my capote I thought I was going to faint from the pain. I remembered the fight I had seen in Mexico City, when Pablo "Macho" Verano was fighting three weeks after surgery on his balls.

I forced myself to think about that as the fight was coming down to the last bull, my bull. Nothing worked, no amount of thinking about another man's nuts could help me. I wanted do the arrucinas, the molinetes, the pase de pechos, the fancy muleta passes, but I couldn't overcome the pain in my side. All of the pases demanded body twisting and I couldn't cut it. **Unfortunately.**

I barely managed to kill my first bull because my sprained wrist got banged up trying to push the sword into the space between his shoulders, his withers. I wouldn't've been able to kill the second bull at all if it hadn't been for Miguelito, Antonia and Paco, my cuadrilla.

Antonio could see what my problem was----"just get the sword in, Azuca', we'll do the rest."

I never took such careful aim at anything in my whole life. When I cited the bull for his charge, I crossed over the right horn as well as I could and Miguelito, Antonio and Paco ran the bull around in circles to try to have the sword cut through a vital organ. Antonio even reached in under his cape and jammed the hilt of the sword down deeper into the bull's body.

The public, La afición was outraged! Before the bull kneeled on the sand, hemorrhaging from the mouth, the public was throwing cushions and curses at me. Miguelito snuck up behind the bull like a burglar and slashed his lights off. The cushions and curses followed us into the callejón, echoed through the exit tunnel.

"Salsero!" "Salsero!" "Salsero!" "Salsero!" That was one that stuck in my ears. They had started off chanting "A-zu-car!/Sugar!" and ended up calling me a "salt shaker!"

There was nothing anybody could say in the car taking us back to the hotel; they felt bad because I felt bad and no one could do or say anything to ease that pain.

"Nacho" clamped his right hand on my shoulder.

"We will have the doctor in the hotel come up to your room to re-wrap your ribs," That was all he said. I made it straight to my room, ignoring all of the curious eyes following me through the hotel lobby.

I laid on my bed and cried like a baby when I got to my room. All of those Black people had come to see me and I let them down. Terrible feelings, that kind of feeling.

Who knows? Maybe it was Maya's Guanajuato...presence on the scene, or I just got lucky. Or maybe it was the beautiful bulls from San Mateo. In any case, I "gave the bath" to the other two men fighting on the same bill. My triumph was so great that, after giving me ears and tail from both of the bulls I fought and killed so well, La afición, that always fickle public, carried me around the bullring on their shoulders.

No doubt about it, I had scored a triumph in Guanajuato. I still had sore ribs and my wrist was still sensitive but I was young, in good shape and I healed fast. I felt bad about not being at my best in Vera Cruz and I made a secret vow to go back there at a later date and give them an experience that they would always remember.

We had to rent rooms on different floors of the Hotel Guanajuato because, as Maya explained – "This is still a small basically conservative place. I have several wealthy art patrons here. They may all know about us, but if we play the pretense game, act the way they think is cool, all will be ignored."

I went along with the program. What else could I do? But I thought it was a bunch of hypocritical bullshit. I couldn't think of anybody in Mexico who didn't know about me and Maya. Word of mouth would've done it.

In our case it was the photographers, the paparazzi. I was totally tripped out to see our pictures on the cover of a tabloid newspaper. "Azucar" with Maya Xochitl – an item?"

The Black Matador, "Sugar"

All my life I had read about celebrities who had tried to stop stories/photos from being put out there about them. I had never sympathized. Shit, if you're a movie star, then you can't avoid being treated like an important person. Now I was one of these having stories made up about him and photographers taking pictures from half a mile away.

None of it mattered a whole lot. We were together and that was all that I cared about. I had five whole days before my next fight in Ensenada (again), Tijuana and then back down to Guadalajara for a festival fight. I made a mental note to talk with Senór Florés again, about another opportunity to show my stuff in Vera Cruz and about money.

But that was all for another day. Now it was Maya Time. We had small, delicious meals in out of the way restaurants, went for drives in the hills surrounding the city, sneaked from her floor in the Hotel Guanajuato to my rooms and vice versa, to share as much loving as we could stand.

It became obvious to me that we were both afraid of being the first one to say – "I love you." I couldn't put my fingers on why I felt that way. Maybe it had something to do with who we were, what we were trying to do. Maya were already up there, with works and a rep. And I was climbing fast. I don't think either one of us was willing to detour our ambitions; she obviously wanted to be a great artist and I wanted to be a great bullfighter, we didn't want to be a great married couple, we wanted to be great lovers. And we were.

———◆◆———

Our few days and nights were a mellow blur, fused together by times when we simply lay besides each other, staring into each other's eyes. We didn't force any conditions on each other, we didn't make long range plans, we just wrapped ourselves around each other and lived in the moment.

I didn't want to hear about her ex-husband, and she didn't seem to care if I was hauling around any emotional baggage from other times. The problems we faced didn't come from each other, they came from the outside.

"Azuca', did you see this?"

One of Guanajuato's biggest daily newspapers had a great photo of us kissing in "The Alley of Kisses," a street with a local legend that said if you exchanged kisses there you would live fifteen years longer and have a lot of other good things happen. It was also obvious the Mexicans press/media didn't quite know what to do with us. They couldn't really nail down the angle they needed to hang a real story on. I don't think the L.A. Times, the Sentinel or any of the U.S. papers were paying me any attention at all. Who in hell cared about an African-American bullfighter and a green eyed Mexican artist?

We were lovers, that didn't seem to send people into the tail spins they might've gone into way back when. It was all of the speculation that spooled off the spin offs; were we going to get married? Would Maya Xochitl become the bullfighter's loyal and faithful wife, giving up her own career? Was "Azucar" Negro going to become a Mexican Citizen?

We laughed at some of the wilder speculations, and we frowned at some of the raunchiest stuff. There were fringe hints of racism in some of the stuff, but it never reached the level of anybody suggesting that this African-American and this Mexican shouldn't get it on. Never went there.

Guanajuato was over, we had done Guanajuato. We shared a very satisfactory feeling about that.

"Chester, Azuca', you've given me a Guanajuato that I would never have known, if I hadn't been here with you."

"And I can definitely say the same for you."

"We'll always have Guanajuato..."

"And Guadalajara."

"And yes, always Guadalajara."

We were so fuckin' mature about our us, about our scene, it almost felt weird. We were just flinging everything we had at each other, emotionally, no holds barred, and crushing all of the negative shit in the embryo stage.

"Azuca', Chester, do you wonder about us, about our ability to sustain what we have?"

"Maya, I don't think that's a fair question. I think, as long as you're the way you are, I'll be able to hold up my end. What are you asking me, for real?"

"I don't know. We just seem to be so well built for each other, emotionally, physically..."

"Yeahhh, I know what you're saying. Like I said, as long as you're the way you are, I'll able to hold up my end."

My comment provoked the kind of humorous physical response from her that seemed to give our love life a kind of surreal feeling. Whilst I was inside of her (or was she inside of me?), and we shared these "In" jokes; I couldn't imagine lovemaking without punch lines, humorous chicuelinas? Has anyone ever written a book that compared elements/sections of the bullfight to love making? Aşe...

Yes, realistically; I had spent enough time in enough chauvinistic locker rooms to know that there were dudes out there who saw the whole business as" – I lured her onto the pic, I did banderillas on her ass and then I fucked her with misleading cape proposals and then I killed her." How many times in my young life had I heard about dudes who boasted? – "I took the bitch to the killing flo' the first night."

Maybe there were a number of white brothers who would've described their activities in a different way, but the notion that they subscribed to would've been elevated to the same basement.

It was not like that with me and Xochitl, with Maya. There were moments when I felt totally dominated by her psyche, by her movements, by her comments. When she said – "Ooh Azuca', I love fucking you so much." And she was the one on top at that moment. Did that mean she was "The Man"?

It didn't matter with us, our pleasures with each other had nothing to do with sexual norms. For long moments I licked her engorged clit, the lips on each side of her vagina like they were candy strips and when she orgasmed on my tongue wipes, I felt as though I had caused a kind of heaven to happen. Did that cue me into Lesbianism? Well, under the circumstances, who in the hell cared?

"So, after this, you're off to Ensenada (again), Tijuana and back down to us in Guadalajara for the Festival fight?"

"Yes, that's the schedule. And I've also scheduled myself for another meeting with Senór Flores, about money."

"So, how much are you receiving now, per bull fight?"

Truth be told, she sounded like my Daddy.

"Maya, I don't want to get off into talking about business with you. Why don't we put together an agenda of things we're concerned about when I come to Guadalajara?"

"When are you returning to Guadalajara?"

"Ensenada, Tijuana, Guadalajara, get ready, babe, "Azucar" is on the way."

She gave me a very strange look, a kind of insulting look maybe, but I really couldn't approve of what her look was about, either positively or negatively. It was like I was in my own ayuhuesca, my hallocegenic bubble. I was beginning to feel that I could do what I wanted to do, with bulls or people.

Doing what I thought I would be able to do with the bulls depended on the their level of cooperation. They did a sort of bi-polar thing with me in Ensenada.

My first bull, "Cubano" was a large, ugly bastard. One of his horns, the right one was slightly lower than the left, but his eyesight was good and he charged like "a nun on rails." I made music with him. He was that rare animal that makes some ignorant people ask – "is that bull tamed?"

"Tamed?", No M'am, not tamed, "Cubano" was one of the classic cases that made me want to force the less educated members of the afición to understand a mystical thing. The wild bulls are not trained, but can be given specific instructions that they will be willing to follow, if the matador is able to give those instructions specifically. The bull is not about or into ambiguity, he is into direct action. If you give him ambigous instructions, he will gore you.

I was clear with "Cubano" and when the Moment of Truth came, and he sighed/died on the point of my sword, I felt that both of us had achieved somthing. Something.

"Justicia/justice was a bull of another type. He was from one of the best bull ranches in Mexico: Coaxamalucan (Felipe Gonzales) and he should've been beautiful, built and all of that, but he wasn't. Maybe he had been a result of some kind of wayward animal engineering. It wasn't like he wasn't beautiful, he was. But his behavior was terrible.

Can you imagine fighting a bull who behaved like an autistic child? It didn't matter all that much to me, my ribs didn't hurt very much, my sprained wrist was holding up and I had this insane notion that I could read "Justicia's" mind. Crazy, huh?"

I played the bull perfectly and, I must say, I played the crowd pretty well too. I was finding out a lot about what to do with the across the border bullfight crowd. With the Ensenada-Tijuana crowd I could play the bull so close to me I could wipe sweat off his brow; and it wouldn't mean anything. But if I did serpentinas and reboleros, large, fancy passes with the capote and afarolados with the muleta, they went nuts.

The one thing I couldn't play with was the kill. I don't want to sound blood thirsty at this late date, but I had developed a feel for the kill. After the proper number of pases, after a definite sequence of things had happened: the pics, the banderillas, a bit of close in work with the muleta, it was time for Senór bull to die. I was very clear about that.

A couple images helped me a lot. My Dad was a huge fan of the late Sugar Ray Robinson, an African-American boxer that most boxing fans, including the great Muhammad Ali, usually called "pound for pound, the best fighter who ever lived". He didn't seem to go into the ring with any specific plan to knock somebody out in a particular round, he just gave the other guy everything he had and when it was time for the other dude to go, everybody knew it.

I put that image on my mind. My killing sword thrust became a deadly right jab. I stuck it right where I wanted it to go. "Nacho" gave me one of his rare compliments....

"Azuca', you have become deadly in a short time, this is a good thing."

The other thing that worked for me was the computer/kill the bull video that Dad had designed for me. When I lined the bull up, it was almost as though I was lining him up as a target in my eyesight. Matador, bull killer was really beginning to have some real meaning for me.

Tijuana was another triumph for me; the bulls were the exact opposites of the ones I had fought in Ensenada. The first bull was large, with beautifully curved horns, the kind that bullfighters feel much safer with than the others, the wide, needle point antlers.

But he was a gruesome animal to fight. He came into the arena to survive. Maybe some hipster in the bull world had passed some info to him, out in the pastures, about what went on in the bullring. He charged dishonestly, that is to say, he wouldn't charge unless he really felt that he had a chance to gore me.

I actually felt afraid of him, but I channeled my fear, I made it work for me. It would be almost impossible to describe how I took my fear and contained it, bottled it in a manner of speaking. I talked to the bull and myself as we went through our time together.

"O.K., Senõr, you want to play games with me, huh? Well, how about this?" Low, slow naturales with the right and left hands, pases de pechos. I even did the mirando al publico act, the pase that "Manolete" made famous, where you lead the bull past your body as you look up into the crowd. I did it facing the people in the sunny side and I did it facing the affluent types in the shade.

It wasn't 'til after I killed him with one big thrust that I realized the blood on my shirt front was not his, it was mine. During the course of one of my close passes his right horn had sliced through my shirt front like a piece of paper. It was a clean, neat slice and it didn't hurt until twenty two stitches had been used to sew the edges back together. But that came later, after the fight.

My second bull had antlers, was ugly to look at, but he came to my cape and muleta as though he wanted to please me. We blended, we bonded. My blood was hot and I felt that I could do what I wanted with him. Because he charged so straight, I did a whole series of behind the back passes with him. I had the crowd screaming in fear, horrified that he was going to ram a horn up my butt. I didn't feel anything like that could happen and when I dropped him with one cold, right handed jab with my sword, I felt something very spiritual had happened.

I was making a name for myself, but I wasn't' being paid. And there was nothing spiritual about that.

CHAPTER SEVENTEEN

The Festival in Guadalajara was to honor an Aztec goddess. That's what Maya told me; "But they've substituted the Virgin of Guadalupe, just to keep the Catholics from getting pissed off."

It didn't matter all that much to me, I was in town to be with my girlfriend and kill a bull. There were six matadors on the bill: Manolo Marquez. I knew him and he remembered me as the espóntaneo who had interrupted his fight in the Mexico City bullring.

"So, you are now a matador, huh? Like me"

"Yes, I am."

"Suerte, good luck, amigo."

Carlos Mayano "Suaves" and Pablo Verano "Macho", guys I had once seen on TV back home in Chicago, didn't seem to be too pleased to see me. I excused "Macho" because he had been gored in the balls earlier in the year and I think he was still feeling a little pain in the jewels.

A local boy, Eugenio Espinõsa "Bombero", was supposed to be the current "hottie". We would see what we would see.

Mario Martinez "Claro" showed a clear disliking for me by ignoring my presence. I didn't really give a shit about his attitude. Like I said, I was in town to be with my girlfriend and kill a bull. I was also going to have a post fight meeting with Senõr Flores about dinero.

Maya and I had decided that we wouldn't hook up 'til the fight and my meeting with Flores was over.

The Guadalajara Festival was not one of those wild Brazilian things, but there were parades up and down the main street.

Miguelito, Antonio, Paco and myself stood on the balcony of our hotel and did little lottery picks of the beautiful women who walked and rode up and down. But the vibe of the Festival was basically conservative, no public drinking, weed smoking, stuff like that.

Two hours prior to the fight "Nacho" and the members of my team melted away. It had started casually after my first fight, my way of preparing my head for what was about to happen. I would take a shower and lay down, maybe to take a nap or simply to think. "Nacho" would come into my space two hours before the fight to help me put on the form fitting "suit of lights", the traje de luz, and give me a chance to kneel in front of my private altar, a large glass of water and a white candle.

Yes, I was saying prayers regularly. Maybe it had something to do with having a little nip in my right leg that took fifteen stitches, a razor blade slash across my chest that needed twenty-two stitches and six recently, almost healed ribs. I still felt damned near invincible most of the time; being young helped that attitude, but I was also aware that stuff could happen. Why not throw up a prayer or two?

They had placed me in the number two spot, after Manolo Marquez. I guess promoter (Senōr Flores again) wanted to milk a little drama out of the fact that I had started my career by doing the espóntaneo bit on a bull that Manolo was fighting. Number two was cool with me, it would give me a chance to do my thing and study the ones coming after me.

<hr />

What's the word they used to use a lot? – "a riot". The bullring was a riot of colors, perfumes, Cuban cigar smoke (I could see Senōr Flores in his shady side box), people calling out to each other, a festival atmosphere. We were going to fight one bull each. "Nacho" was enthusiastic about the bulls.

"These are La Punta bulls, a blending of bulls from Saltillo and Vistahermosa, plus San Mateo blood, excellent bulls, Mexico's best."

"Nacho's" critique of the bulls was always 100% on the money, but he didn't have to fight them.

Twenty minutes later, after a couple politicians had said a few words (the public wouldn't allow more) the ritual was on. The huge wooden doors were opened, we blinked at the blinding sunlight and started our struts across the bullring. There is no magic like the magic of the bullring. The people, the audience, la afición is there to see bloodshed, to see a bull or a man die, no doubt about that.

But there is also this artistic thing about the scene. The people want to experience something beautiful, maybe even sensual, before the ugly part happens; death, the ultimate blow job, someone once called it.

"Nacho", a kind of natural philosopher, had run it down to me like this.

"Now, I have to tell you that what I'm saying does not hold true for all men or for all women, but I think, for many, it is true.

Lots of women leave the scene of a successful corrida with damp panties. You know what I mean? As a man I cannot suggest that I know the real reason why this happens, but I have had, uhh, various ladies say that the sight of a man with the imprint of his balls showing through his pants and the way he goes about sticking his sword into the bull causes them to, uhhh, you know, feel very warm and juicy down there."

"And for the men?"

"For the men, we are the ones they would like to be. I have read, somewhere, that the bullfighter is supposed to be a symbolic female, with the glittering clothes, the slender bodies, the capes of deception and all that. I could never buy that interpretation because symbolic or non-symbolic females do not have cojones, balls.

Talk to "Macho", "Verano" and others who've been spiked in the nuts about "symbolic femaleness". I think we are like superior males for some men; we are the ones who are willing to challenge wild animals with cojones that are bigger than our own, and have horns to defend those cojones. I can't talk a lot about this because I don't understand a lot about it; but I do know that whenever the bullfight public, la afición, gets what it came for, there is no better feeling in the world for the matador or those who have witnessed the event.

Someone else would talk about these matters in a spiritual way. I can't do that, I can only say that we must be the best of ourselves when we go to the bulls, 'specially if they are the best."

La Punta bulls. I studied the first bull to come out, Manolo Marquez's bull, "Fino", was like a perfect example of what a fighting bull was supposed to look like. He had classic definitions, a bulky, muscular front, with horns mounted on his head like curved swords, and a slightly slender lower/back with two huge sacs of masculinity. I really took notice of that for the first time – the balls and the horns, that made him a bull. Plus all of the aggressive blood that had been pumped into him by his ancestral DNA. I said a little prayer for Manolo…

"Be careful, pal, and may the Force be with you."

Manolo Marquez had his hands full from the moment he did his first Veronica. "Fino", the bull, dominated the action, the matador looked like someone who was trying to simply survive. "Nacho" edged up to my side as I studied the scene from behind the barrera.

"What do you see?" he whispered.

"I see a man trying to survive, he's doing a lot of wild stuff, he's frustrated".

"Exactly. That is why the bull is dominating, why the bull is forcing him to do this and that. The bull is not giving the man a chance to think clearly. He knows, this bull, that the man is afraid of him – he can sense it."

I think we were more relieved than anything when Manolo was finally able to make the kill after two messy attempts. It wasn't a pretty sight to see the bull, huge and beautiful when he first trotted into the arena, lurch around, hemorrhaging from the mouth.

Manolo had to wait for the bull to sink down to all fours before he used the descabello sword to sever the spinal cord, to put the bull out of his misery. I really felt sorry for Manolo, he had "sponsored" me, in a way, and was friendly from the beginning.

The Guadalajara people were knowledgeable, hip to what had happened. And they we're't kind to Manolo Marquez about his inept performance with a great bull. Large clots of people chanted stuff like, "La Punta was the best" and "Where is the beef?" It isn't hard to sympathize with a fellow bullfighter; there, but for the grace of God go me.

"Vigilante" burst into the arena looking for a fight. A gorgeous bull, black as night, rippling with muscles, beautifully cradled horns.

"Azucá, there is a lot you can do with this one."

"You got that right."

Some might call it a death wish or a suicidal urge, but I felt anxious to get into the arena with "Vigilante". I could barely contain myself when I unfurled my capote for the first series of fluid veronicas. "Vigilante" was alert and well named; he was vigilant and could turn on a dime. I played him into the picador for two pics and requested permission from the president of the event to change to the banderillas. The crowd applauded, they didn't want to see a great La Punta bull worn down by the picador.

Miguelito did a beautiful job placing the banderillas. He rushed back behind the buladero with a big smile on his face after he stuck his last pair into the bull's huge roll of neck muscle.

"He's all yours, matador".

I had Antonio lure the bull to the other side of the arena as I dedicated the bull to the crowd. I was dedicating the bull to la aficion, but Maya knew I was dedicating it to her. She was seated in the fourth row of the shady side seats, her green eyes glistening like jade marbles.

I was going to start my fight from far away, about fifty yards and then work us both closer and closer. I was sweating but I felt very cool, very calm.

"'Ey hey toro! Ey hey!" I called. The crowd was suddenly quiet. It was on. I could see that he had good eyesight, which was good for long range movements. I had to work him closer to see how his sight was for close work.

After the first few rushes at me and past me he had already figured out that something was not correct from his perspective. And he was going to straighten that out. My job was to do as much work with him before his bull-detective work determined that it was not the waving cloth that was his enemy; but the still figure waving the cloth. That's a crucial piece of business for the matador.

Lots of bullfighter's have been gored because they hadn't stayed a few jumps ahead of the bull, that they had forgotten to estimate how long it would take for the bull to figure out the waving cloth from the still figure.

"Vigilante" was a hand full but I had him under control. I forced him to charge by invading that invisible territorial line we both understood. After he had half way run out of gas I took him into a series of en redondo movements, teasing him to follow the muleta around and around my body. He was charging so close to me that his whole body pressed against me as he followed my lead around and around. And then the unexpected happened, a usual thing in bullfights; just as I was turning to release him from the en redondo with a left handed naturale, he pushed against me, I stumbled backwards a couple steps and twisted my right ankle.

I thought he had stepped on my foot with all of his kilos, but lucky me, he hadn't done that. I had just stumbled and got a seriously sprained ankle. "Nacho", all the members of my cuadrilla saw what happened, but what could they do? Nothing. I wasn't on the ground. I was just simply a matador with a seriously sprained ankle. What it meant is that I was immobilized, I couldn't dance around, I had to stand my ground. And that was what I did.

In a far off way I could hear the crowd screaming "Olés!"; but I couldn't respond to them. I had to concentrate on taking little shuffling steps to change from one "statue" position to the next. I pulled it off. And then it was time for the Moment of Truth. My ankle was beginning to swell and hurt like hell. I couldn't cite the bull and go to him, I was going to have him come to me. This method of killing is called recibiendo, receiving the bull's charge.

I lined him up properly, profiled and jiggled the muleta just a teeny bit. "Vigilante" slid onto my sword like a stick of black muscular butter. He was dead before he slowly sank to the sand. The crowd went crazy.

"Recibiendo! Recibiendo! Recibiendo!" they shouted. It was an unusual way of killing; but I had no choice, I had to wait to "receive" the bull because my ankle wouldn't allow me to take the few steps I had to take to plunge the sword into the bull. The Lord **does** work in mysterious ways.

Antonio, Paco, Miguelito, members of the other cuadrillas ran out from behind the barrera to congratulate me on my kill. They picked me up and one of the strongest mounted me on his shoulders for a lap around the ring. The audience threw flowers, hats, botas, bags of wine, all kinds of stuff. Meanwhile my ankle had swollen like a ballon.

When we finally managed to end my lap around the ring, and I was gently lowered to the ground, I felt an electric pain shoot up from my ankle.

"Oooooh! My ankle! My ankle!"

"Nacho" draped my arm around his shoulders as he and Antonio helped me hop through the callejon to the infirmary.

"Ooohhh! My ankle! My ankle!" I moaned. "Nacho" smiled at my pain.

"Better a twisted ankle than a horn twisted into your guts, huh?"

I stopped complaining.

I missed the rest of the Festival fighters being taken to the hospital for ex-rays.

"We have to make sure you don't have any broken bones."

They brought me two ears and a tail, -- to the hospital from 'Vigilante', the brave bull who had given me such a great fight. The head nurse placed my trophies in a plastic bag.

"You can get these on your way out." She looked pleased.

The x-ray showed no broken bones. All they had to do was put a tight A-bandage on my ankle and give me a cane. A cane? I felt ridiculous. Me, a twenty year old matador walking around, leaning on a cane. O well. At least I didn't have a bandage on my mouth and I was determined to speak my mind to Senŏr Flores.

He welcomed me, as usual, in the penthouse of the hotel we were staying in, always in the penthouse. "Nacho" had excused himself.

"Ahh hah, Azucá, come in-come in, please sit. I know your ankle is hurt. So, how are you feeling? You had a tremendous faena this afternoon, tremendous! Everyone is talking about it. You know the Festival de Guadalajara was transmitted to Mexico City, and they may have a chance to see it in the 'States sometime this winter on cable; we are negotiating about that."

Senõr Flores was animated and doing his usual thing; he was coopting my reason for meeting with him by overwhelming me with his own brand of gusto. I was determined not to play his game this time. I had already fought a bull, I was determined not to go for any bullshit.

"Senõr Flores, I've asked for this meeting to talk with you about money...."

It was like I had dropped a stink bomb in the middle of the room, judging from the way Senõr Flores and his two muscle bound bodyguards curled up their noses and pulled the corners of their lips down. Senõr Flores, sitting across from me in his black leather upholstered chair (did he carry it around with him?), leaned forward to open a bottle of Arc d'Triomph Cognac and pour himself a generous two fingers in a cognac glass.

"Too bad you don't drink, Azucá, there are times when a nice cognac will soften things." I could see next to the cognac, a small mirror with white, dusty looking particles on it. Cocaine? More than likely. We were getting ready to have a serious discussion. I knew I was in over my head but I also knew I had some real business to back me up.

"So, you want to talk about money, huh? So, let's talk. What do you want to say?"

He was giving me a chance to make my case. Good, I was ready.

"I wanted to say that I haven't received any money from you in weeks..."

"You know why?" he snarled at me. Uhh ooh, we were headed for deeper waters; I couldn't tell him why?

"No, I don't know why. I thought you would be able to supply the answers to that."

He sipped his cognac, took a hit on his smoldering Cuban cigar, pulled off his tinted glasses to clean them. I had grown to recognize that that was a bad sign. But I was determined to return his piercing bloodshot eyeballs stare without blinking, to see him as a dangerous bull that I had to cope with.

"Well, matador…." The way he said it didn't sound too cool. "Well, matador, since you are asking a question that I can answer, I will answer." He took a-nother sip of his cognac, another hit on his fragrant cigar, gaining control of the moment. He made me so mad I wanted to scream. But I chilled on the points. I could sense that that's what it was going to be about, points.

"Please let me remind you that I was the one who offered to be your manager after your espóntaneo in the Mexico City bullring."

"Because you saw my talent and possible greatness." Suddenly, a whole bunch of the great Muhammad Ali's film clips, stuff that I had watched with my boxing fan father, blipped up in my mind.

Senõr Flores exchanged expressions with his bodyguards. Can you believe this, this kid is challenging me? I took it all in but I held my ground. That's what Muhammad Ali would've done.

Senõr Flores shifted the ground under our dialogue.

"Ah yes, Azucá! I **could** see your possibilities, which is why I put you into "Nacho's" hands." So, now he was going to do a lil' hitting below the belt.

"I could see, after experiencing many, many corridas, that you needed a coach, a mentor, someone who could enrich your understanding of the corrida."

"And I have to say that I am grateful for 'Nacho'".

"O, so you are saying that 'Nacho' has been of some benefit to you?"

"Yes, but I also feel that he had fertile soil to work in."

"You are speaking of yourself?"

"Yes, of me, myself."

Everything became quiet for a few beats. I caught the vibe that Senõr Flores was under the impression that I was going to bitch a bit, and go on back into the fields.

"So, now I give you my house in Polanco to learn the art…"

"I already knew **something** about the corrida, Senõr Flores."

"So, I give you someone who can improve your **immense** knowledge of bullfighting…"

"Senõr Flores, I didn't have an **immense** knowledge of bullfighting when you put 'Nacho' into my life. I didn't have an **immense** knowledge of anything, but I was willing to absorb/learn. I am willing to learn."

Senõr Flores didn't replace his glasses, he simply stared at me. The look said – "Are you talking back to me?"

"So, now, where are we?"

I didn't feel it was my business to keep him on track, I just sat there and waited, my ankle throbbing like hell.

"You are coming to me, to ask that I should pay you?"

"People usually get paid for the work they do."

"So I've heard," he said with a sarcastic sneer and took a sip of his cognac. I was beginning to feel very uncomfortable. It had to do with the body language of Senõr Flores's bodyguards and the casual way Senõr Flores was treating me.

"Look, Senõr Flores, I don't think I am asking too much of you to receive some compensation for what I'm doing. I mean, after all, I'm risking my life very time I go into the arena."

He put his cognac snifter down on the table in front of us, took a big hit on his cigar and blew the smoke into my face. He was really mad, really mad. He looked like his face was going to explode. He didn't shout at me, he just started talking real fast and his voice got deeper.

"Now you listen to me closely, young man, because I'm not going to repeat myself. You say you risk your life every time you go into the arena? That may be true, but you go into the arena for yourself, for the excitement and glory you seek. I've given you the opportunity to do this. Do you know how many Mexican boys would be willing to take your place on any Sunday? You should consider yourself very fortunate, instead you come to me whining…"

"I'm not whining…"

"The hospitality of my home in Mexico City, the benefit of a teacher like Ricardo Ortega, 'Nacho'. I bought you four trajes, very expensive ones; I have fed you well, you've stayed in the best hotels, I have paid the members of your cuadrilla. I have paid large bribes to supply you with the visa you need to work in Mexico."

"And I'm grateful." I could feel that he was turning the tables on me and I didn't know how to stop him.

"Right now, at this very moment, I'm deeply involved in an action to defend your right to be called a matador. I believe I spoke to you about how unhappy some of the people in the Bullfighter's Association are about you. Number one, they are unhappy with you as a foreigner who is lapping up the glory that one of their own should have. Two, big questions are being asked about you. Who is this guy? Where did he come from? Where did he receive his alternativa to be a fully accredited matador?

Who was the padrino for his alternativa? Up to now I haven't bothered to tell you about all of these things; but now that you have become so arrogant that you question my judgment and you think I owe you something, I think it is time for you to understand that I don't owe you shit, you owe me."

"I owe you?" Duhhh. I felt like the village idiot.

"Yes, you do. What did you think? You were getting a free lunch? No free lunches in Mexico, amigo. Hahhahhah."

"I owe you?"

"That's right, you owe me. I can give you the exact figure with one call to my accountant; but I can tell you off hand, we are somewhere in the 40 – 50 thousand dollar range, not pesos, dolares."

Senõr Flores stood to signal that our talk was over. I didn't know what else I could say and one of the bodyguards was strolling in my direction, it was time to go. Senõr Flores clamped his big right paw on my shoulder as I limped across the huge penthouse front room.

"So, how is your ankle, think you will be able to show the aficion in Tijuana a thing or two this coming Sunday?"

"I don't know, right now, as you can see I'm using a cane."

"Hah! You're young! A little sprained ankle, what's that?! You'll be ready."

It sounded more like a command than a question. And that was that. He almost pushed me out of the door. I stood outside of the door, felt tempted to knock on the door with my cane and when he opened it I would cuss him out. Well, thank God my better judgment grabbed hold of me. I already had a sprained ankle, the last thing I needed was a broken head.

———◆———

Maya was waiting for me with a table loaded with little snacks, tapas, she called them.

"You've had a very busy day, I thought you might like a little something to eat."

One shrimp and fifteen minutes later I had managed to hop-limp upstairs to her bedroom.

"Be careful of your ankle."

"**You** be careful of my ankle".

Being in Maya's arms was the best place for me to be at the moment; I could'nt've prayed for a better way to push the bad memory of my meeting with Senõr Flores into the background. Afterwards, after we had emotionally and physically bankrupted ourselves with each other, we laid in bed, draped around each other like vines. She had discovered a way of snuggling up into my right arm pit that made me feel that she belonged there.

We didn't say anthing for a long time, we just simply enjoyed the warmth of our bodies being close together. From somewhere the sound of a man singing…

"What's he singing about?"

"Oh, the usual, how his heart is filled with emptiness, how much he wants to be with his beloved Maria again."

"I wish him luck."

"So do I."

We exchanged kisses, and continued listening to the night sounds of Guadalajara.

"People seem to sing a lot here, especially in Guadalajara."

"People don't sing in Chicago?"

"Well, I'd have to say yes and no. Yes, people do sing in Chicago 'specially us Black folks. But it's usually in the summer time, and usually in some kind of formal setting, not just on the streets, anywhere like here."

"What about the White people, do they sing?"

Once again Ihad to think hard.

"I'm sure they do, but to be honest with you I'd have to say that they're not quite as spontaneous as African-Americans."

I felt kind of strange giving out my big time opinions about who did what in Chicago. In a few short months I was beginning to feel that I didn't know anything about the place.

Five minutes later, Maya nudged me gently in the side.

"Be careful, my ribs…"

"Azucá, what's wrong?"

"What makes you think something is wrong?"

"I can tell."

I didn't see any point of denying that I had a serious problem, what purpose would that serve? I told her about the whole scene without going super dramatic or anything. She listened closely and after I finished she asked…

"What are you going to do?"

"Right now, I can't say. I haven't thought this out yet. One thing I do know is that I'm going to have to knock off this relationship with Senõr Flores."

She nodded in agreement.

"I'm taking a month off, from Thanksgiving through Christmas to go back home for a visit, my Mom and Dad want to make sure I'm still alive."

"Next Sunday, after your fight in Tijuana – are you going to be able to perform with your ankle and all?"

"Senõr Flores is **not** a nice person. Come, let's go downstairs…"

"No, you stay here, I'll bring a tray of tapas up here. Would you like juice, a soft drink, tea, coffee?"

"If you have tamarindo juice I would like that."

"For you, I have tamarindo."

She gave me another luscious kiss before she got up. I loved the unself-conscious way she got up in front of me, naked. I looked at her as though she was a work of art. She pulled one of her gauzy yellow see through night gowns from her walk-in-closet, winked at me and tripped downstairs to get our food.

I sprawled out in the oversized bed, flexing my toes, gently trying to turn my injured ankle from left to right. It hurt like hell. I stared up at the giant fan in the ceiling. A beautiful person, a beautiful woman. Do I love her? Does she love me? We hadn't even mentioned love, but it was totally obvious that we loved loving each other. It was sort of like a magic bubble we lived in when we were together, as though we didn't have to burden our relationship with a lot of ordinary stuff.

I told her that I was going to have to knock off my relationship with Senõr Flores. So, how was I going to do that?

Damn! I'm hot as a stolen two dollar pistol, right in the middle of my first season and I had to figure a way out of it or else I would just be a bullfighting slave. A slave. The word dancing through my head made me sit up straight in bed.

A slave. Slaves didn't get paid for their work; they got some food, water and shelter, if they behaved themselves and had a "good" master. A slave.

Maya interrupted my negative thoughts with a large tray of delicious tapas. Food. I was young and full of vinegar, I could solve any problem, but first let's eat.

———————◆◆◆———————

The Tijuana bullring, a few minutes before our strut across the arena to begin the ritual. "Nacho" and the members of my cuadrilla had been slightly cold to me, I could feel it. I had no doubt that they knew about my session with Senõr Flores and that they had probably been told to take sides – " If you're with him, you're against me." Or however Senõr Flores would've fed it to them.

I was trying hard not to let all of the emotional politics play on my head. I had to face two bulls and there was no room for a lot of distracting junk to clutter up my mind. Aside from the emotional stuff, my ankle was still in bad shape but after hours of Epsom bath crystal soaks and gentle massage from "Nacho" I could walk without a cane.

I had developed a hip lil' dip to hide my limp, but there was nothing I could do to give me more agility, more mobility, I would have to do the best I could do with what I had. I prayed that the bulls wouldn't be too big or too dangerous.

My prayers were not answered. I was fighting in the second spot, which gave me a chance to "acclimate". The Tijuana crowd was full of beer and bad behavior. The police came and dragged a couple of guys out of the arena who had dumped buckets of ice on the picadores as they entered the ring. A trio of college girls threw their panties into the arena before the first matador, Manuel Solorzano, came into the ring. Solorzano stood next to me, watching one of his cuadrilla place the banderillas.

"Who are these animals?" he whispered, glancing around at the crowd.

"Bullfight fans in Tijuana, that's who they are."

"Trash", he mumbled, "They wouldn't be allowed in the Plaza Madrid". And then he went out and gave a beautiful faena. He didn't do a lot of creative stuff, but he definitely gave all of us a lesson in how to control a hard charging bull with his techniques. And too soon it was my turn.

"Azucá, your ankle?" "Nacho" showed his concern.

"I'll be o.k., if I don't have to do a lot of running."

"These bulls are monsters, I don't know where they got them from. I'll signal the picador to bear down hard on the lance, to sap the bull's strength as much as possible."

"'Nacho', don't do that, the bull is still going to have horns, can the picador take the strength out of those too?"

He gave me a big hug. "You are a torero, Azucar, a real torero."

After the pics, after the banderillas, it was time for the muleta, for the close work. I discovered, by moving slowly, carefully planting one foot after another my ankle didn't hurt so badly; but I couldn't run backwards at all, a very important thing to be able to do with an aggressive bull.

I really learned the deeper meaning of the word – "aguantar" – to stick it out, to endure. Like being forced to wait for the bull to complete his charge without moving a muscle. The first bull was called "Misionero" and I gave him every stationary pase I could think of. I heard the crowd screaming as I did four "pèndulos" in a row. The muleta is held in front of the bullfighter's body to cite the bull and then, when he charges, the man swings the muleta behind his back; and, hopefully the bull swooshes past behind him.

I did four arrucinas, the Carlos Arruza invention, where the man holds the muleta with his right hand around behind his back, with just the end of the muleta held out to provoke the bull's charge. Four arrucinas. I sucked my stomach in so much it hurt my ribs. I did pase de pecho, sanjuaneras and slow motion naturales with both hands.

I did two spinning molinetes and ended the whole sequence of pases with a swirling serpentine that left "Misionero" positioned in place as though I had frozen him to the spot. It was time for the truth. The crowd was going crazy until they saw me lining the bull up and profiling for the kill. Like somebody had put his finger to his lips and said, "hush!" they went completely quiet.

I took my time, I wanted this over and done the first time, no repeats. Dad's video helped me focus on exactly the right spot, like my eyes had become bomb sights. I zeroed in up to the hilt of my sword and "Misionero" took exactly six steps backwards and crumpled down on the sand. It took twenty minutes for the crowd to calm down for the next fight and a sea of white handkerchiefs awarded me both ears, a hoof and the tail from "Misionero". My cuadrilla carried me on their shoulders for a victory lap around the bullring. They even gave the bull a lap around the ring, a rare thing.

And then back to the business. My cuadrilla had warmed up a lot.

"Azucar, that was a great faena" Coming from "Nacho", that was more than a compliment, it was like a medal I could put on my mind. Antonio, Paco and Miguelito came in right behind him.

"Beautiful faena, matador, beautiful!"

I almost felt pity for Pancho Vincente "Pedres" when his turn came. He had the misfortune to follow my performance. He would've been wise to do his own thing, to fight his own fight; but he didn't do that, he tried to compete with my performance and he almost got gored three times. And finally he messed the whole thing up with a butchershop kill. The fans booed and whistled.

In rotation, Manuel Solorzano, the arrogant Spaniard who had called the Tijuana crowd "trash", did a few routine pases and killed his bull as soon as possible. The crowd was screaming "Olés" before I did my first veronica with a wonderful little bull called "Chachao". I don't mean that he was physically small, but it was the way he responded to my capework.

If I was almost immobile for my first bull it was like my feet were planted in cement for my second one.

My ankle was cold, chilled by the afternoon, locked. I could barely shuffle from one position to another. I think a lot of the aficion thought I was into another style of bullfighting. It wasn't that at all, it was simply a matter of having a very stiff ankle.

I've looked at my performances for those two fights in Tijuana (video taped by Maya with "special permission" from Senõr Flores), many times and, until this very day I can't really tell you how I did what I did.

We've all been told about people who've lost the ability to use something, to develope a handicap, and how they turn to something else. I'm thinking about the blind dude who developed his sense of touch and smell 'way beyond the normal. I think that's what happened to me that day in Tijuana. A frozen ankle is the last thing you want to have in a bullring, facing an angry bull. But you don't want to have a headache, a distraction of any kind, an upset stomach, **none** of that.

But, getting back to the bullfight. Since I couldn't do agile, gymnastic stuff, I had to "aguantar", to stick it out.

I forced the bull to charge me by shuffling into his territory, giving him a greater shot at goring me. The fifteen minutes of my faena seemed to last for an hour, and I wasn't bored by any of it for one second. "Chachao" made me substitute brain power for rapid movements.

And once again, when it came to the kill I was ready and able. I heard a scream from somewhere when I plunged the sword in – "hasta la bola" – up to the hilt. I thought that it was the bull who had screamed, but that would've been impossible. Bull's don't scream when they're killed, do they? I was the one who had screamed.

I felt drained as I stood in front of the dead bull. I had challenged this great bull, shuffling around the arena on one leg, basically, and I had survived. I didn't feel like I had conquered him, I felt that I had survived him.

"Nacho" and my crew carried me around the arena for my reception of applause, hats, bota bags of wine – Miguelito and Antonio almost got drunk spurting wine into their mouthes – panties from the college girls, a small bag of marijuana – yes, a small bag of weed. Antonio looked at me, palmed it and it had disappeared just like that. I was given two ears, two hooves and the tail from the bull "Chachao".

Just a lil' aside here: I never felt at ease with the custom of the bullfighter being awarded bits and pieces of the bull to celebrate a "victory". The ears, the tail and all of that reminded me of the time when lynch mobs in the U.S. cut off Black ears, penises, fingers, toes, to congratulate themselves for doing the evil shit they did.

But I had to remind myself that I was in Mexico, where no one had ever had a cross burned on his lawn. And people may have been lynched, but there was no systemic record of people being lynched just because they were "people of color". Just saying all this to say that the body parts award system was not ever cool with me.

I went along with it, I'm ashamed to say, because I couldn't think of a sensitive way to go against somebody else's cultural stuff.

After Tijuana, I was taking a break, going home, going back to my roots, Chicago. I felt a need to take a month away from the bull madness.

⸺◆⸺

I didn't tell anybody what day or what time I was coming in; I just wanted to land and be there, and we would take it from there. From Mexico City to Chicago. On one level, it was simply like going from one modern city to another. But there were differences. I wasn't coming into a place where ancient civilizations, Aztec or otherwise, played any part in the life of the average person.

In Mexico, I had discovered, the history of a people was embedded in the way people looked, the way they looked at life/death, their attitudes, the food they ate, why they loved the bullfight so much. I knew I wasn't coming/going back to anything like that. Maya and I had discussed things.

"Do you think they will see you as a heroic figure?"

"I can't imagine that. Most African-Americans don't know anything about bullfighting, and could care less."

"How long will you be there?"

"About a month, from Thanksgiving to Christmas."

We traveled from Tijuana back down to Mexico City, stopping at every reasonably large town to make love. It got to be almost an addiction, our love making.

On the outskirts of Mexico City, in Xochimilco, at a small swank boutique hotel, I suddenly reminded myself of José "Cantinflas'" uncle and aunt for a brief, very shy conversation. I didn't really know what to say to them and they didn't really know what to say to me.

"José gave me your names and address and told me to be sure and connect with you when I came to Mexico."

"Ahh, José he is a good boy."

And that's about as far as it went. I played with the idea of taking Maya with me to see the gang in Tlaltelolco, but decided not to. All I could imagine is that there would be a whole bunch of negative vibes.

We checked into the Maria Christina Hotel, right off the Paseo, for a night of passion and conversation.

"So, what have you decided to do about Senōr Flores?"

"I haven't decided anything yet; I'm just letting it stew around in my head for the time being."

I got a very vague vibe about us, it was like, she wanted to say – Well, what about us? – and I wanted to say the same thing, but it never reached the vocal level. The next morning I had to take a taxi to the airport…

"It's best we do it this way, otherwise we'll have camera flashes popping in our faces from every direction. Call me if you feel like talking."

"I will. Take care, Azucá."

"You too, Maya."

Next stop, O' Hare field, Chicago, Illinois.

———◆◆———

It had snowed, the piles of sooty snow and slushy patches of water told me that. But, thank God, it wasn't one of those typical freezing cold Chicago days. Two days before Thanksgiving. I had to smile, thinking of something Maya had said.

"Well, at least here in Mexico we don't give thanks for the Spanish conquest of our people."

"The indigenous people in America don't give thanks either."

"Well, who celebrates then?"

"The White people certainly."

"What about African-Americans? Your people?"

I hated to admit that we wre guilty of joining the conquerors in their celebration of victory over the Native Americans.

"But I don't think that we think of it in those terms, for most of us it's just an opportunity to eat a lot and watch a football game."

I asked the taxi driver to drive around the Southside for a few minutes.

"Where to, buddy?"

"Oh, just anywhere, Hyde Park."

The driver, a White guy, looked relieved. I think he was afraid that I was going to ask him to drive down 47th Street; or maybe 63rd Street. Hyde Park was on the Southside, but it was the semi-bohemian neighborhood next door to the University of Chicago. Cool.

We were two blocks away from Dondisha's place, my former home. I had half an urge to drop in but cancelled it out. It was better not to jump in on people with surprises. I had told my Mom and Dad that I was going to be coming in for Thanksgiving, now I was two days ahead of time. Well, I could count on them being happy and pleased with my early arrival.

After a brief tour, time to go home.

———◆◆◆———

Mom met me coming up the front steps with a big hug and kisses on both cheeks. A big Christmas tree reef on the door.

"My goodness! What a nice surprise! We were lookin' for you next week." A ten foot tall Christmas tree in the living room. Chicago people, As usual they had put up the Christmas tree before Thanks-Giving and probably wouldn't take it down 'til after the New Year's Day.

"I had a break in my schedule so I thought I would take advantage of it" They were doing well, despite the economy and all, I could tell.

It took us about fifteen minutes to settle down, to sit at the kitchen table for a cup of the best coffee in the world. She dashed into the dining room to make two phone calls. I listened with a smile on my face.

"He's here, Chester, he's here, he just got in an hour ago. No, you don't need to do anything but close up the shop before six o'clock 'n bring your hips on home. Awright, good, 'bye baby."

"Hello, Dondisha, I knew you'd be home. I just had a feelin' – well, guess whose in town? Uhh huh, your first guess is your best guess. We're gonna have a lil' dinner for him this evenin'; you feel like comin' over? Oh kay, good – see you about seven."

My mother was such an arranger. And I loved her to death for being the way she was. My sister popped in a couple hours later.

"Well, well, look whose here?! El toro himself."

"Louise, el toro is the bull, I'm a torero."

"Same ol' Chester, always gotta be different," she spoke with a smile on her face. Sis looked good, a little tired from working and going to school; Mom had already told me, but I could see a more serious set of her jaw, a more aggressive way of walking.

"Louise is doin' real good now, now that she managed to shake that vampire off…"

"The guy she was dating?…"

"Yeah, that one."

Dad must've closed up shop long before six o'clock because he was parking his car in the drive way a couple hours later. I met him in the doorway. He dashed up the steps of the front porch and grabbed me in a python grip. For a minute I was afraid he was going to crack one of my fragile ribs. After his bear hug, he held me away from him and looked me up and down real hard.

"You're a man now, son, you're a man, I can see it."

That's all he said as he draped his arm over my shoulders to lead me into the house. He made me think of "Nacho". "Baby, I'm home," he called out to Mom.

Mom and Louise were already busy in the kitchen. I could smell delicious food smells. Dad steered me into his office/library/rec-room. He had a nice little bar with a small fridge behind it.

"I'm gonna have a couple of shots of this Chivas Regal, can I pour you?…Oh, I forgot you're not a drinkin' Man."

"I'll have one of what you're having."

I could see that he was pleased to sit and sip with me. I had no idea what effect two fingers of Scotch would have on me.

"Well, here's to us."

He took a sip and I took a sip. And we started talking about something. And we sipped some more. And that's where it faded to black for me. It wasn't a dream filled sleep, it was just a fade to black.

Dad was gently shaking me by the shoulder an hour later – "Chester, wake up almost time for dinner. I put your stuff upstairs in your room. You want to change clothes or something before we eat?"

I nodded yes, feeling like I was coming out of a deep fog.

"Guess jet lag and that Scotch kinda got to you, huh?"

"You can say that again. Be right down in a minute."

I dashed upstairs to take a quick shower and put on my black guayabera, the hip Mexican shirt and a pair of black jeans. On my way back downstairs I looked through the banisters at a warm family scene. Dad was sitting at the head of the table, of course, with Mom on his right and Louise on his left. And a gorgeous, dark skinned woman next to Louise. Dondisha?! I didn't recognize her. Honestly.

They were sipping glasses of Mom's favorite sweet wine and Dad had another snort of Scotch in his glass. Dondisha? Unreal. Louise announced my appearance by waving her white napkin in my direction.

"Oyé! El toro is back with us again."

"Good", Dad announced, "Let's eat, I'm starving."

Dondisha stood and walked into my arms. I was dying to find out what she had done to herself. The woman was absolutely gorgeous. In just six quick, short months she had slimmed down to a beautiful body. She always had a beautiful face, with her big doe-deer eyes; but now the face/the head rested on a slender neck that led my eyes down into a lovely cleavage, a small waist and beautifully flaring hips. Was it my mother who had told me in one of our long distance conversations? – "Dondisha has gotten fine, Chester, really fine."

It had turned cold outside, but there was a lot of warmth in our place to counterbalance it. Mom had made beef stew, seasoned with anise and had slabs of rye bread to sop up the juices that bled from the beef, the whole potatoes, the carrots. I noticed that Dondisha and I didn't have seconds. And we turned down the Haägen Daz for dessert. Dondisha turning down her favorite ice-cream? She really had changed.

After another Scotch for Dad and a bit more sweet wine for the ladies, it was time to talk about the bulls. Dad kicked it off.

"Chester, what's it like, really, to be down on the ground with a crazy, wild bull?"

"Well, first off, I have to say they may be wild but they ain't crazy. The people fighting them may be crazy, but the bulls ain't crazy. Take my word for that."

I decided to keep it light, slightly funny. I glanced at Dondisha as often as I could, trying not to stare.

"Chester, you remember my girlfriend Pearline?"

"Uh yeah, I remember her I think."

"You know, the one who used to laugh at you waving that blanket/ cape around all the time, when we lived over on Bowen."

"O yeah, I remember her."

"Well, she called me up one day last week to tell me that she had seen a documentary, or some kind of travel program that had you in it. She said it came from Guada- something or other."

"The Guadalajara Festival, that was my last fight in Central Mexico before my fight in Tijuana."

"The way she described it was like the announcer described you as being 'great'. Are you great?"

Nobody but my sister could ever think of asking a question like that. Was I great?

"People exaggerate a lot. Joselito was great, Gaona, Belmonte, Manolete, Arruza, people like that, they were great. Me? I'm still in the first grade." That was my answer.

"What's the kick behind this thing, where do you get your satisfaction from?"

Dondisha surprised me by answering that one.

"The satisfaction comes from doing a beautiful piece of work with the bull; and then giving him a quick, merciful death. Isn't that the way it is, Chester?"

"I couldn't've said it any better."

We exchanged winks. She had asked me that same question one

Friday night, watching Alfredo Leal do a beautiful piece of work and afterwards, he made a quick, merciful kill.

The evening was coming to an end. It gave me a real good feeling to be back at home; I hadn't realized how much I had missed our family circle. Dad seemed to have mellowed a bit. Mom was full of practical ideas and knew how to get things done. Louise was becoming more than a sister who annoyed the hell out of me.

But the star of the evening so far as I was concerned was Dondisha Phillips.

"I really want to thank you for a delicious dinner, Mrs. Simmons."

"Dondisha, I'm gonna knock you up side your head if you keep calling me 'Mrs. Simmons'".

We had a good laugh about that and hugs all around. Dondisha was leaving.

"Wait a sec, I'll get my coat and walk you to your car." Thank God she was parked at the curb in front of our house; I wouldn't've enjoyed walking a block away with her. It was cold out there. We stood on the driver's side and kissed. It started as a peck on the mouth and developed into foreplay.

"Chester, I've really missed you…"

"I've missed you too." What else could I say? It was the truth.

She unlocked her car door, got inside and stared up at me. "How long will you be in town?"

"'Til a couple days after Christmas."

"Well, I guess you know I'm on holiday break 'til after Christmas. You can come over, if you have time."

"How about tomorrow afternoon?"

"Great, I'll look forward to it." And she slid away from the curb; she left me trembling with excitement and the cold.

———◆———

I e-mailed Maya an hour later. Was I feeling guilty? I don't think so, I just had an urge to connect with her. She got back to me a couple hours later with a review that was written by the bullfight critic of the Guadalajara Times.

"Juan Negro, 'Azucar' has brought another kind of element to

The Black Matador, "Sugar"

Mexican bullfighting. This past Sunday in the Plaza Guadalajara, at the Fiesta de Guadalajara, with the bull called 'Vigilante', 'Azucar' took us back to the old days. He played 'Vigilante' like a well tuned guitar.

Seldom have we seen a young man (barely twenty) show such templé. He started us off with a series of veronicas that were sculpted especially for this particular animal. In a fight that could have been a disaster because of the bull's characteristics, he took control of the situation and presented us with a faena that was warm, passionate and filled with elegance.

Like some of his spiritual ancestors he was able to use the muleta as a device to open the bull up, to persuade 'Vigilante' to cooperate with him in giving us an opportunity to see what could be done with the muleta. And when the inevitable moment of truth came, he killed recibiendo, receiving the bull on the point of his sword with complete authority. Once again we are forced to refer to 'Azucar's" youth. We are not often privileged to see young matadores who know how to bring the business to a brilliant conclusion. Later, we found that he was almost crippled by a sprained ankle during the course of his work with 'Vigilante'.

I'm sure that the other matadores on the bill, Manolo Marquez and the Spaniard Solorzano, would gladly be willing to suffer sprained ankles if they thought it would give them the capability to fight and kill with the elegance, courage and skill that Juan Negro, 'Azucar' demonstrated in his faena with 'Vigilante'. We look forward to seeing more of this one."

I had to smile. Mexican bullfight critic's were almost bi-polar, they could be way up on you, or way down. This one was way up. I e-mailed my thanks to Maya for sending me the review.

———◆———

Mom had a big smile on her face when I told her I was going to hang out in Hyde Park for the day.

"Just give me a ring if you should decide to come home for dinner, o.k.?"

"For sure, see you later."

There was a one hundred percent chance that Mom knew that I was heading straight for Dondisha's pad, and she was obviously pleased. It would be hard to say what Dondisha had done, other than turning herself into a fine lady, that turned the corners for her relationship with my mother, but there it was, full blown.

A cold, clear, sunny day in Chicago. I was tempted to jog from our place in South Shore to Hyde Park but the first icy blast from the lake cancelled that notion. I got the bus.

Dondisha met me at the door with a hot cup of tea and a much warmer kiss. Fifteen minutes later we were in the same bed we had shared before I left her for Mexico. Prior to us racing to get in bed together, she asked only one question.

"Do you have a condom?"

"I have several of them."

An hour later, after our hunger for each other had been momentarily satisfied; waking up after a brief sexual catnap, it was time for a little pillow talk. I stroked the side of her face, her neck, her shoulders, her breasts. I couldn't keep my hands off her body. And I was terribly curious to find out what had happened to her during the six months I was away.

"What happened?

"You mean about my weight?"

"Well, yes, that's a good place to start…"

"After you left me…"

I couldn't help but cringe a bit at that. – *"After you left me…"*

"After you left me, I decided to take a cold blooded look at myself. I may be a kindergarten teacher; but I still have a brain."

We shared smiles at that one. I had once asked her if teaching munchkins was bringing her I.Q. down.

"I was fat and out of shape. I didn't feel good about myself. I felt that I could've held onto you if I had made some effort to get my act together."

"Some men like full figured women."

"More men like women with the kind of shape I have now and I'm gonna stay this way." Her jaws snapped on that.

"Uhh, how did you do it? I mean, what did you do?"

"I stopped stuffin' myself with ice cream, potato chips, cookies, and all those wonderful o' greasy fried foods that I grew up on. And

I started going to this Capoeira Angola Class at the International House on the U.C. campus."

"Capoeira Angola, that's the Afro-Brazilian martial art, right?"

"That's it."

"Hey, that shit is hard. I've seen documentaries about it."

"It **is** hard and I gave myself up to it. For the first three months I was so sore and tired when we finished our sessions I would just stagger home and soak in ten pounds of Epsom salts. But I lost damned near five pounds each workout and I was eating five pieces of lettuce and a cucumber for lunch."

"That's all."

"Sometimes, on the weekend, I would have a piece of baked fish and some fruit."

My hand drifted down to her stomach, it felt like an ol' fashioned washboard.

"Nowadays, I give myself permission to eat a little more, but I've learned how to balance it off with workouts three times a week."

"Woww, that's what I call discipline."

"I've noticed that you've had a few body changes too."

She ran her well manicured hand across my chest, tracing the path of the twenty two stitches that cinched a horn slash together.

"The saying is, 'If you play with the bull, sooner or later you will get the horn.'"

"And here too?" She felt the inside of my right thigh, the fifteen inch wound.

"Sometimes you get the horn if you play with the bull."

I tried to lighten the mood but I thought I saw tears in the corners of her eyes as she kissed each stitch traced across my bony chest. I wanted to tell her that the greatest wound was not being caused, had not been caused by the bulls, but my my manager, Senõr Flores, who had turned me into a bullfighting slave. "A slave", isn't that what you call someone who doesn't get paid for his labor?

⬥

I called Mom to tell her that I wouldn't be coming home for dinner.

"Uhh, don't worry about me, I ran into an old friend whose taking me to this Chinese place for dinner."

"I'll leave a piece of fish in the fridge for you, if you should happen to want a bite when you get in."

It was a neat lil' diplomatic game. Who were we fooling? Definitely not Mom. And definitely not Dondisha. I got with her in the intimate kitchen — dining space we once shared. She had lit the table with a couple candles and lit some incense over there. She had prepared a delicious Porto Bello Mushroom, garlic omelet. Doused with powered mint and oregano.

"I still eat meat, but I don't feel the need for it at every meal. Is this cool with you?"

"Oh yes, this is very cool with me."

I felt completely satisfied after our dinner. That's what a good dinner is supposed to do, isn't it? Satisfy you? She gave me a sweet Moroccan tea for dessert and sat across the table from me, looking like a chocolate goddess.

"Chester, have you been with another woman since you left me?"

"Dondisha, you've asked that a couple times now, I didn't leave you, I went to the bulls…"

"So, it's like a calling, like being called to preach, huh?"

"Something like that, I guess you could say." I could hear "Nacho's" voice in the back of my head. " 'Azucá, many are called, few are chosen – Comprende?"

"Chester, have you been with another woman since you left me." She repeated the question.

"You want the truth?"

"Have I ever asked you to lie to me?"

A moment of truth for real. But I had to fight back.

"Yes, I have. What about you?"

She sipped her tea and smiled brightly at me, cancelling out all possible bad vibes.

"It was a one night stand; well, acturally two nights because he couldn't really get it up the first time. And no, no, it wasn't here, I wouldn't disregard what we've shared like that."

Dondisha was thumping a concrete forefinger against my forehead. What the hell had I missed the first time around?

"Are you in love with her?"

The sister was forcing me to take a hard look at stuff that I hadn't given a lot of thought to.

"I don't know, we've never discussed it. I don't really think so." She nodded as though she understood what I was saying.

The candle lights flickered, supplied surrealistic shadows, made us kiss. Truthfully, when I had been with Dondisha the first time around, I felt that I was using her, taking advantage of her "fat girl complex". It was different now, totally. She was asking me to come to her with honesty, truth, love. Maybe her Capoeira Angola class was responsible. I made a date to go to a class with her.

"You're welcome, Mestre Yves and Mestre Cedric welcome visitors. A matador! O my God! They might make you an honorary Capoeirista or something!"

But before the Capoeira Angola class we made a date to go tango dancing.

"This weekend, over on the Northside, at the Club Argentine, we're gonna kick their asses!"

Dondisha? Shy, reluctant, hesitant, less than confident Dondisha. She was gone, had been replaced by a different being. I liked the new Dondisha.

———◆———

The tango dancing date at the Club Argentine was a booty buster, for them, not for us. On the Friday evening we went, the place was full, not packed tight, but full. We attracted attention right away because we were the only African-American couple in the club. And I have to admit, at this late date, we played with the Argentine tango head for awhile. Dondisha had a glass of white wine and I ordered a ginger ale with two cherries.

"A ginger ale with two cherries, sir?"

The dance floor was one of those beautiful dark mahogany things, waxed just right. We had a ringside table, given to us I think, as a way to put us on exhibit. We both thought it was a nice gesture. Live music, live.

We sat, sipping our drinks for about three numbers, enjoying each other's company, enjoying, critiqueing the dancer's techniques.

"She's too much into herself."

"He needs to learn how to turn properly."

On the fourth number I stood and did a torero strut onto the dance floor, Dondisha strutting behind me. After the first series of movements, a few people dancing near us simply slunk off the scene. And then a few more. 'til it got down to us and another couple. There was no competition, we were simply the best and we knew it.

Midway through the set, just to show you what a groovy set it was, we switched partners right in the middle of the dance. The house exploded with applause; it was like being in the bullring. The guy's name was Giorgio, we found out afterwards, and his lady's name was Sophia.

Dancing with Sophia was like holding a cloud in your arms, she drifted wherever I wanted her to go. We gave a good show of pretending to be loving tango dancers; but it was all about technique. Dondisha gave Giorgio as much stuff as he could stand.

"You are phenomenal, Madam", I heard him whisper as we changed back to our original partners. And they insisted on having us join their table after our dance demonstration was over.

"Please, please, come! You must sit with us, you must!"

There were six ladies, excluding Dondisha, at the table who were anxious to dance and it became Giorgio's job and my job to dance with them. Giorgio explained it…

"Look, my friend, these women don't want to dance with inferior dancers after they've seen us, after they've danced with us."

It was a gorgeous evening of tangoing. I think the tango ensemble really got caught up in our stuff because they played and played and played. The dude playing the accordion **really** got into it. People sent bottles of wine over to your table, and called out, while we were dancing – "**This** is the tango."

"How did you learn your tango? Where?" – was the question on everybody's tongue.

"We learned our tango from 'Raul', who learned it from Rudolph Valentino."

"O yes, he is the best dancer they have in the Argentine Tango Group."

I was puffed up with pride to hear that my friend was so well known. And then I heard something that will always stick in my memory. Someone called out – "Azucar! Azucar Negro!"

The word traveled through the top and bottom levels of the club as we were leaving – "Azucar! Azucar Negro!" Evidently there were a few bullfight fans in the house and they had recognized me. I was flattered. Dondisha was stunned.

"Wow! They're talking about you. Is that what they call you in Mexico?"

"Yeah, just about everybody has a nickname in bullfighting. My manager named me Juan Negro, 'Azucar'. He explained that Chester just didn't sound like the right name for a bullfighter."

Later that night, as we laid in each other's arms, she whispered, "Chester, I'm so proud of you – Azucar Negro, my Azucar Negro."

———◆◆◆———

Her Capoeira Angola class was exhausting, just to watch. Mestre Yves and Mestre Cedric were an odd couple, but they made a good match.

"Mestre Yves is a French Jew of Hungarian descent and Mestre Cedric is an African-American from east Texas; they make a good team."

The vocal and instrumental music was hypnotic and the movements deceptive and strenuous. There were twenty five men and women in the class, about equally divided, and I could see that Dondisha was one of the top five.

"Young people are not as motivated as they should be."

Dondisha was what, twenty-five, twenty-six? Young people?

After the class she introduced me and we went to the International House Cafeteria for coffee. Dondisha had given me a good character analysis of her two instructors. They **were** an odd couple, but a good team.

Mestre Yves was pencil slim, intense and slow talking. Mestre Cedric was pure east Texas, slow talking, quick thinking, fast as a rabbit. It was a kick to sit and chat with them. When we hugged at the end of our time together I wanted to thank them for turning my girl into a beautiful body. But I didn't have to say anything that obvious.

Mestre Yves spoke in a voice that sounded like rusted sand paper – "Capoeira Angola can change a person."

Mestre Cedric looked off into a distant corner as he spoke, "Angola is what we eat, that's what Mestre Pastinha once said."

———◆◆◆———

I settled into a nice little routine after my first week back on the scene. I took myself down to the local YMCA for two hour workouts and on the weekend I went jogging with Dad. I had to give it to him, he was in damned good shape.

"Shit, I used to jog in my cell, when we had lock-downs, by the hour. You hear me? By the hour, c'mon! I'll race you to that big tree!"

I can honestly say, for the first time in my life, I was actually enjoying my father's company. He was a man I could talk to, someone I could trust, a man I could confide in. I didn't open the door all the way on the Señor Flores thing, but I gave strong hints that everything was not cake'n cream. He was philosophical about the problem.

"You know I think that's one of the hardest things to come to grips with in life, when you realize somebody is tryin' to fuck over you; and what you should do about it.

"Ches', I know you're a man now, and a man has to do what a man has to do. But I'm sayin' this to you, straight up…don't take no unnecessary shit from those people down there. Remember, long as we got a home, <u>you</u> got a home."

Dad made me feel real good, real good, saying something lie that. And he left me huffin' 'n puffin' a full city block behind him.

———◆◆◆———

Just an aside here: Mom was slightly ticked off at me because I had refused to say the traditional Thanksgiving blessing over the turkey and all of the stuffings.

"Sorry, I just can't make myself offer blessings for a meal that celebrates the genocide of Native Americans."

A couple distant cousins who had tripped in from Milwaukee or somewhere looked stunned. Mom was the one who took up the slack, she said a few brief things and that was that.

Later, while we were all hunkered around the TV, watching "The Game", Dad signaled for me to join him in his "inner sanctum" during the half-time.

I didn't know if he was inviting me to a fistfight or what; but after he freshened his drink he turned to me and said. "You know something, Chester, I completely agree with you. I guarantee you we won't be having any more long winded prayer sessions over a dead bird in this house anymore."

I almost cried because I knew what a stubborn, hard shell Dad was. I took a half finger of Chivas Regal with him, to celebrate the declaration. It didn't send me all the way into the Black Hole; but I definitely thought the football game was funny as hell afterwards. My sister smiled at me. And the cousins didn't know what to think – how couild anybody laugh at "The Game"?

The days and early evening belonged to the family; the late evenings and nights belonged to Dondisha. We planned some things, we let other things happened.

"Chester, the Dance Group from Harlem is in town. Let's go."

"Dondisha, you like Egyptian music?"

"I don't know, let's find out."

It was a real cultural bang for your buck living so close to the University of Chicago. There was stuff happening all the time: Koto concerts, a sarod concert by a disciple of Ali Akbar Khan, African and African-American dance groups up the yingyang, plays, art exhibits, cold walks on the lakefront and afterwards, hot tea and love.

"Dondisha, I didn't know you dug all of this kind of music and stuff."

"I didn't know myself, until I put that potato chip bag down hahhahhah…"

She had such a beautiful sense of humor about herself and we could laugh at the same stuff. We almost died laughing about a very stiff-stick-up-the-ass-kind of singer, who sang a whole program of German and Italian songs with her wig half screwed around. It was after the concert of course.

It went to another level the day before Christmas. We had just come back from a tango expedition at the Argentine Club, where we had worn their asses out with our "Raul" learned steps. She had brewed me a cup of Jasmine tea and was sipping a cognac. We were sprawled out on the bed.

"So now what, Chester, what're your plans?"

I had been doing a lot of thinking about that particular question.

"I'm going back to Mexico after Christmas to work some kinks out with my manager. If we can't get our heads together on certain matters, then I'll have to see what I can do for myself in Spain."

"Spain?"

"So far as I'm concerned that's the Vatican of bullfighting, it's either Mexico or Spain."

She didn't say anything. She just nodded her head in agreement. I wouldn't be spending New Year's eve with her.

———◆—◆—◆———

Mexicana Airlines, from Chicago to Mexico City.

I stared out at the colorful buildings on the Paseo de las Reforma, the great avenue that slices through the heart of Mexico City, the Zócalo, the masses of people who looked like ants swarming from place to place.

I felt good, a little bit full of myself. I had worked out for a whole month and my ankle was well. I had re-connected with my family – "Chester, just call me if you need anything" – and re-discovered a girlfriend who seemed like much more than a girl friend this time around. I had some issues to deal with, with Senõr Flores, but I felt pretty sure that we would be able to work things out. I needed him and I'm sure he didn't want to lose a cash cow, no matter how many other "cows" he had.

And then there was Maya. I was definitely looking forward to being with her again. Did I feel a bit guilty about going from one woman to another? I would have to say no. when you're twenty years old I don't think you give a lot of thought to moral stuff. And besides there was only two of them, it wasn't like I had a girl in every town in Mexico, or girlfriends all over Chicago.

"Raul" had e-mailed me while I was in Chicago.

The Black Matador, "Sugar"

"Yo Matador Negro!

So, you're back in Chi for the holidays. Hope you're enjoying yourself. Had a chance to see your work in the Festival de Guadalajara, it was shown in a documentary about Mexico. I take my hat off to you, brother, you were great!

Too bad we couldn't hook up while you were in Chicago. Maybe next time. We're going to start the New Year off with a two week gig in New York, and from there to Europe; England first, then France, Spain, Portugal, Itally, Germany, the Scandinavian countries and finally we'll finish in Moscow. It'll be six months of dancin'-n'-prancin'. I'm looking forward to it. Well, that's it for the moment. Stay up, your amigo in Buenos Aires.

Leo Anderson a.k.a. 'Raul'"

I felt just a tiny bit of envy. Brother "Raul" was having a chance to run all over the place. Well, I could do the same thing if I had some money.

———◆——

CHAPTER EIGHTEEN

I called Maya and left a message on her service – "Maya, I'm back. I have some business to take care of with Senōr Flores, if I can catch him. And then I'll be with you. Love, Azucar"

I hung up the phone wondering if I should've said "Love".

O well, too late now. Off to the big house in Polanco. "Nacho" was the first one to greet me.

"Eh, Azucá, good to see you…"

They were having some kind of party for something. I never did find out for what, and I didn't give a shit. There was a buffet, a couple open bars, beautiful people sashshaying around. Expensive cars parked in the driveway.

"Nacho, I need to see Senōr Flores."

"You're in luck, he is here. There, upstairs behind that door."

A number of people nodded and smiled in my direction as I marched up the stairs. I wasn't in a smiling mood. I had hit the ground determined to get some kind of reasonable understanding with this guy. I was not going to be jammed out this time.

One of the bodyguards opened the door a few inches to see who was knocking and called back over his shoulder – "Azucar". I heard Senōr Flores call out.

"Tell him to come back in ten minutes."

So, I was left to pace up and down in the hallway for ten minutes. I was getting madder by the minute. Who did this fat asshole think he was? Twenty minutes later four gangsters strolled out. That was the only name I could think of for them. They looked like gangsters, complete with dark suits and lots of bling bling. They smiled at me. Well, why not? I was Juan Negro "Azucar", the matador.

The largest of the two Rottweiler looking bodyguards gestured for me to come in. The scene was obvious at a glance. Senōr Flores was dealing cocaine or was it heroin? I would've been blind not to see ten kilo, cellophane wrapped bags in a cover behind Senōr Flores's desk. Always a desk. He was wearing his tinted glasses and was fat as ever. He didn't say anything to me, he just simply gestured for me to sit down on the chair in front of him.

I had decided not to do the school boy thing again, to seat myself in front of the teacher, and get a jive lecture. I decided to stand in front of the teacher's desk. I was obviously in a rebellious mode.

"Senōr Flores, I think we need to talk about this money issue again."

"Oh, are we back to that? I thought we finished that matter off at our last meeting?"

"No, you finished it off, I didn't."

I tried to sound as respectful as possible; but my words were definitely not respectful. Senōr Flores' right side body guard started massaging his ham sized fists.

"So, Azucar, you're not satisfied with my management, huh?"

"I'm not satisfied with not having any take home pay for risking my life in the arena. Slaves work for nothing, Senōr Flores, not free men."

He took off his glasses to clean them, the way he did when he was angry. He was angry. I had to control a slight trembling in my knees. Maybe I should've started off sitting down. Too late now.

"You have a lot of nerve, you know that? I took you under my wing put you in the hands of an excellent instructor. You agree "Nacho" is a very good teacher, no?"

I could see that he was trying to lead me back up the same ol' path, I decided to head him off at the pass.

"Senōr Flores, we all know the facts that you gave me a great opportunity, a great trainer, food, shelter, all that good stuff; but I have to repeat – I haven't been given any take home pay even if it's only thirty-five percent of the gate."

A mean looking smile warped his already evil looking face. He made me think of a crocodile.

"So, you're saying – if I don't give you some percentage of the gate you won't perform?"

To be honest, I hadn't even thought about anything like that; a strike? I was just trying to get paid, something.

"Uhhh, well, I don't think it would make much sense for me to continue to risk my life for bread, water and a hotel room."

From somewhere outside the window to my left I heard the sound of a bird chirping. The room was well lit, but the shadows seemed to dim the scene. Senōr Flores took one of his fragrant Cuban cigars from a box on his desk and lit it. He puffed on it a few times. And stared daggers at me. I knew that drug dealers, in general, including Mexican drug dealers, didn't hesitate to kill people they weren't pleased with.

"So, let's say you don't get a percentage of the gate, what then?"

"Well, uhhh, I guess I'll just have to take my skills elsewhere, to Spain maybe."

The croc smile widened a bit. I've never felt so threatened by a smile in my whole life. One of the bodyguards cracked his knuckles. Senōr Flores leaned back in his plush chair.

"No, no, my young friend, you're not going to Spain with your skills – I will see to that. Perhaps you are unaware that I have a great deal of influence in the bullfight world, all over.

And from this day forward you will **not** be fighting bulls in Mexico either. I gave you a chance to become something and you've betrayed me by being arrogant and disrespectful, I cannot tolerate that kind of behavior. Do you understand what I'm saying to you?"

I gave him a dumb nod nod; what else could I do?

"Now then, concerning money. I checked with my accountant just this morning and he gave me a complete rundown on the expenses, the money I've spent on your behalf; the hotels, the hospital fees, your food, payment for "Nacho", the cuadrilla. You owe me $50,000. That is fifty thousand dollars, not pesos."

I took a deep breath and swallowed hard.

"Fifty thousand dollars?" It could've been fifty million. I had about

$1,200.00 to my name.

"I will repeat -- $50,000. That is what you owe me, that is how much it will cost you to clear the decks with me. Believe me, my young friend, I'm letting you off easy. If I didn't like you at all, I wouldn't even allow you to re-pay me.

Now then, since we are in the middle of the holiday season I'm going to be very generous with you and give you a full month to re-pay me. You have the first month of the New Year, January to make your payment. After January I will be forced to charge you 10% interest on the money you owe me. Is that clear?"

I nodded yes, yes, that's clear.

"Good. If you have any questions, please feel free to contact me. "Nacho" will know how to reach me. Oh, incidentally, you will not be allowed to leave Mexico until this matter is settled. I wouldn't attempt to do anything stupid, if I were you, if you value your life."

He put his glasses back on, leaned back in his chair and puffed on his cigar. That was it, I was dismissed. I tried to strut out of his presence with as much dignity as I could manage. $50,000.00. Where in the world could I get $50,000.00?

"Nacho" saw me coming down the stairs, staggering down the stairs I should say, and walked me to the front gate. He looked very sad.

" 'Azuca', listen to me. Many things are not fair in this life, in this world, but a man must maintain his dignity until his dying day because there is no telling what is going to kill him."

I couldn't do anything but stare at him. I didn't really understand what he was saying.

"I feel that I lost my dignity when I let myself get pulled in under Señor Florés thumb. I was a bullfighter who had lost his nerve, his will to fight the bulls. Señor Florés gave me "the opportunity" to remain close to the bullfight by using my knowledge, but it has cost me a lot."

Suddenly I was seeing "Nacho" in a different light.

"You owe him money too?"

A sad little smile pulled the corners of his mouth down.

"Maybe I owe him more than money, maybe I owe him my soul."
That's all he said and strolled back into the house.

I took a bus to Guadalajara. I wanted to move slowly, to give myself time to think. Nothing to do on a bus trip but stare at the passing scenery and think. I ignored the trio of singers in the rear of the bus, the pretty senõrita who sat next to me, all of it. All I could do was think of what had happened to me.

I was no longer Juan Negro, "Azucar", Matador. Senõr Flores had pulled my foundation from underneath me. The trip from Mexico City to Guadalajara only took a few hours, but it seemed to go on for days. I'm sure it was my state of mind that made things drag on. I had been pulled from my pedestal with one hard yank from Senõr Flores.

Fifty thousand dollars, the price I would have to pay for my freedom. Weird. I suddenly felt that the country called Mexico was holding me hostage…*"You will not be allowed to leave Mexico until this matter is settled."*

I thought about trying to hire a "coyote" who would take me across the border. Who was brave enough to run the risk of defying Senõr Flores?

I thought about just taking a bus to Tijuana and walking out of Mexico, across the border, but I had to scrap that idea. Getting across the border was no big deal, I was, after all, an American citizen. But that wouldn't stop Senõr Flores' hit-men from killing me. The forces of revenge didn't stop at anybody's border.

I thought of trying to blend into the Mexican population, maybe somewhere, in some small village on the west coast of Mexico. That idea was killed by a number of Mexican bullfight fans who popped on the bus and saluted me with tips of their sombreros and broad smiles. They didn't crowd up next to me asking for autographs, but they recognized me. Once upon a time that would've been an ego trip, now it was a problem.

What could I do in Mexico to earn $50,000.00? I thought about holding up a bank. I could just imagine the headlines in La Opinion – *"Juan Negro, 'Azucar', up and coming star in the taurine world, arrested on bank robbery charges."* It didn't take a lot of thought to laugh that one away.

The Black Matador, "Sugar"

I thought about asking my parents for the money –
"*Dear Mom, Dad,*
Please send me $50,000.00 before February 1st, so that I won't have
to pay 10% on $50,000.00." Or get my neck twisted backwards.

How could I ask them to bail me out of some shit that they never thought I should've been in, in the first place? And I'm sure that sending me fifty grand would've been a serious drain on their resources.

I felt like a zombie when I got off the bus in Guadalajara. I'm sure I must've looked like a zombie when Maya picked me up from the bus station. I was spent from thinking so hard.

"Azucar, welcome to Guadalajara."

I wanted to tell her – hey, you may as well start calling me by my real name because Senōr Flores has taken my other name from me. But I was too numbed out to even say that. I felt like a zombie without a name. Senōr Flores had really done a number on me.

"So, how was your holiday in the north?"

"It was a holiday in the north. What can I say?"

Thank God she didn't press me. I might've gone on a crying jag or something. I couldn't pin my feelings down. I wasn't Juan Negro, "Azucar", matador, anymore. But I was the only one who knew that at this point in time. The word would get out pretty soon, but for now, no one else knew about my demotion but me.

Maya, beautiful Maya; she had prepared for my arrival. There were tapas, the candles, the gorgeous musical tidbits – "I know you like all kinds of music – this is from some lil' people in the Congo, I think they are called Ituri Forest Pygmies. We don't really know what they call themselves because no one has ever asked them; a typical Western imperialistic thing."

And there it was, once again, our relationship with each other. It took three days of me moping around before she started pressing me.

"Azucá, don't you want to go out somewhere? Maybe listen to some music?"

"No, I'd rather stay here and listen to music."

It really hit the fan with one simple, logical question.

"What does your schedule look like for the coming season?"

"I won't be having a schedule for a coming season."

———— ◆ ◆ ◀ ————

It was a relief to tell her the whole story, to unburden myself.

"I have to tell you, I've often heard rumors about your Senõr Flores being connected to the drug business; about him being a bad person. Now I know it's all true. What are you going to do now?"

I just broke down and started crying. I didn't know what to do. I felt totally helpless. I felt powerless. I felt sorry for myself. Maya held me in her arms and comforted me. That just made me feel worse. The matador, Juan Negro, "Azucar", was being petted and stroked like a small boy who had scraped his knee.

After a few minutes I got a grip on myself, I had to. What good would it do to waste time crying? Maya gave me a sweet little kiss and excused herself.

"Azucá, I have to do a little errand; I'll be back in an hour".

I filled in the time she was gone by e-mailing Mom and Dad.

"Back in Mexico. Everything is going well. I'm pretty busy right now so I won't make this a long note. Hope all is well with y'all.

Love, Chester."

I thought it would be better to tell a little white lie, rather than burden them with the madness I was involved with. I was curled up on the downstairs sofa when Maya returned, trying to force my brain to think a way out of my dilemma. She glided over to me, gave me a kiss and placed a black briefcase beside me.

"What's this?"

"Open it."

I thought my heart was going to stop. The brief case was packed with neatly banded bundles of one hundred dollar bills. I looked from the briefcase to her, to her and back to the briefcase.

"There is fifty thousand there, the money to pay that bastard for your freedom."

I've heard the words a zillion times but I really had no idea what they meant 'til that time. I was speechless. Maya was bailing me out.

"Maya, thank you. It's gonna take me a while to re-pay you, but I promise you, I will re-pay you."

"I'm not worried about you, I know you are a man of honor. Senõr Flores is the one who worries me, he and all those of his type almost make me feel ashamed to be a Mexican."

I cell phoned "Nacho" in Mexico City.

"Nacho, this is 'Azucar', I'm trying to reach Senõr Flores. You have any idea where he is?"

"He is here in the house, Azucar. He will be leaving for Europe in the morning."

"I have to see him before he leaves, it's very important."

"Well, he is here for now."

"See you in a little while."

Maya had changed into striped slacks and a cool bolero jacket almost before the conversation with "Nacho" ended. She was ready to roll.

We jumped on #15 at twelve noon, shot through Morelia and were on the outskirts of Toluca/Cuernavaca, just a few miles north of Mexico City in three and a half hours. I had never seen this side of Maya. She was pissed.

"I love my country, I love everything about it but the hyenas who feed on our people."

I directed her to the big house in Polanco. "Nacho" came out to meet us. I noticed that he avoided looking me in the eye.

I introduced him to Maya.

"I am honored to meet you, Senõra, your work does great service to Mexico."

"Thank you, Senõr."

We had to wait for a half-hour to get inside of Senõr Flores' space. As usual he was finishing up a meeting with a collection of thugs. He seemed a little surprised to see Maya.

"Ahh, Azucar, so good to see you. And one of Mexico's finest artists. Senõra, my house is honored by your presence."

Maya's smile looked close to being a frown.

"Thank you, Senõr."

"Now, Azucar, what can I do for you?" No cigar this time, almost a gentleman. Or was he just putting on a front for Maya Xochitl de las Reyes? I suspected he was just putting on a front. Only one bodyguard for this meeting, no bundles of cellophane wrapped dope in the corner. We sat in chairs in front of his desk.

I did a little drama with the briefcase by placing it squarely in front of him on the desk.

"I've come to pay you the money that you say I owe you."

I opened the briefcase slowly, enjoying the effect it made on him. He actually looked surprised.

"Well, I must say this is a pleasant surprise."

I wasn't feeling very congenial, all I wanted to do was pay up and go. Senõr Flores snapped his finger at his bodyguard who picked up the briefcase, took it to a nearby coffee table and started counting the bundles of hundred dollar notes. No one spoke. Maya sat in the chair next to me, looking like an inscrutable Aztec Indian with green eyes. The body guard counted the money out onto the table and returned the briefcase to me.

"It is correct", he mumbled to Senõr Flores. Senõr Flores stood slowly, as though to signal that our business was over.

"Well, if there is nothing else…"

Maya's words almost crackled when she spoke.

"Two things, Senõr Flores. The contract that 'Azucar' signed for you to manage him and a receipt for the money you have just received."

"Hahhhah, I can assure you that my word is my bond, I give you my word…"

"The contract and the receipt, Senõr Flores, if you please."

"If you insist, Azucar."

"He does insist, Senõr."

Once again I was seeing another side of Maya. She could be cold. Senõr Flores walked across the room to a large portrait of somebody in a fancy uniform with mutton chops covering up his ears. The portrait was on hinges, he swung it aside and dialed into a wall safe. I noticed that he kept his back to us as he shuffled through a sheaf of papers to find my contract. I felt the urge to run up behind him and smash him in the head with my fists. Maya gently placed her hand on mine. I could just imagine the rotten contract he had in his safe for the boxers, for members of my cuadrilla, for a whole bunch of people.

"Ahhhhah, Juan Negro, 'Azucar', I overlooked it." He pulled my contract out with his thumb and forefinger, as though he was handling something nasty. He walked back across the room and dropped it on the desk in front of me.

"And your receipt…"

He pulled a large receipt book out of his desk drawer and smiled his familiar crocodile smile in our direction.

"Shall I write, money received from Senõra Maya Xochitl de las Reyes or matador Juan Negro, 'Azucar'?

Sarcastic asshole.

"Write, received from Chester Simmons, Jr., also known as Matador Juan Negro "Azucar".

I could tell he didn't like that, Senõr Flores didn't like to be given instructions. I could imagine, if Maya hadn't been with me, he would've given me a lecture on respect and the proper way to talk to him. Or maybe had his bodyguard do a bit of homework on my jaw.

It seemed to take him a long time to write the receipt.

"There you are, your receipt. Just as you demanded."

Sarcasm again.

I felt that he should've said something – "Well, sorry things didn't work for us, Azucar" – something. But that was just my feeling, not his. I took one last glance at the pile of bills on the coffee table and had to grind my teeth together to keep from saying something. Greedy ass bastard. I had made him money in the bullring and paid him to release me from a rotten contract to make him more money. It was a lose-lose situation for me; but I came away feeling colder, more experienced. I would never let anything like this happen again.

"Nacho" met us on the first floor and walked us out to the car.

"Azucar, I can tell you this openly, as a friend. If you had been given the right circumstances, within a couple of years, you would have been great."

I was stunned to hear "Nacho" say something like that, he wasn't the type to blow smoke up your butt, to inflate your ego.

"Nacho", thank you for saying that, it makes me feel much better."

We did the hearty Mexican male embrace, he shook hands with

Maya and gave me the section of a newspaper he had in his back pocket.

"I think this will be of some interest to you."

We took the newspaper section and got off the grounds of Senõr Flores' property as fast as possible. Maya suggested a little celebration at a restaurant she knew in the Zona Rosa district.

"It's in a ritzy area but the people are real and the food is very good. I could use a glass of wine."

"I'm with you, sweet thang."

"I like that, I like that 'sweet thang' very much."

"I do too."

The Chalet Suizo was not a hole in the wall. As a matter of fact it was somewhat fancy, but she was right, the people were real. They greeted us like old friends.

"Senõra de las Reyes, such a long time. And Matador Negro, we welcome you." They gave us a choice table in the window, to see and be seen. After Maya's wine was served, hot Oolong tea for me, and our food ordered, she opened the newspaper that "Nacho" had given us.

A columnist in El Diario wrote:

"Senõr Miguel Flores, Juan Negro, 'Azucar's' manager announced yesterday that 'Azucar' had retired. Senõr Flores suggested that 'Azucar' may have retired for 'purely personal reasons'. No other reason than that was given. It will, of course, be quite interesting to hear what 'Azucar' himself has to say about this matter.

We hope that 'Azucar's' sudden announcement will simply be the result of an impulsive nature. I am certain that my readers will agree with me when I say that 'Azucar' brought a whole new dynamic to the Mexican bullfight scene.

If you were privileged to see any of his fights during this past season, his first season, then I do not have to waste a barrel of ink describing his elegant work with the capote, his brilliant improvisations with the muleta and the definitive way he killed.

There were only a few low points that I could point at concerning this phenomenon from the North; that were definitely overshadowed by his courage and distinct style. We should hope that Juan Negro, 'Azucar' will resolve those 'purely personal reasons' and return to the corrida, to give the afición further demonstrations of his unique capabilities."

"Senõr Flores is a dirty rotten snake dog beast!"

"I think you've said it all, I would like another glass of wine."

We weren't prepared to deal with the newspaper reporters and the paparazzi who ambushed us outside the restaurant.

"Don't tell them anything", Maya whispered to me. "We've just gotten rid of Senõr Flores, we don't want him back in our lives again."

Believe me, it takes a lot of effort to say, "No comment!" No comment!" When you want to scream something, but she was right. No doubt in anybody's mind, if I had let the real story out, about how Senõr Flores had tried to turn me into a bullfighting slave, we would've had some serious problem with Senõr Flores. I had to chomp down and bite the bullet.

They tried to get me on television to talk about my reasons for "retiring". I declined the honor. The newspapers wrote all kinds of crazy stuff; "*I had lost my nerve. My fiancée, the well known artist-sculptress, Maya Xochitle de las Reyes, had forced me to stop because she had dreamt of my death.*"

There was lots and lots of speculation out there, but only a few of us had the truth and we weren't giving it up. I had decided to wait a few years, after all of the hullabaloo had died down and write this book. What the hell, I was only twenty, I had lots of time to tell my story.

———◆◆———

New Year's Eve 1983. We had decided to see the New Year in on the coast, at Puerto Vallarta.

"My family has owned a beach house there for ages."

A "beach house?" A gorgeous four bedroom, Oceanside villa with a private pier.

"We'll have the ocean to ourselves for the New Year; everybody else will be in the cities, drinking and being muy Mexicano."

The day before the New Year we strolled on the beach, casually talking about our future, hers and mine. Bright, clear, sunny day.

"Maya, I have to go back to the states…"

"I know, I know."

"I mean, now that I've had my career taken away from me by that, that dog, there's nothing I can do here to earn my living."

"I understand."

"My Dad is the general manager of Gelman Tech, computers and all kinds of next century technology. He's promised me a place in the organization. I wouldn't be making a lot of money to begin with, but I'm sure I'll be able to advance pretty rapidly. I want you to go back with me."

I don't know if what I said shocked her or what; but we both sank down onto the sand.

"Azucá, it would be a very big step for me to take, to leave my country. Aside from that, I have been commissioned to do a number of large works; it would be very difficult for me. I hope you understand. It's not that I wouldn't want to be with you; but I need some time to think about this."

"No problem, think as long as you have to. I just wanted to let you know that I love you and I want us to be together."

"I love you." Where did those words come from? Just goes to show you what will come out of a young man's mouth when his raging hormones are properly fired up.

"I love you too, Azucá."

So there we were, we had outed ourselves, and had no place to go. At midnight that night, when we heard the sound of distant church bells we kissed, sipped glasses of Piper Heidseck and made love.

———◆———

I felt like turning the plane around as we left Mexico City, heading for Chicago. I really wanted to stay in Mexico; but I couldn't stand the idea of being a rich woman's man. I had to have my own pesos. Maya had put it to me straight up.

"Azucá, listen to me. My parents left me land and a name and, as I've told you, a pre-nuptial agreement with a terrible husband who destroyed himself trying to knock a tree down on the Paseo left me with a fat bank account. Plus, thank God, the Mexican art lovers **and** the government have been very gracious to me. What else can I say?"

"You have yours, Maya, I have to make mine, that's just the way I am."

"I understand, I really do."

So, we had agreed to take our time about things, to see how we could work things out. Strangely, the closer I flew toward Chicago the more I started thinking about Dondisha.

<hr />

Mom and Dad treated me like the Prodigal Son. I had finally come to my senses and left the bull business alone. I didn't bother to take them through the Senōr Flores madness, it was over, why beat a dead horse?

Everybody kicked in, even my sister.

"Chester, look, you're a smart dude, you oughta think about becoming a doctor."

"Louise, that's something to think about."

Dad had me on the Gelman Tech payroll as his personal assistant at the end of my second week in town.

"Technology is the key to tomorrow, check it out."

Mom made my favorite dishes.

"I made that lamb stew you like…"

But I think the biggest and best surprise of all was Dondisha. She started doing some serious talking with me from the first night we spent together.

"Chester, I don't know anything about the Mexican woman and I'm not gonna make myself grey trying to figure anything out. All I do know is that you've come back to me and I love you; I want to be with you.

But we're gonna have to do a few things: Number one, I'm very uncomfortable with the idea of rubbers. I know you've been careful and so have I, but it wouldn't hurt to have ourselves checked out again, so we can get back into that natural groove."

"No problem."

"Number two, I want you to move back with me. I can't tell you how much I missed having you in bed next to me."

"That won't be a problem." I felt very free, very loose. I wasn't on a rigid schedule, going from one place to another, training in between times, stealing private moments from time to time. Now it was like time had slowed down. And when I went down to the store to learn the ropes from Dad, I wasn't in danger of being killed.

I kept a pretty tight personal training schedule going on because I had grown accustomed to being in good condition.

Dondisha tried to lure me, seduce me would be a better way to say it, into her Capoeira Angola class. I went with her as often as I could but there was something missing for me. I enjoyed the music, vocal and instrumental, and the clever movements; but it lacked an element that I had become used to, the kill. I couldn't tell anybody that. I had become a killer and the experience had changed something in me.

I think back to this time as a sort of schizo section of my life. Later on, I could see it as a transitional period. I was coming down from a fabulous high. I had been Juan Negro, "Azucar", for a few hot months and suddenly I was Chester Simmons Jr, again. It took a moment for me to adjust to that.

And, of course there was Maya. She didn't pester me and I didn't pester her. I tried to explain – via e-mails – something of what my life was like in Chicago. But I had to leave out some details. I couldn't, for example, tell her about Dondisha. That was a biggie. I can't think of any woman who wants to hear that a man she has professed love for is with another woman.

No guilt trips here, none of that. I just saw myself as a dude who was actually in love with two different women. I think that vibe offered me a justifiable connection to both of them. And they made a lot of stuff easy for me. Maya saw herself as the woman that I was in love with, in Mexico. And Dondisha saw me as the woman I was living my life with, in Chicago. It was like they were giving me as much polygamous rope as I needed. After all, they weren't threats to each other, really. And that's how the early stages of our lives together played out. It got a little stickier later on, but that took awhile. I mean, after all, when I left Mexico I had asked Maya to come with me. But now I was living with Dondisha and there was no way in hell I could imagine us living happily ever after as a trio, a ménage a trios.

CHAPTER NINETEEN

What was I doing? Hard to say, just sort of skimming on the surface, I guess. 'Til the afternoon I heard the trumpets go off in my head. I was sitting in front of one of Dad's super fast computers, just noodlin' around, when I heard the trumpets. Well, there wasn't any actual sound, but in my mind I heard the trumpets, the fanfare-prelude that they do just before the gates are opened and the bullfighters strut across the bullring to salute the president of the event.

I heard the trumpets and I saw dollar signs click up in front of my eyes. A bullfight video game. A bullfight video game. I settled back in my seat and took a deep breath. It took an hour for me to think out the program I would have to develop for the game, but it would definitely be a way to feed on my own experience as a matador. I would design a video game that would give every boy, every girl, anybody who ever wanted to be a bullfighter, a matador, an opportunity to do their thing without worrying about being gored. No, I would design being gored into the program too. If you mess up, made the wrong move, then you would be gored.

———◆———

Chester Sr. and Lillian, an old husband and wife team, sat across from each other at the Sunday morning breakfast table, casually reading the Sunday edition of the Chicago Tribune, "updating their knowledge of the latest tragedies".

"Chester?"

"Uhh, yeah baby?"

"Stop hidin' behind your paper for a minute…"

Chester, Sr. couldn't prevent a slight smile from creasing his lips. God, this woman knows me like a book.

"Hidin? Whose hidin'?"

"You are. You've been hidin' since Thursday evening."

"Hidin' what?"

"I don't know, you tell me. All I know is that something is bothering you and we haven't talked about it."

Chester, Sr. folded the newspaper section he was reading into a neat square, took a deep breath and vented.

"Your son…"

"Our son, Chester Simmons, our son…"

"Our son is fluffin' around on the job; he's not doing his work properly. I've been forced to have a couple other people do some stuff he was supposed to have done. If he wasn't my son I would've fired him a week ago."

"Have you talked to him about the problem, about what he should be doing?"

"Well, not yet…"

"So what's the problem?"

"Chester is off into that bullfight shit again."

"O my God no! He's not going back down to Mexico again is he?"

"I don't know what the hell he's gonna do, all I know is that this is about a video game, I've seen him working on it."

———◆———

Out of the corner of my eye, I saw Dad standing in the door. How long had he been there? Who knows?

"Uhhh, Chester, it's six o'clock. Remember, your mother is fixin' some spaghetti and fryin' red snapper for you and Dondisha this evening."

"Give me a few more minutes with this, Dad, I'll be right with you."

I'm sure he was surprised because I was usually the last to arrive and the first one to want to leave Gelman Tech. I had to pull myself away from the mouse and the screen fifteen minutes later, but my brain felt like it was on fire. I would have a chance to fight the bulls again and make some money. I would be able to re-pay Maya. Maybe they already had a bullfight video game out there somewhere but I'd never heard of one.

I definitely knew that they didn't have a Black bullfighter-video game. Where could I sell it? Well, Mexico, Spain, Columbia, Peru would be primary markets. And, who knows? Maybe even America and Europe, people were always interested ;in new stuff. If I could get a few top flight celebrities to endorse the game, if. . . ? Lots of ifs. . . .

"Chester, you want another piece of fish?"

"Huh?"

Louise did that cock-eyed look thing in my direction, one of her favorite ways of teasing me, of indicating that I was "out to lunch."

I said, "Do you want another piece of fish?"

"Uhh, no, Mom, I'm full, thanks."

What the hell do you say to people, to "normal people", when your brain is on fire with an idea?

I loved the way Dondisha handled me that particular evening. She thanked Mom and Dad for the delicious food, complimented Louise on her good grades, and steered me out to the car like I was an absent minded o'l man. By this time Mom was completely at ease with our domestic set up. She didn't bug me about "shacking" with Dondisha, she just accepted what was in front of her and let it go at that. I'm sure she expected us to get married sometime in the future; but she wasn't trippin' any more.

I couldn't wait to get home to design an outline for my game. In my head I had started calling it "Matador Negro". Yeah, "Matador Negro". Take that Señor Florés!

The bulls came first. I sat in front of the screen, designing the prototype of every bull I had fought. I would use the circumstances they put me in as the raw material for the videos. Out of the gates/my memory, they charged hard and fast: "Yambu," the first bull I had ever faced in my life as an "espontaneo". "Bongo", my first bull in the Tijuana bullring. And the "Gordito", the fat one. "Bigote", the bull I had to kill for the Venezuelan Francisco Torres, "Minuto".

"Rojo", the dull reddish colored bull in the Acapulco bullring. Followed by "Cachuco", fighting with busted ribs in Vera Cruz, a triumph in Guanajuato, ears and tails from both bulls. "Cubano" and "Justicia" in Ensenada, running from one bullring to another, sometimes sleepy and tired, the Festival in Guadalujara.

The wonderful bull called "Vigilante" in Guadalajara, I could create a whole video of him alone.

"Chachao", in Tijuana again. I did the whole thing, from the beginning to the killing of the bull. I wanted to create the scene and milk the emotions from it. Should I eliminate the picadores? No, keep that in, that's a part of the whole scene, it would be incomplete without the picadores.

For the next week I rushed downtown to Gelman's to do what I had to do with Dad, test the ideas that I was working on, and then jumped right back to the drawing board at home.

Dondisha was there, somewhere in the background, a blurred figure who gave me fresh fruit to nibble on, cups of Jasmine tea from time to time. I had to smile, listening to her talk to my Mom on the phone.

"Lillian, I don't know what he's workin' on, but I can tell you this – he's working!"

No doubt about it, I **was** working. I felt driven, the way I felt when I had decided to become a bullfighter. The vision was so clear in my head I felt like I was hallucinating. After a hot six weeks I was ready to "go public". I decided to start off with Dad.

"Uhhh, Dad, would you come in here for a minute? I'd like to show you something."

I didn't give him a lot of razzle dazzle, I just laid the whole program out in front of him and stood back to get his reaction. By this point in time he knew a little bit about bullfighting from talking with me, doing some reading on his own and, after all, he had created the program that helped to make me a better killer.

"Dad, what I'm doing, basically, is building on what you gave me, your program to make me a better matador." I think that information put a little puff in his chest.

"Who you aiming this at?"

"I think my primary markets would be in those countries where bullfighting is common; Mexico, Spain, Venezuela, Peru. And then I'm looking at off brand places like Japan and China. The Japanese, as you well know, love anything having to do with swords."

"You think they would dig a Black Matador?"

"We could rearrange the facial characteristics and the color to suit the market. Look at what they did with the Barbie doll over the years."

He was doing veronicas and media veronicas with the mouse as he asked me questions, he was getting into it.

"How would you deal with the people who would come out of the woodwork, the ones who would say that you're teaching children how to kill animals?"

"My attorney would argue that there are already war video games on the market that have soldiers gunning each other down, big time. Games that kids play every day."

I thought he was going to twist himself off of the chair when he did his first body cape wrapping chicuelina antigua.

"Damn! This comes close to being virtual reality. You thinking about that?"

Now he had switched to the muleta and was doing slow motion naturales with his right and left hands. Olé! Olé! Olé!

"I can't believe a bull would go for a red cape."

"The bull is color blind, the cloth could be green or purple, he goes for the movement, that's why the bullfighter must be so still."

He was talking to me and I was talking to him, but I could see that his attention was fixed on the bull. After a few spectacular spinning molinetes and four manoletinas he was ready to try to kill the bull. He read the "Moment of Truth" instructions that scrolled across the bottom of the screen.

"That's nice", he mumbled as he made the bull's hooves parallel, gained the bull's complete attention and plunged forward for the kill, "crossing over", leading the bull past his right thigh with the muleta and stabbing into the bull's withers. Pinchazo! The sword hit bone and popped out.

"Damn! I missed!"

"But you didn't get gored."

"You got that programmed into this too?"

"It's part of bullfighting."

"So, that gives the game an element of danger?"

"Correct."

He lined the bull up again, took aim and plunged straight into the right place. His "moment of truth" had only lasted three minutes. He sat up straight as a stick as the bull sank to his knees. A jerky figure in black crept up behind the bull to slash the back of the neck, sever the life-line.

"Who is that?"

"That man is called the Puntillero, he gives the bull the Coup d'grace, to prevent him from suffering too much."

"You might have to have some of these terms translated."

"I'm thinking about that, but I can tell you right now, I'm not too inclined to translate too much. When you go to a Japanese restaurant, they don't translate Yakitori for you, or Sashime or Sushi. That's what it's called and that's that."

He was smiling his ass off, pleased as he could be.

"You've thought it all out, huh?"

"Not completely."

"How long would it take you to put a business plan together?"

"About a month, I've already started working on one."

He rubbed his clean shaven chin and stared real hard at the screen for a long time.

"Chester, son, I think you've got something here. Look, ol' man Gelman is at his home in the South of France, a place near Cannes. I'll wait until you finish that business plan and we'll fax it to him.

Meanwhile, I'll throw a little bait out to him with a phone call, you know, as a teaser."

"Ol man Gelman? What's he got to do with this?"

Dad gave me that shrewd, jailhouse learned look out of the corner of his eye.

"Ol' man Gelman is going to bankroll this, how much money do you think it would take to kick it off?"

"Uhh, I hadn't really, I mean, I haven't figured that out yet."

"Well, figure it out. Gelman would be good for a mil or two, easily. But he likes to know exactly where his money is going. One of the reasons why we've done so well together is because I don't try to cook the books, embezzle, cheat in any way. He pays me a decent salary and I'm straight up about things with him.

What he's gonna ask me, first off, is, "Mr. Simmons, you believe in this?"

"I'm gonna say, 'Yes, Mr. Gelman.'"

"'It's not because this is your son?' he's gonna say. And I'll say, 'No, because it's a good idea, a good investment.' In your business paln if you can show him how he can keep on sun bathing in the South of France and gambling in Monté Carlo he'll be willing to supply you with the capital.

It wouldn't take a lot of effort to hire a couple more people here, re-tool a section of this place and we would be off and running."

I felt my shoulders droop and my body sag a bit. I had been in such a state of tension for weeks. Ol'man Gelman, Dad's employer, my prospective angel. This business plan was on the way.

━━━━◆◆◆━━━━

I tried to keep "Matador" as close to my vest as possible, but I couldn't stop myself from sharing the good news with Dondisha.

"That's a damned good idea, baby, go for it!"

And, of course, if Mom was told about the game, then Louise knew. And Louise had to tell her girlfriends. It didn't really matter all that much, it was going to go global anyway, I just didn't know how soon.

A week later, five working days later, Dad came up behind me while I was putting a few more features into the game.

"Spoke to ol'man Gelman yesterday evening, laid the program out in front of him and what did he ask me?" ' "Mr. Simmons do you believe in this enterprise?"

"Yes, Mr. Gelman", that's what I said to him."

"It's not because this is your son, is it? "He asked me.

No, its not that at all; I think it's a damn good idea and a good thing for Gelman Tech to invest in."

"Very good. How soon can you send me the business plan?"

"Very soon."

"Good, I'll look forward to it. Incidentally, me and Gertrude went to the bullfights at Nimes, the border town between France and Spain, last weekend."

"I didn't know you were a bullfight fan, Mr. Gelman."

"Lots of things you don't know about me, Mr. Simmons. I've been an aficionado for many years. Let's have a look at that business plan. Aside from this new development, how're things going otherwise?"

He didn't have to say another mumbling word, I stood up and we embraced and started doing a lil' soul waltz around the room. A few weeks later we faxed the business plan to Mr. Morris Gelman.

"Chester, you can relax. Even if he digs the plan from the first sentence onward, he's going to take ten days to reply, that's just the way he is."

I had laid out a precise plan covering every base I could think of, and some that Dondisha thought up.

"Is there any humor in the bullfight? Any crazy shit?"

The opening package would cost at least one mil, 1,000,000. Dad suggested that I pump it up to a mil point five, for the sake of "contingencies." You never, never know what's going to happen when you go into a new area." So, that was the business plan-package we sent to Mr. Gelman.

Exactly ten days later, Mr. Gelman faxed a concise well crafted reply.

"I'm going on record in support of "Matador Negro", a video game that was invented by Chester Simmons, Jr. And will be issued and distributed from/by Gelman Tech. I'll be sending my attorneys to meet with you to iron out all of the details.

I'm only taking a 10% cut of this pie, in order to keep my capital gains within reason. I don't think I need to make more money at this state of my life. I think I need to be in a position to give more away. My wife and I reached an agreement about this after my last heart attack."

We were in business, just like that. I found the whole thing hard to believe, on one level, but then my sister Louise took it to another level by saying. . .

"Aww c'mon, Chester, you've been livin' out a fantasy life for years, that's why you wound up in Mexico, fightin' bulls, in the first place."

———◆———

CHAPTER TWENTY

Maya

Mom and Dad helped me form the Matador Corporation. Lots of stuff had to be done before we could step out. Patents, copyright, forms for this and that. The biggie for me was having a business bank account with 1.5 million dollars in it. One point five million dollars. I was chairman of the Board, Mom and Dad were senior members of the corporation and I "persuaded" Dondisha to do publicity and public relations. The truth of the matter is that I wanted to snatch her out of her kindergarten classroom and make some money with her.

"But Chester, you don't understand, baby, I like my job, I like teaching the munchkins."

"Fine, good, wonderfull. Help me put this game over and we can start our own kindergarten."

Maya. Our communication had gotten a little spotty. Maybe it was my fault because I had reached the point where I was just e-mailing some inane, jive bullshit about the weather, the lake front in Chicago, how nice everything was. And she was counter-responding with pretty much the same.

'Til one afternoon I just simply decided to be a man about the situation. Me and Dondisha had bonded, no doubt about it. I mean, it had reached the point where we were finishing off each other's sentences and stuff like that.

"*Dear Maya, as you know, I had this girlfriend in Chicago when*

I first met you. And when I came back here she was here for me. I'm not going to try to do some gauzy stuff about where things are, I'm just going to be straight up with you. It looks like this is the "Moment of Truth" for me, for us.

I know that I'm not going to be begging you to come to Chicago anymore. It wouldn't make any sense and it wouldn't work. I'm sure you must know that I'm digging deep inside of myself to say what I'm saying, but I feel that I owe you this kind of honesty.

I've gone into the videogame business and it seems to be taking off. I'm still into bullfighting as an art, but I've created a game that will allow me to repay you for your generosity. I hope you will be kind and not think of me in any kind of negative way. Please, let's remain friends but please remember that I have committed my emotions to someone else."

It was a very difficult e-mail. A very difficult e-mail. I was shocked to get a response to my e-mail, hours later.

"Dear Azucar" (I had to look back at who I had been.)

"Your e-mail explains a lot of things. I respect the relationship you have established with this woman in Chicago. I can only wish you the best. I hope you feel the same way about my relationship with Rodolfo Fuentes, III..."

I had to take a deep breath. Well, I'll be damned! I hadn't been gone two year and I had been replaced. But it was about much more than that.

"...Azucar, it's very difficult to tell a man who must leave a place that you are pregnant. Trust me..."

Pregnant!? The word flared up in front of me like a neon sign. Maya? Pregnant?

"...Fuentes is an unusual Mexican male. He accepted the idea of my pregnancy. And when I made it absolutely plain that it was <u>your</u> baby, not his, he didn't flinch." " 'It is of you, Maya, it is of you, that's what is important to me.' ".

No matter how blasé I wanted to be about it, the idea of Maya having another man in her life was, well, a bit unsettling. I never expected the woman to remain celibate for the rest of her life or anything, but to receive info that Maya had my baby was a shock. What should I do?

I think she solved the problem by explaining: *"...please don't feel compelled to do anything. I can well afford a child and I feel good about us. You came to me honestly, and I have been honest with you, so we have nothing to be ashamed of.*

Rodolfo is going to be the adoptive father, but there is no question about who the biological father is. It might mean, in the years ahead, that you will have the opportunity to meet this son of yours. (I had the scan and they told me it was a boy growing inside of me.) How you explain us to the woman who shares your life now is your own affair. Please feel free to communicate with me and always remember – we had Guadalajara."

I was in a strange kind of daze for a couple of days. A baby, a son with Maya, the most unexpected piece of news I ever expected to have. I made a decision to keep this secret in my personal closet. No need to tell Dondisha anything about this. The day would come, but meanwhile let sleeping dogs sleep. Surprise, Surprise, As a P.S. Maya let me know that she and Señor had had a daughter too. *"We thought that our son Juan needed company."*

———◆———

We had a small, very intimate wedding. Dondisha Phillips-Simmons and me, Mom, Dad and Louise for me; and Dondisha's mother and father bussed up from Miss'ssippi. A few close friends.

"Why didn't they fly?"

"These are country folks, Chester, flying is for the birds, far as they are concerned."

Let me tell the truth; I think that I asked Dondisha to marry me for my mother's sake, more than anything else. But it doesn't matter now, it was one of the best decisions I ever made.

It took almost three years for the video game "Matador Negro" to find it's place in the market place; but when it did it went through the roof. I re-paid Maya and I've taken a couple quick trips to Mexico to see my son, Juan Fuentes. He's six years old now and according to Maya, he's already crazy about the bullfight. I'm afraid that I'll have to keep Little Juan a secret until this book is published and then I'll tell Dondisha the whole story. I don't think we'll have a problem, she's quite mellow now, money helps.

The Black Matador, "Sugar"

Oddly enough it was ol'man Gelman's idea to write a book about how I got into bullfighting, my short, unhappy relationship with Señor Flores, the cultural foundation of the corrida.

(I was not totally surprised to read that Señor Miguel Flores had been machine gunned to death by a rival drug cartel in downtown Culiacan. Play with the bull and sooner or later you'll get the horn.)

"Chester, I think it would make fascinating reading, in addition, as the creator of "Matador Negro" it might do a lot to help boost sales of the video game." I agreed. "Futhermore," he suggested, "why not bring it out in Spanish first? Because that's where your major markets are. I just happen to know Salvador Catalán, the owner/CEO of Libros Catalan. I think Libros would be the Spanish equivalent of Random-House or Little and Brown, one of those places, what do you think?"

I had never thought about a book about my life as a bullfighter, but I could definitely see his point. Shrewd ol' dude, Mr. Gelman.

I could easily understand how he got to be rich. He had a great imagination and he was willing to back up his ideas with cash. Aside from that, he wasn't all up in your butt, breathing down your neck. All he wanted from me was his 10% and a fair shot at any other games I would come up with.

One day I received a registered letter to Chester Simmons, Jr. – Juan Negro, "Azucar":

"Dear Juan Negro, "Azucar", please allow me to introduce myself. I am Francisco Obregon, manager/promoter/entrepreneur. Your video game "Matador Negro", compels me to contact you. I think it is a wonderful piece of work, but that is not the only reason why I am contacting you.

I am of the opinion that your return to the bullring would be a great financial and artistic success. Indeed, I can say to you, Matador, that the aficion hungers for your return. I am aware of some of the difficulties that you experienced with Don Miguel Florés, and I can assure you that we would not be troubled by such matters with me.

Please reply at your convenience, but remember, the aficion eagerly awaits the return of Juan Negro "Azucar".

No need to bullshit about it, the letter caught me off balance, had me feeling that urge to hear the olés! Experience the excitement of fighting again. I was still young enough, still had the nerve and equipment to do it. I knew I could.

I went around for a few days with the memory of what I was, what I had done, sloshing around in my brain. I was still in a serious maybe mode when I e-mailed Francisco Obregon, manager/promoter/ entrepreneur – "*I would like to speak with Ricardo Ortega, "Nacho", before I make my decision concerning your proposal, please send me an address or e-mail for him – gracias, Juan Negro, 'Azucar'.*"

A day later I was absolutely stunned to read: "*Unfortunately, Ricardo Ortega, "Nacho", was shot dead in Culiacan last year. It had something to do with drugs. We are still eagerly awaiting your positive response to our note. I can give you my personal assurance that we will give you the best possible representation. I remain, Francisco Obregon, manager/promoter/entrepreneur.*"

I was pushed out of the maybe mode by this unwelcome news of "Nacho's" death. It was really hard for me to process the idea that my former teacher, my friend was dead. But there was a proverb that he used to say that stuck with me, that put the clincher on my – "Thanks, but no thanks" – note to Señor Francisco Obregon – "Remember, Azuca, the fire you want to go back to is always ashes".

———— ◆ ————

I thought "Matador Negro" was going to be it for me, the video game of my life time, 'til me and Donisha went to Ghana for our honeymoon. It was May, the beginning of the rainy season, hot and humid. We pulled into one of those local bars they seem to have all over the place. This was in a section of Accra called Osu.

"I think we could use a couple cold beers." We weren't drinkers but some folks who had been there told us – "drink beer, drink beer, it's safer than the water."

The drinking bar was called The Shalizar Bar and the beer was cold and served in frosted glasses. Delicious, while we were chillin', Dondisha glanced through the wooden slats of the window next to our table. There was a vacant lot shaded by a huge tree.

"Chester, look…"

A small circle of Ghanaian school girls in their brown and egg yellow uniforms were playing some kind of footsie game. They did a rhythmic clapping and then two of the girls would jump up and down and suddenly one or the other would land and slide one foot or the other toward the other one. We couldn't make heads or tails of the thing. What was it called? Did they keep score? What was the point of the game? We called the bar owner over.

"Madam, can you explain this to us? What is it called?"

"Oh! This one is called ampée, all of the school girls play it."

"Only school girls?"

"Only school girls. After the buds are gone, no one wants to bounce up and down. Are you getting me?" She winked at Dondisha. Dondisha winked back. I get it.

It was very easy to give us the name of the game and who did it, but hard as hell to explain the point system. It made as much sense to me as the scoring of a cricket game. It didn't really matter whether I understood it or not, the important thing was to put it out there. I hired Madam Betty Kotey, owner of the Shalizar Bar as the technical consultant for our Ghana Ampée video game on the spot.

The Matador Negro Corporation had become a boutique game operation. I jumped from Ampée to wari (the board with the scoops, marbles, a counting game) straight into Capoeira Angola.

I pulled Mestre Yves and Mestre Cedric in as technical consultants for the Angola game. Twenty six years old, in the middle of the worse economic down town since the Great Depression, somebody told me. Maybe that had something to do with people buying "Matador Negro" in Mexico, Spain, Venezuela, Peru and Japan, a game they could play at home.

For some crazy reason Ampée caught on big in Sweden, Denmark, Norway, Scandinavia. Mr. Gelman thought it had something to do with the African girls bouncing up and down. We hadn't created any 38 C cups or anything that obvious, but we had tweaked the bustlines up just a bit. Madam Kotey gave her approval – "I think this is very clever and also good for business."

Wari maintained a profile but it didn't break any records, hard to say why. But the Angola game hit big, 'Specially in Brazil. That was kind of puzzling because we thought, with it's history of Capoeira Angola, that they wouldn't be too receptive to a video game about the game. Our marketing people scratched their heads about it for awhile. We sent Mestre Yves and Cedric down to Bahia, to the core, to see what the deal was. They came back with a surprising number of angles.

It seems that a lot of the young people, even the ones who're doing Angola, play the game because they see that it helps to improve their physical game."

"Same thing for the older set. It seems that they're using the game as a sort of testing ground for techniques and stuff."

"And finally, at the end of the day, it's technology and they love technology."

◆━◆━◆

Leo Anderson a.k.a. "Raul" came into the lobby of our condo with a copy of "Matador Juan Negro, 'Azucar' " tucked under his armpit. We had a grand reunion. He had five days in town before he whizzed off to Japan. He stayed with us.

"Japan?"

"Yes indeed, Japan. The Japanese love the tango and our Argentine Tango Group is gonna give it to' em. Right between the eyes."

Chicago in the Spring can be pure magic. We took him to the Club Argentine and turned him loose. "Raul" had it, that glow/aura that some people have who have developed their art to a peak degree. I sat back and watched "Raul" dance with Dondisha and it was a command performance. I know he was shocked at the New Dondisha, at her movements, her flow. This was the girl he had once called "clumsy".

The Club Argentine wouldn't let us leave until they closed at 4:00 a.m. "Raul" danced everybody into the ground. And after the Club, a walk along the Point at 57th Street, on the Lake front. Dondisha, poor baby, stretched out in the back seat of the car.

"Go' head on, walk. I'm gonna take me a nap."

"Don't worry, we won't be too far from the car."

She gave me a small smile – "Don't worry, baby, if anybody tries to get up in here with me they're gonna have 130 pounds of Capoeira Angola in their nuts."

We strolled, not saying anything for a few yards.

"Chester, I really dug your book, man. Maria found it in our local bookstore. I was really puzzled to see it in Spanish first."

"That was a business decision, my advisors thought it would reach a more receptive market in Spanish. And then we had Zola Salena, the artist-linguist do the translation."

"Beautiful job. I like the fact that she didn't try to jazz it up with a lot of hip shit, you know what I'm sayin?"

"Yeahhh, in some ways I think she improved on what I was trying to say."

"I know Dondisha read it."

"A half dozen times."

"And how did she take the part about Maya and the baby?"

"She was cool. We had had little talks, you know, about lots of <u>real</u> things before we got married. So, how is it with you? You found that ultimate Tango Partner yet?"

"Not yet, my brother, not yet, I'm still taking applications. And I'm in no great hurry to put anybody in the main slot yet."

The sun was slowly rising up on the lake horizon, it looked like a giant lollipop.

"Did you ever think that we would've been able to pull this off?"

"You mean, you with the bulls and me with the tango? -- coming straight off the Southside."

I nodded, the sky was opening like a beautiful blue, cloudy tapestry.

"I would have to say yes, yes. I can't answer why I would have to say yes, but it just seemed like we had no alternative. That's what we had decided to do."

We turned to re-trace our steps back to the car.

"So, you're retired from the bullring. Do you ever think about going back into it?"

"I did, for awhile, after Señor Flores was gunned down but I decided that I had had enough. I lit my fire, I poured olive oil into my skillet and I cooked, for one great season, enough time to live a part of my dream. I think that's what it's all about, living your dream."

"I gotta agree with you. I think you did a wise thing. I think I would've given up the tango long ago if I had run into a partner with horns."

We laughed and draped our arms across each other's shoulders. Dondisha had taken her nap and was outside of the car doing stretches.

"Raul, you're on your way to Japan, for how long?"

"Six weeks; Tokyo, Yokohama, Kamakura, here'n there."

"While you're there, think about a market for a Tango Video game, I'll make you the technical consultant."

"I'll get on it as soon as I get there."

I looked back over my shoulder, at the sun. Yeah, I lit my fire, I poured olive oil into my skillet and I cooked. And I still had a lot more fish to fry. Meanwhile Dondisha has just informed me that she has twins "baking in the oven". Looks like we'll be starting our own kindergarten pretty soon.

END

The Beginning